Developing Country Debt
(Pergamon Policy Studies—36)

Pergamon Policy Studies on Socio-Economic Development

Barney *Global 2000 Report to the President of the U.S.: Entering the 21st Century*

Carman *Obstacles to Mineral Development: A Pragmatic View*

Chou/Harmon *Critical Food Issues of the Eighties*

Demir *Arab Development Funds in the Middle East*

Fritz *Combatting Nutritional Blindness in Children: A Case Study of Technical Assistance in Indonesia*

Golany *Arid Zone Settlement Planning: The Israeli Experience*

Goodman/Love *Integrated Project Planning and Management*

Goodman/Love *Management of Development Projects: An International Case Study Approach*

Gould *Bureaucratic Corruption in the Third World: The Administration of Underdevelopment in Zaire*

Grundy/Hughes/McHale *Evaluating Transnational Programs in Government and Business*

Kidd *Manpower Policies for the Use of Science and Technology in Development*

Morgan *Science and Technology for Development: The Role of U.S. Universities*

Morris *Measuring the Condition of the World's Poor: The Physical Quality of Life Index*

Renninger *Multinational Cooperation for Development in West Africa*

Stepanek *Bangladesh— Equitable Growth?*

Thomas/Wionczek *Intergration of Science and Technology with Development: Caribbean and Latin American Problems in the Context of the United Nations Conference on Science and Technology for Development*

PERGAMON POLICY STUDIES ON SOCIO-ECONOMIC DEVELOPMENT

Developing Country Debt

Edited by
Lawrence G. Franko
Marilyn J. Seiber

Pergamon Press
NEW YORK • OXFORD • TORONTO • SYDNEY • FRANKFURT • PARIS

Pergamon Press Offices:

U.S.A.	Pergamon Press Inc., Maxwell House, Fairview Park, Elmsford, New York 10523, U.S.A.
U.K.	Pergamon Press Ltd., Headington Hill Hall, Oxford OX3 0BW, England
CANADA	Pergamon of Canada Ltd., 150 Consumers Road, Willowdale, Ontario M2J 1P9, Canada
AUSTRALIA	Pergamon Press (Aust) Pty. Ltd., P O Box 544, Potts Point, NSW 2011, Australia
FRANCE	Pergamon Press SARL, 24 rue des Ecoles, 75240 Paris, Cedex 05, France
FEDERAL REPUBLIC OF GERMANY	Pergamon Press GmbH, 6242 Kronberg/Taunus, Pferdstrasse 1, Federal Republic of Germany

Library of Congress Cataloging in Publication Data
Main entry under title:

Developing country debt.

(Pergamon policy studies)
Bibliography: p.
Includes index.
1. Underdeveloped areas—Debts, Public. I. Franko, Lawrence G. II. Seiber, Marilyn J., 1945-
HJ8899.D48 1979 336.3'4'091724 79-11161
ISBN 0-08-023864-5

Printed in the United States of America

Contents

Foreword

> The world is very different now. For man holds in his mortal hands the power to abolish all forms of human poverty and all forms of human life.
>
> John F. Kennedy
> January 20, 1961

Eighteen years ago John F. Kennedy's belief in the unlimited power of the United States to determine the future course of world economics, as well as world politics, was shared not only by the nation he sought to lead, but also by the world he aspired to mold. Two and one-half decades of unrestrained expansion had resulted in the unquestionable superiority and dominance of American economic system. The world then stood on the threshhold of the "last frontier." All that was required to establish a world order of economic health was the exercise of the tremendeous power of the United States with wisdom.

Two decades later it is again valid to observe that "The world is very different now." No longer do economists, politicians or world opinion believe that our world is approaching a final era of economic harmony and stability. The events of the past twenty years have again altered the political and economic structure of the world as profoundly, if not as cataclysmatically, as the two world wars which fashioned the American empire of 1960. The proliferation of nation states and nationalism, the insatiable energy consumption of the Western industrialized countries, and the dramatic demonstration in 1973 of the helpless dependence of the United States upon OPEC have created the new realities which now confound the world order.

The chapters in this volume present the most comprehensive and cogent analysis of the revolutionary effects of the post-1973 OPEC oil pricing structure on the world's economic system. The authors have dramatically demonstrated that the problem of developing country debt is no longer the limited concern of multilateral lending institutions and the various organizations and scholars concerned with the economic development of less developed countries, but is now inexerably involved in the successful functioning of any future world economic system. For the first time in history, the successful management of lesser developed country debt is essential to the successful functioning of the world economic order. Because of the unparalleled growth of debt due to the imperative of recycling post-1973 petrodollars, the poor countries of the world have now become full partners of the rich. This critical new reality so insightfully detailed by the authors of this volume has gained only creeping cognition of the world's bankers, politicians, and policy makers. Familiarity with the facts and policy alternatives contained in this volume will be essential to the proper fashioning of future public policy.

The essential reality which the people of the United States and their government must acknowledge is the altered role of the United States from that of the determining force of the world economic system capable of working its will; to that of the major but limited partner in a vastly more integrated and complex system. The authors have invaluably detailed the structure of the new system and more importantly provided the insights necessary for the future policy decisions needed to accommodate that structure.

The most important lesson to be learned from these brilliant authors may well be that the emergence of the phenomena of large debt among the developing countries of the world has at least created the imperative necessary for the creation of an economic system both committed and capable of achieving the ageless goal "to abolish all forms of human poverty...."

The Honorable John J. Cavanaugh

U.S. House of Representatives
January 1979

Preface

A decade ago, the phenomenon of developing country debt would have been thought an improbable international economic issue. Even the most astute observers of the global economy did not contemplate the emergence of the less developed countries (LDCs) as large-scale borrowers in international capital markets. But by 1976-77, developing country debt had taken on sizable and unprecedented proportions. Moreover, it was accompanied by unprecedented controversy.

The immediate concern, especially within the framework of a "stagflationary" world economy, was whether the high indebtedness of developing countries was dangerous to the solvency and stability of the lending banks and thereby the international financial system. Thus, developing country creditworthiness, bank risk analysis, and the size of LDC debt became central issues of debate. Those who were not so pessimistic - notably creditor bankers - hastened to assure and persuade those with alarmist views that no "debt problem" existed. Indeed, no major developing country had defaulted, nor did a massive chain reaction of defaults occur.

Out of this controversy grew many articles, pamphlets, and pages of congressional testimony. But few books, if any, comprehensively examined this phenomenon. Developing Country Debt attempts to fill this gap. This collection of articles presents a variety of views and perspectives on the topic of developing country debt. As the biographical notes for this book point out, the contributors have academic, business, and government backgrounds. Many have been participants in the operational and policy processes related to LDC debt. More than gathering a variety of views, however, we also have assembled serious analyses of LDC debt and presented the range of proposed solutions to debt servicing problems.

Our chosen route has been to begin with an overview,

followed by disaggregated country analyses and a review of proposed solutions to debt relief and their constraints. We conclude with an examination of the debt issue as it relates to the world economy and public policy.

First, in Part I, Neil J. McMullen presents historical perspectives on developing nations' debt starting with the debt experiences of the now developed countries prior to World War I. He then reviews the external debt picture of the 1920s and 1930s, and brings the debt experience to post-World War II. Next, Robert Solomon provides an aggregate analysis of recent LDC debt since the 1973 OPEC price increases and of the developing countries' abilities to carry debt. His conclusions are optimistic. Developing countries' ventures into the Eurocurrency market and the consequent ballooning of private debt are then presented by Marilyn J. Seiber. And, finally, in this section, Charles S. Ganoe offers a banker's view on the myths of debt.

Part II provides a disaggregated analysis of debt and is introduced by Ganoe's commentary on risk analysis - a process, he advises, that is more than a numbers exercise. Then a series of case studies reports the economic and political conditions of selected countries with substantial debt and varying degrees of economic difficulty. The analysis of the Philippines by Seiber and of Jamaica by J. Daniel O'Flaherty demonstrates the wide differences that can exist among debtor nations; and the "package picture" of Turkey, Portugal, Peru, and Egypt by Robert N. McCauley points out the often critical role of the IMF when debt problems, among others, arise.

Part III follows with an examination of proposed solutions to debt burden problems by Seiber, and an examination by Jane D'Arista of United States congressional attitudes toward developing nations and United States economic assistance to them. D'Arista's appraisal indicates that congressional commitment to support developing countries' objectives has not strengthened in recent years. Third in this section is Carl R. Neu's response to the proposal that the International Monetary Fund take on greater direct responsibilities - perhaps as a lender of last resort - when emergency debt problems occur. He makes clear that neither the IMF's purpose nor resources would enable it to assume such a function.

Finally, the concluding section, Part IV, places the analysis of developing country debt in a broader, global context. First, Robert W. Russell presents the differing perspectives on debt of the borrowing LDCs, the lending banks, and the national interest of the United States. William A. Noellert then assesses debt in a framework of the global economy and international adjustment problems rather than the traditional framework of "development" or "financial stability." Last, Lawrence G. Franko concludes by examining what could be done about LDC debt in the context of global problems of growth, trade, and energy.

One fact will become apparent to the reader. The current and increasing magnitude of developing countries' external indebtedness has become an important international policy issue with major implications for both developed and developing countries. The World Bank estimates that developing countries' demand for external financing will increase from $63 billion in 1975 to $276 billion in 1985, and half of these funds would be used in repayment of loans and interest to developed countries. As various contributors to the book point out, such external financial requirements have significant effects on policies concerned with such issue as trade, economic growth, multilateral financial institutions, resource and technology transfers, and domestic regulation of international banking activities.

The specific stimulus to gathering the collection of works contained in this book came from the International Studies Association which asked the editors to organize a panel on developing country debt for the association's Annual Meetings in February 1978. Thanks are therefore due to the International Studies Association for triggering the actual production of this work. Also, our thanks and appreciation go to the contributors for lending their expertise and efforts to this project.

As the reader will see, countries always have borrowed externally to supplement their capital resources. However, in recent years developing country debt has come to public attention because of its magnitude, rate of growth, concentration, the condition of the world economy, and the increased participation of LDCs in international fora. The exact amount of debt is not known - as varying figures throughout these pages illustrate. Yet it is widely agreed that the economies and policies of the industrial countries, the petroleum pricing policies of OPEC members, and the character of growth and development in the developing countries will largely determine how much debt is too much.

Lawrence G. Franko
Geneva, Switzerland

Marilyn J. Seiber
Washington, D.C.

January 1979

I

An Aggregate Analysis of Developing Country Debt

1 Historical Perspectives on Developing Nations' Debt*

Neil J. McMullen

THE EXPERIENCE OF THE UNITED STATES, CANADA, AUSTRALIA AND NEW ZEALAND IN THE ERA BEFORE WORLD WAR I

It is sometimes forgotten that foreign investment played a large role in the economic development of the United States in the nineteenth century. Canada, Australia and New Zealand are additional examples of successful development, and these countries were even more dependent on foreign investment inflows than the United States. Typically, a developing nation lacks capital relative to its endowment of labor and natural resources, including arable land. Under these circumstances, successful economic development along a noncommunist pattern has implied the import of capital from abroad and the accumulation of foreign debts.

Estimates of the foreign indebtedness of the United States in the nineteenth century have been made and, when related to the size of the economy incurring the debt, are similar to the debt levels of many twentieth century developing countries. For the United States, total foreign indebtedness as a percentage of GNP is estimated to have been 40 percent in the 1830s,(1) 24 percent in 1869, 20 percent in 1899, 18 percent in 1914, and 8.5 percent in 1929.(2) This is gross indebtedness and, if foreign liabilities are offset by foreign assets, the

---

*From "Perspectives of Developing Nations' Debts" (Washington, D.C.: Committee on Changing International Realities, National Planning Association), forthcoming. Printed with permission.

percentages decline more sharply after 1869. Net indebtedness as a proportion of GNP is estimated to have been 15 percent in 1899, 10 percent in 1914, and -7.9 percent (foreign assets exceeding liabilities) in 1929.(3) This sharp decline in the net foreign indebtedness of the United States was a result of successful development and indicates the increasing financial maturity of the United States. By the end of the nineteenth century, the United States was lending abroad and repaying foreign debt faster than new foreign capital was flowing in. The big turnaround in America's foreign position occurred during World War I. In 1914, foreign obligations totaled $7.2 billion, with assets equal to $3.5 billion for a net liability of $3.7 billion. By 1919, this situation had reversed itself; assets rose to $7.0 billion, liabilities fell to $4.0 billion, and the net position was $3.0 billion of foreign holdings.(4)

Foreign loans to the United States in the 1800s were not without risk. Though data is fragmentary and incomplete, it is well known that there were periods in which American states, local governments and private borrowers defaulted on foreign loans in sizable numbers. Large borrowings by American states for canal and railroad construction in the 1830s were defaulted in 1841 and 1842 as the price of cotton collapsed and foreign exchange was not available to make debt payments. Nine states in all defaulted but, by 1845, with a revival of cotton prices, all but two states resumed payment, effecting settlement on all or part of their debts.(5) In the 1870s and 1890s, there were some defaults on foreign bonds by railway companies and municipalities and, as late as 1915, a French loan to the New Haven Railroad was in default. On balance, however, foreign investors as a whole derived gains from their American investments that made their losses through default seem insignificant.(6)

In reviewing the trends of investment flows into Canada and Australia, the pattern is similar, but the timing is somewhat different. Foreign capital flows into these areas reached a peak in the years prior to World War I. The total amount of British foreign capital invested in the Dominions rose from $11 million in 1830, to $63 million in 1854, $450 million in 1870 and $7,400 million in 1914.(7) Of this, $2,778 million had been invested in Canada up to 1914. Foreign capital invested in Canada totaled $1,200 million in 1900, $2,480 million in 1910 and $3,700 million in 1913.(8) About 20 percent came from the United States, 75 percent from the United Kingdom and 5 percent from elsewhere.

Comparing estimates of Canadian GNP with net foreign indebtedness in the years of the twentieth century shows a very high level of debt. In 1900, net foreign debt totaled 114 percent of Canadian GNP; in 1910, this ratio was 111 percent; and, by 1920, the proportion of debt to GNP was 88 percent. By comparison, the figure had dropped to 42.7 percent in

1960. These figures are higher than those for the United States, indicating a greater dependence on foreign capital inflows throughout the Canadian growth process.

Australia and New Zealand followed the Canadian pattern of economic development with strong emphasis on foreign capital inflows. Up to 1914, Australia and New Zealand had together received some $2,435 million(9) in foreign investments, which represented about $400 of external debt per person. The comparable figure for Canada in 1914 was about $500 per person.

These figures shows that Canada, Australia and New Zealand were heavily dependent on foreign capital for their development and growth in the early 1900s. The ratio of external debt to GNP exceeded 100 percent for Canada and was probably close to 100 percent for Australia and New Zealand. By comparison, none of the key nonoil developing countries had a ratio of foreign debt to GNP that exceeded 45 percent in 1976. Two important qualifications must be considered. The first relates to the external debt that is being compared; the Canadian, Australian and New Zealand figures include direct investment in local firms, whereas the external debt of the nonoil developing nations generally does not. Thus, there is an incongruity in definition which would reduce the difference between the ratios compared. A second important difference relates to the nature of the economies being compared. Canada, Australia and New Zealand were sparsely populated lands with vast amounts of underutilized natural resources and unsettled arable lands in the early 1900s. Development strategies would be expected to be more capital-intensive for these countries than for nations that had large supplies of labor available for employment in mining, manufacturing and agriculture. From this perspective, it is not surprising that, relative to output, external capital was larger for the newly settled British Dominions in the early twentieth century than for the developing nations in the last half of this century.

The experience of the British Dominions shows that very high foreign debt levels can be sustained and are compatible with long-term economic growth. Where foreign loans are utilized productively, where their repayment is properly planned, and where world trade continues to expand, historical experience shows that it is possible to service very high levels of external debt. Nonetheless, there are enough important differences between historical events and current conditions to make past experience an imperfect predictor of the features.

Experience prior to World War I indicates that, in an expanding world economy, foreign lending is both remunerative to the creditor and productive for the borrower. There are clearly risks to be faced and, on occasion, repayment may be tardy or partial but, over the long haul, there are tremendous gains to be made by both sides.

FOREIGN DEBTS IN THE 1920s AND 1930s

After World War I, the United States became the world's leading foreign investor. Net foreign assets held by Americans rose from $3.0 billion in 1919 to $6.7 billion in 1924, $8.1 billion in 1929, and then declined to $7.4 billion in 1935. The interwar period was a time of great financial and economic dislocation and provides the most recent experience of large-scale defaults of foreign debts. After the buildup of foreign lending that occurred in the 1920s, the economic depression and sharp decline in world trade in the early 1930s resulted in widespread defaults by Latin American and Eastern European nations.

By January 1932, the problem was evident as defaults on a total of $2.6 billion had already occurred.(10) It was noted that the "income of every government has been drastically decreased, although the debt charges have remained stationary."(11) Table 1.1 demonstrates the magnitude of the

Table 1.1. Debt-Service Ratios

	Percent of Government Revenues	Percent of Export Earnings			
	1931	1930	1931	1932	1933
Argentina	36.9	18.2	22.5	27.6	30.2*
Bolivia	72.7*	13.5	24.5*	50.0*	38.5*
Brazil	25.0*	23.5	28.4*	41.0*	45.1*
Chile	32.2*	18.0	32.9*	102.6*	81.9*
Colombia	32.0	14.0	15.6	21.8*	29.6*
Cuba	NA**	6.1	13.4	18.1	22.4*
Peru	34.3*	9.5	16.3*	21.4*	21.7*
Uruguay	NA**	9.7	22.4*	36.3*	31.3*

*Years of partial or full default on outstanding foreign loans.
**NA = not available.

Sources: Max Winkler and Maxwell S. Stewart, "Recent Defaults of Government Loans," Foreign Policy Reports 7, no. 22 (January 6, 1932): 397; and Dragoslav Avramovic, Debt Servicing Capacity and Postwar Growth in International Indebtedness (Baltimore: Johns Hopkins University Press, 1958), p. 194.

problems faced by various Latin American nations. In 1931, estimated debt service costs for principal and interest payments were running at approximately one-third of government revenues in Latin America, and totaled 72.7 percent of Bolivian government revenues.

Table 1.1 shows that, as a proportion of export earnings, debt-service costs rose sharply from 1930. This was principally because of declines in the prices of the commodities exported by these nations. Prices of coffee fell from 18.5 cents per pound in 1929 to six cents in 1931. Tin prices dropped 55 percent, from 45 cents a pound to 20 cents a pound in 1931. Sugar prices halved, going from six cents a pound in 1929 to three cents a pound in 1933. A general index of primary products indicated that prices fell 60 percent from 1929 to 1931.(12) The result was a devastating decline in the value of exports for the countries which specialized in the export of primary products. From 1928-29 to 1932-33, the value of Chile's exports fell 80 percent; Bolivia, Cuba and Peru suffered export declines of 70 percent and Argentina and Brazil had declines in excess of 60 percent.(13)

In a period of falling prices, "the burden of debts and accrued interest is much greater in terms of commodities or services than was originally intended" and debtors in effect are repaying much more than the value they received.(14) Due to depressed volume and falling prices, the value of world trade fell from $34.3 billion in 1929 to $27.9 billion in 1930, $20.00 billion in 1931, and $13.5 billion in 1932.(15) In such circumstances, governments lacked the foreign exchange to repay their debts, and, even where debtor entities set aside local currency in the amount of their obligations, there were no United States dollars available to fund the external payments.

The key elements in the series of defaults by developing countries in the early 1930s were the collapse in world trade, the decline in the prices of their exports, and the resulting unavailability of foreign currency to meet external debt payments. A crucial factor in these defaults was the rapidity with which export earnings declined and debt servicing ratios rose. It is not just a high debt-service ratio that makes a default more likely, but a sharp and unexpected rise in the ratio. Estimates indicate that, in the early 1900s, Canada, Australia and Argentina were able to service higher debt burdens than those which were in default in the 1930s.(16) In the earlier era, the debt burden had built up slowly, and was planned for by the borrowing governments and firms. Frequently, these investments were self-financing and self-adjusting in that they represented ownership in an exporting enterprise. The sales of the operation generated the needed foreign exchange and, during unprofitable years, no return on the investment was expected. This resolved problems of obtaining foreign exchange and meeting payments during cyclical downturns that proved insoluble for many debtor nations in the 1930s.

The key elements that led to defaults in the 1930s are largely absent from the world economic scene in the 1970s. The world economy is not in depression and continues to recover from the sharp downturn experienced in 1974-75. World trade has grown in value each year throughout the 1970s, even if the exports of the petroleum-producing countries are excluded. Table 1.2 presents the annual figures for world trade growth from 1970 to 1976.

Table 1.2. Exports in the 1970s
(in billions of US$)

Year	Exports of Non-LDCs	Exports of Nonoil LDCs	Exports of Oil LDCs	World Exports
1970	228.0	35.9	18.3	282.2
1971	255.1	37.2	24.1	316.4
1972	303.2	44.7	28.8	376.7
1973	417.5	67.4	39.1	524.0
1974	556.1	97.7	118.1	771.9
1975	592.2	93.4	109.4	795.0
1976	656.7	118.3	131.8	906.8
	Annual Growth Rate (percent)			
1970-1976	19.3	22.0	48.5	26.3
1974-1976	8.7	10.0	5.6	8.4

Source: International Monetary Fund, International Financial Statistics, various issues.

Much of this increase is inflationary rather than real growth, but the effect is to put foreign exchange in the hands of exporters and to reduce the burden of past debts. Thus, the key elements that led to defaults by developing countries in the 1930s are not only absent in the 1970s, they are reversed. The value of world trade has not declined, rather, it has grown by leaps and bounds, more than trebling in seven years. The value of oil exports has grown fastest of all since 1970, but the exports of the nonoil developing countries have expanded faster than exports of the developed countries. Prices of primary agricultural and mineral products have not generally declined as they did in the 1930s. The price of exports from nonoil developing countries has increased 95 percent(17) since 1970 on average. There can be little doubt that price deflation, a key element in the widespread defaults of the 1930s, is working in reverse in the 1970s.

Another important difference between the 1930s and today is the existence of international institutions - such as the International Monetary Fund, the World Bank, and the regional development banks - that were absent during the depression era. These institutions provide a number of functions, which make it less likely that debt servicing will become an overwhelming problem for a developing nation. They provide concessionary loans and grants to the less creditworthy nations, with the result that debt costs are lower for these countries. The international financial institutions make foreign exchange inflows more stable than when the inflows depended entirely on export sales, and they put international purchasing power in the hands of buyers helping to stabilize demand for goods and services in international markets. These institutions also assist developing countries with technical advice on both specific projects and the monetary and fiscal management of the development process. In sum, the international institutions provide a broad range of services which assist developing nations in acquiring and utilizing resources in the most efficient way and thereby make defaults much less likely in the current period than they were in the interwar years.

During the post-World War II era, institutions, mechanisms and procedures have developed which allow debt payments to be rescheduled without a default being declared. Since the 1940s at least 16 developing countries have faced serious debt problems at one time or another. Between 1965 and 1972, 26 multilateral reschedulings were negotiated.(18) The framework within which such negotiations take place consists of a group of lenders meeting with a borrower and working out a repayment program that is as satisfactory as possible to all concerned. These reschedulings have come to be known as "Paris Club" meetings, and provide a forum for discussion, conciliation and action that was totally lacking in the 1930s.

Short of a full default a developing country with debt problems has a variety of possible alternatives to consider. These include continuing with partial or delayed payments, arranging a rescheduling of debt payments, or requesting new loans which in effect stretch out the repayment of principal without having to negotiate a full rescheduling.(19) In contrast, during the 1930s, when the lenders were principally small bondholders and no international forums for debt negotiation existed, full or partial default was the only alternative to immediate payment.

It is widely recognized that the last few years were very different from the 1930s. Borrowers are much more creditworthy, the dollar value of world trade is growing rapidly, the dangers of widespread default are well understood, the international financial institutions provide a range of services for developing countries that make defaults less likely, and the mechanisms for debt rescheduling are in place, giving debtor countries a range of alternatives more attractive than outright default. Thus, a comparison of the early 1930s with the current era reveals more differences than similarities.

INTERNATIONAL INDEBTEDNESS IN THE POST-WORLD WAR II ERA

The years from 1946 to 1977 can conveniently be divided into three periods for purposes of analyzing international capital flows: 1) the reconstruction period from 1946 to about 1950, 2) the growth and development period from the early 1950s until 1974, and 3) the post-OPEC period from 1974 to the present. The first period was dominated by efforts to reconstruct the European economy. Between 1946 and 1950, the Western European nations received $16.4 billion in public grants and $14.4 billion in public loans(20) primarily from the United States. Over the same period, countries outside Europe and North America (including Australia and Japan) received $5.5 billion in public grants and $3.0 billion in public loans. (21) This represented gross payments, with offsets on loan repayments reducing the net flows. The net impact of public lending between 1945 and 1950 is shown in Table 1.3. For the "developing" countries, there was very little change from 1945 to 1950 and, for Japan, Australia and South Africa, repayments exceeded new loans. After 1950, net lending to Westerns Europe became negative as reconstruction neared completion and repayments began on past loans.

During the period of reconstruction, international indebtedness did not become a problem. The data in Table 1.3 shows that, from 1945 until 1950, the net public indebtedness of the developing nations rose only slightly from $1.8 billion to $2.1 billion. Thereafter, developing countries' net public debt began to grow but, by 1955, it totaled only $4.2 billion. In real terms - i.e., adjusting for inflation in the dollar values of goods - this debt was only $2.8 billion in 1945 prices, so there was little growth in the real indebtedness of the developing countries and certainly no debt problem.(22)

The net public indebtedness of the European countries increased very rapidly, rising from $3.6 billion in 1945 to $12.1 billion in 1948.(23) Repayments more or less offset new loans through 1955, when the debt level was $11.7 billion. European indebtedness never became particularly worrisome as it leveled off after three years of sharp growth from 1947 to

Table 1.3. Estimates of External Debt (in billions of US$)

			Developing Countries			
			Avramovic	National Planning Association	World Bank	
Year	Western Europe	Japan, Australia and South Africa		Estimates	All	Nonoil Exporters
1945	3.6	2.3	1.8			
1950	12.3	1.8	2.1			
1955	11.7	2.4	4.2	6.8		
1960				13.1		
1967				33.9	35.8	31.4
1971					59.9	50.0
1972					68.9	56.8
1973					86.2	66.8
1974					100.2	82.3
1975					121.0	100.0

Source: Data for 1945-1955 from Avramovic pp. 162-3. NPA series is Bitterman (see Overseas Development Council) adjusted by 0.70. World Bank data is <u>World Debt Tables I</u>, September 1977, vol. I, p. 78.

1950. Thereafter, European net public debt declined until it was essentially repaid in the early 1960s. The European economy required a ten-year injection of capital and then was able to achieve self-sustained growth. This growth combined with inflation to reduce the burden of repayment. Another important element in reducing the debt burden for the European nations in the 1950s was the large concessionary element in the capital injection due to the emphasis on grants in the Marshall Plan. In 1946 and 1947, loans to Europe totaled $9.0 billion, while grants amounted to only $3.5 billion; starting in 1948, grants exceeded loans, reaching a total of $19.5 billion; as compared with loans of $9.9 billion for the eight years through 1955.(24) After 1955, the role of foreign public grants and loans became quite small, and was replaced by European domestic savings and private direct investment from the United States.

The second period of the post-World War II era in the

international economy is marked by a tremendous growth in world trade and world income together with increasing emphasis on using public capital for the development of Asian, African and Latin American countries. The period of growth and development began in the early 1950s and lasted until the 1970s. The European nations continued to receive sizable inflows of private capital from abroad but began to export public and private capital of their own to the developing nations. During the years between the end of the Korean War and end of the Vietnam War, the United States directed its efforts to underwriting the growth of the international trading systems and assisting the developing nations with public capital flows. During the 20 years from 1953 to 1973, the developing nations received $75 billion(25) in public grants and net public loans of $81.1 billion from the developed nations. World trade increased from $75.7 billion in 1953 to $524.2 billion in 1973,(26) an average annual rate of 10 percent. The result was an unprecedented growth in the world economy with the middle-income nations growing the most rapidly. Of the 25 countries with a 1972 per capita income in excess of $1,500, 72 percent grew faster than the 4.2 percent annual rate of the United States between 1960 and 1972, whereas 85 percent of the nations with 1972 per capita incomes between $100 and $1,500 grew faster than the United States.(27)

An unusual confluence of factors - including the availability of low-cost energy, a stable international political order, the liberalization of trade and the expansion of markets, and the relatively unhindered flow of public capital to developing nations and private capital to Europe - combined to create a generation of growth and development in the world economy.

During this period, the indebtedness of the developing nations increased substantially. Table 1.3 indicates an increase in outstanding developing country debt from a level of $2.1 billion in 1950 to $121.0 billion in 1975. There is no single series which specifies the debt level of the developing nations for the entire post-World War II era; consequently, three series have been spliced together in Table 1.3. As the earlier estimates probably underestimated the total debt, developing country debt for 1950 was probably in the range of $2 to $4 billion.

Another factor that must be remembered is the emergence of most of the developing world as nations between 1950 and 1967. In the early years of this period, there were fewer independent nations in existence and thus able to borrow internationally. In the main, however, the bulk of the debt represents increased emphasis on accelerating the development process by the lenders as well as the borrowers. An indication of the increase in indebtedness for 22 developing nations over the period from 1953 to 1973 is given in Table

1.4. This presents the "debt-service ratio" - the ratio of public debt-service payments (principal plus interest on public external debt) to export earnings - a key indicator of an economy's ability to service external debt. The data for the early 1950's show debt service as a proportion of gross current-account earnings, including interest on foreign investments and remittances by overseas workers (factor service payments), whereas the data for 1973 exclude factor service payments, including only the exports of goods and nonfactor services, such as travel, insurance, shipping and financial

Table 1.4. Ratios of Public Debt Service Payments

	1952-1954 Gross Current Account and Earnings	1967 Goods and Nonfactor Services	1973
Argentina (1955)	2.0	25.9	18.3
Brazil	4.9	16.0	13.9
Colombia	3.8	14.2	13.0
Chile	6.7	12.6	11.0
Ecuador	3.1	6.7	7.5
El Salvador	0.5	2.6	5.3
Ethiopia	2.5	9.7	6.4
Guatemala	0.3	7.4	3.8
Haiti	1.8	n.a.	n.a.
Honduras	0.1	2.1	3.9
India	0.8	24.9	20.1
Mexico	5.2	23.8	25.2
Nicaragua	4.0	6.4	17.8
Pakistan	0.2	16.7	16.1
Panama	1.3	2.9	16.4
Paraguay	5.5	7.4	9.5
Peru	3.0	11.1	22.8
Philippines (1955)	2.2	7.2	6.3
Sri Lanka		3.5	12.6
(Ceylon)	0.4		
Thailand	1.0	3.6	2.6
Uruguay	3.3	17.0	30.1
Zaire		2.4	7.0
(Belgian Congo)	1.2		

n.a. Not available.

Source: Avramovic, pp. 44-45.

services. However, this variation in definition is not important as few of the developing countries had large factor service incomes in the 1950s. Mexico and the Philippines are two possible exceptions and their debt service ratios for the 1952-1954 period may be understated slightly.

The picture that emerges from Table 1.4 is one of a sizable increase in the debt assumed by all 22 of the developing nations between the early 1950s and 1973. The smaller nations do not seem to have borrowed as extensively over this period but, without exception, these developing countries have increased their indebtedness faster than they have increased their export earnings.

During the period of growth and development lasting from the early 1950s until 1973, the debt of the developing world increased substantially but, for a variety of reasons, it was not felt that indebtedness was a serious pervasive problem. Debt levels in 1950 were very low and part of the observed borrowing was clearly a return to a more normal pattern that had been interrupted by two world wars and the subsequent dislocations. A comparison of debt-service ratios in 1973 with those shown in Table 1.1 shows that, by historical standards, developing country debt was high, but in general not excessive. A comparison of 1967 and 1973 indicates that debt-service ratios fell for 10 of the 22 countries, including most of large ones. Incomes, exports and prices were rising in the early 1970s, reducing the real burden of debt on the developing nations and enabling them to raise living standards, invest and repay past loans. Continued net flows of foreign investment were forthcoming from governments, financial institutions and business corporations in the developed countries. Finally, the international financial system had evolved to the point where countries facing repayment difficulties could work together with the lenders and the international institutions to resolve problems in a mutually satisfactory way. Between 1956 and 1973, some 15 developing nations faced debt-repayment difficulties that were serious enough to lead to multilateral renegotiations of debt payments.(28) The causes of these difficulties were generally related to problems specific to particular countries, such as excessive short-term indebtedness, a sharp deterioration in the terms of trade, insufficient export earnings, and other particular factors. The experience gained in handling these separate cases and the institutional framework now available provide an important alternative for those countries that will face difficulties in the years ahead, and lend stability to the system of international development finance.

NOTES

1. "Cleveland and Britain," New York Times (Financial Section), Sunday, May 29, 1977, p. 1.
2. Cleona Lewis, America's Stake in International Investments (Washington, D.C.: The Brookings Institution, 1938), p. 560 (debt data); U.S. Department of Commerce, Historical Statistics of the United States September 1975, p. 224 (GNP data).
3. Lewis, America's State, p. 605.
4. Ibid., p. 168.
5. Ibid., pp. 25-26.
6. Ibid., p. 168.
7. A. G. Kenwood and A. L. Lougheed, The Growth of the International Economy, 1820-1960 (London: George Allen and Unwin, 1971), p. 43.
8. Jacob Viner, Canada's Balance of International Indebtedness, 1900-1913 (Cambridge, Mass.: Harvard University Press, 1924), p. 299.
9. Kenwood and Lougheed, Growth of International Economy, p. 42.
10. Max Winkler and Maxwell S. Stewart, "Recent Defaults of Government Loans," Foreign Policy Reports 7 (January 6, 1932): 403.
11. Ibid., p. 397.
12. Charles P. Kindleberger, The World in Depression, 1929-1939 (Berkeley: University of California Press, 1973), pp. 88, 188.
13. Ibid., p. 191.
14. Winkler and Stewart, "Recent Defaults," p. 396.
15. Kindleberger, World in Depression, p. 172.
16. Dragoslav Avramovic, Debt Servicing Capacity and Postwar Growth In International Indebtedness (Baltimore: Johns Hopkins University Press, 1958), p. 194.
17. International Monetary Fund (IMF), International Financial Statistics, various issues (see line 74d of the various country tables).
18. Gordon W. Smith, "The External Debt Prospects of the Nonoil-Exporting Developing Countries," New International Economic Order Research Project (Washington, D.C.: Overseas Development Council, Summer 1977), p. 15.
19. For a fuller discussion of these points, see David O. Beim, "Rescuing the LDC's," Foreign Affairs 55 (July 1977): 721-27.
20. Avramovic, Debt Servicing Capacity, p. 6.
21. Ibid.
22. Using United States GNP deflators for 1945 and 1955 as price indices.
23. Avramovic, Debt Servicing Capacity, p. 162.
24. Ibid., p. 6.

25. OECD, p. 253.
26. IMF, International Financial Statistics, Annual Data Supplement, February issues for various years.
27. New International Realities 1 (July 1976): 9.
28. Neal P. Cohen, "Econometric Debt Early Warning Systems," Consultants Paper for U.S. Treasury, August 10, 1926, p. 4.

2 A Quantitative Perspective on the Debt of Developing Countries*

Robert Solomon

Since 1973, when the price of oil was raised very sharply, developing countries have incurred heavy debts. This paper looks at their ability to carry debt, first by examining the balance of payments and external borrowing of all developing countries that are not oil producers in general. It then focuses on a group of ten advanced developing countries that account for the bulk of the borrowing from private sources that has given rise to widely expressed concern.

The analysis that follows leads to an optimistic conclusion about the capacity of the ten countries not only to carry their present debt but to expand it. It does not follow that decision makers in private financial markets will come to the same conclusion. Thus attention is given also to supplementing private lending with resources supplied by the International Monetary Fund (IMF). Furthermore, questions are raised about what could go wrong - what international developments could make the outlook less rosy for the heavy debtors.

---

*Originally published by the author as "A Perspective on the Debt of Developing Countries," in Brookings Papers on Economic Activity, Arthur M. Okun and George L. Perry (eds.) Vol. 2, 1977.

The author wishes to thank George Henry Gonan Ohlin, and Edwin Truman; the discussants Allan Greenspan and John H. Karekin; and Arthur M. Okun and George L. Perry, the Brookings Papers editors for helpful suggestions on earlier versions of this chapter.

THE ENLARGEMENT OF CURRENT SURPLUSES AND DEFICITS SINCE 1973

The current-account surplus for countries of the Organization of Petroleum Exporting Countries (OPEC) and the corresponding deficit of oil-importing countries is being financed in large part by the creation of international debt. The OPEC surplus (on goods, services, and private transfers, the concept used throughout this paper) increased from $6 billion in 1973 to $67 billion in 1974; it fell to $35 billion during the recession of 1975, rose again to $41 billion in 1976, and is expected to fall only slightly in 1977.(1)

The members of OPEC have been unable to sustain the rapid increases in imports of 1974 and 1975. Whereas the dollar value of OPEC imports rose about 64 percent in 1974 and 65 percent in 1975, the increase was only 24 percent in 1976, according to data from the International Monetary Fund. As is well known, the OPEC members with the largest output and largest oil reserves - those on the Arabian peninsula - have a limited capacity to absorb increased imports. However, as other OPEC members move into current-account deficit, the aggregate surplus of OPEC will decline even if Saudi Arabia and its immediate neighbors continue to run large surpluses. Just when the OPEC surplus will disappear and give way to deficit is uncertain. For the purposes of this paper it is assumed that the surplus will persist, probably on a declining scale, for a number of years. Consequently, the process of international debt creation will also go on for some time. As long as the imports of OPEC members as a group fall short of their export proceeds, a corresponding deficit must be incurred by the rest of the world. Unless they are directed at cutting oil consumption without depressing total output, efforts to depress this deficit will tend to reduce the aggregate demand either of the countries making the effort or of their trading partners.

Conceivably, these surpluses and deficits could be financed without debt creation. The OPEC and other surplus countries could acquire direct investments or equities in the deficit countries; or the IMF could issue special drawing rights (SDRs) in a volume large enough to permit the financing of deficits by countries that would otherwise exhaust their reserves if they did not borrow; or the countries in surplus could make grants to the countries in deficit. In fact, OPEC and other surplus countries have made some direct investment and purchased equities since 1973. And the OPEC group has provided some grants - mainly to military allies - while the industrial countries have continued to make development assistance available partly on a grant basis. To a major extent, however, the imbalances have been financed by borrowing on the part of countries in deficit and by the acquisition of securities and bank deposits on the part of countries in surplus.

It is also conceivable that the countries in surplus, while accumulating repayable claims, would lend directly to countries in deficit. If this practice were followed, the intermediary role of banks would be eliminated and, with it, the concern that has arisen about the ability of banks to continue this role. But, it seems clear, the countries in surplus have preferred to place most of their growing claims on the rest of the world in what they regard as secure and relatively liquid financial assets: United States government securities, other official and private securities in developed countries, and bank deposits. Countries in deficit, in turn, have issued securities in these markets and have borrowed from these banks.

Under the circumstances, questions have arisen about the debt burden that is accumulating, especially on the part of developing countries. Though less subject to publicity, many - in fact most - industrial countries have also been heavy borrowers. Only a few industrial countries - West Germany, Japan, the Netherlands, and Switzerland - have current surpluses; but they are sizable, totaling almost $17 billion in 1976. As a result, the rest of the world has incurred a current deficit equal to the OPEC surplus plus the surplus of these few countries. As noted, a large part of that deficit has been financed by borrowing. Net external borrowing by nonoil developing countries in 1974 and 1975 financed about 70 percent of their combined current-account deficit. In 1976, these countries borrowed an amount greater than their current-account deficit and added substantially to their reserves. In the three-year period, about 80 percent of the borrowings were on a long-term basis, about half from official sources and half from private sources. Short-term borrowing (less than one-year maturity) from private creditors, at about $5 billion in 1974-75, accounted for about one-fifth of total borrowing.(2) Of the total debt of nonoil developing countries outstanding at the end of 1976 ($140 billion), all but about $20 billion was either borrowed by official entities or officially guaranteed.(3)

This process is likely to continue and it is easy to demonstrate that as long as OPEC members in the aggregate remain in surplus, funds will be available from the proceeds of that surplus to finance the deficits of oil-importing countries in the aggregate. The OPEC surplus provides the means for its own financing.

Such aggregative analysis leaves many observers uneasy. Isn't it possible, they ask, that the growing debt of some countries will threaten to become unmanageable (a concept to be examined below) and that lenders - those who are intermediating between the OPEC and other surplus countries on the one hand and the large number of deficit countries on the other - will stop lending or be left with bad debts? This type of question tends to focus on those nonoil developing countries that have been borrowing heavily from banks.

The sizable increase in debt by developing countries in recent years is a more complex matter than the financing of the OPEC surplus and the corresponding "oil deficits" of oil-importing counties. As noted above, the nonoil developing countries increased their reserves in 1976, and they did so by more than they increased their debt to private creditors. Furthermore, their enlarged deficits have results not only from the increase in oil prices but also from the impact of the recession and subsequent slow recovery in industrial countries. Real output in the industrial nations was unchanged in 1974 and fell 1 percent in 1975, while in nonoil developing countries output increased 5.2 percent in 1974 and 3.4 percent in 1975 (see Table 2.1).

Table 2.1. Growth of Output, Trade, and Debt, Nonoil Developing Countries, Pre-1973 and 1973-76 (percent)

Growth Item	Pre-1973	1973	1974	1975	1976
Real GNP	6.1(a)	6.7	5.2	3.4	5.1
Exports	6.5(b)	8.0	4.5	0.0	13.0
Imports	5.5(b)	15.0	8.0	-6.0	1.5
External public and publicly guaranteed debt (in 1970 prices)	9.8(a)	-11.4	-10.7	25.4	8.1

(a) Compound annual rate of growth, 1967-72.
(b) Compound annual rate of growth, 1962-72.
Sources: International Monetary Fund, Annual Report of the Executive Directors for the Fiscal Year Ended April 30, 1977, pp. 7, 9, except the last row, which is computed from row 10, Table 2.2, below.

As a result of these and other influences, the current deficit of nonoil developing countries increased from $11 billion in 1973, to $30 billion in 1974, and to $38 billion in 1975; in 1976, the deficit declined to $26 billion and it is estimated at about the same level in 1977 (see Table 2.2).

Table 2.2. Selected Debt-Related Data on Nonoil Developing Countries, 1967 and 1971-76(a) (in billions of dollars)

Debt-Related Item	1967	1971	1972	1973	1974	1975	1976
1. Trade deficit (fob)	4.6(b)	8.6	7.0	6.6	22.8	29.1	15.5
2. Exports to OPEC	n.a.	n.a.	n.a.	2.3	4.7	6.4	6.1
3. Imports from OPEC	n.a.	n.a.	n.a.	8.1	23.1	22.8	25.9
4. Trade deficit with OPEC	n.a.	n.a.	n.a.	5.8	18.4	16.4	19.8
5. Current-account deficit (c)	7.1(b)	11.4	9.2	10.9	29.5	38.2	25.8
6. Total external public and publicly guaranteed debt(d)	28.7	47.3	53.8	63.5	77.2	94.7	116.1
7. Private nonguaranteed debt(d)	n.a.	n.a.	n.a.	15.0	18.8	20.9	24.0
8. Total external debt(d)	n.a.	n.a.	n.a.	78.5	96.0	115.6	140.1
9. External debt to private creditors(d)	7.8	n.a.	16.2	35.9	46.9	58.2	71.9
10. Total external public and publicly guaranteed debt in 1970 prices(d)	31.9	47.3	50.8	45.0	40.2	50.4	54.5
11. Total external debt in 1970 prices(d)	n.a.	n.a.	n.a.	55.7	50.0	61.5	65.8
12. Total reserves	12.2(b)	15.8	21.6	29.6	32.5	31.1	42.7

(a) Annual or year-end data.
(b) Annual average, 1968-70.
(c) Goods, services, and private transfers.
(d) Debt with maturity of more than one year.
n.a. Not available.

Sources: Row 1 - IMF, International Financial Statistics 29 (August 1976), and IMF, Annual Report, 1977, p. 15; rows 2-4 - United Nations, Monthly Bulletin of Statistics, Special Table C, August 1976, and June 1977; row 5 - IMF, Annual Report, 1976, p. 20 and 1977, p. 15; rows 6-8 - World Bank, World Debt Tables 1 (October 31, 1976):31, 33; and vol. 2, country pages; and other World Bank sources (excludes advanced Mediterranean countries other than Turkey and Yugoslavia); row 9 - same as row 8 except that data before 1973 also exclude Turkey and Yugoslavia; rows 10-11 - rows 6 and 8 divided by export price index (excluding petroleum) of developing market economies, from United Nations, Monthly Bulletin of Statistics, July 1977, p. xx (1976 estimated by author); row 12 - IMF, International Financial Statistics, various issues (data converted from special drawings rights to dollars).

These deficits of nonoil developing countries rose in 1975 as the result of the recession in industrial countries. But the increase from 1973 to 1976 seems to be explainable entirely by the rise of oil prices.

As shown in Table 2.2, the value of merchandise imports to all nonoil developing countries from OPEC members increased from $8.1 billion in 1973 to $22.2 billion in 1975. Their exports to OPEC increased from $2.3 billion to $6.4 billion. Thus their trade deficit with OPEC grew from $5.8 billion in 1973 to $16.4 billion in 1975 and accounted for 47 percent of the increase in their total trade deficit in this period. In 1976, the trade deficit of these developing countries with OPEC, at $19.8 billion, was larger than their total trade deficit. The growth in the trade deficit with OPEC from 1973 to 1976 ($14 billion) exceeded the increase in the total trade deficit of nonoil developing countries ($9 billion). Trade with OPEC countries includes more than oil, so that these results do not give a precise measure of the impact of the change in oil prices and oil consumption on trade balances; but it comes fairly close. (Even for one of the more developed and diversified OPEC countries, Venezuela, petroleum accounted for 94 percent of total exports in 1976.)

Faster recovery in the industrial countries could bring a further narrowing of the deficit of nonoil developing countries. But some of these countries have imposed stringent restrictions on a broad range of imports, and these might be relaxed as export proceeds increase. It is noteworthy that the volume of total imports into nonoil developing countries was six percent lower in 1975 than in 1974, despite the continued, though less than historical, real growth of their economies.

The notion that deficits of nonoil developing countries are abnormally enlarged is contradicted by an analysis of the International Monetary Fund that scales up these deficits for world inflation and real growth. On this basis the average current-account deficit of $8.1 billion per year in 1967-72 becomes the equivalent of $27 billion in 1977 prices and levels of real output. It so happens that this is precisely equal to the fund's projection of the aggregate current-account deficit of nonoil developing countries in 1977.(5)

The conclusion drawn from the fund analysis is that the nonoil developing countries are absorbing resources in real terms from the rest of the world at about the same relative rate as before the OPEC price rise. The big change is that now the OPEC countries rather than the industrial countries have the corresponding surpluses. For purposes of this paper, the IMF analysis is reasonable in broad terms, and the paper therefore assumes that nonoil developing countries as a group should and will continue to incur substantial current-account deficits in the years ahead.

The question is whether or not the debt being incurred by nonoil developing countries is manageable.

GROWTH AND MANAGEABILITY OF DEBT

The literature on debt-financed economic development pictures the process as a race between two variables growing at compound rates: debt and income.(6) Debt is generated by the gap between domestic saving and investment, which can increase in absolute terms over time. As the gap widens and debt cumulates, interest charges also cumulate, and the country must borrow increasing amounts just to maintain a constant flow of net imports. It must also borrow to refinance maturing debt obligations. Income, in turn, grows as a result of the investment process. The capacity to service debt depends fundamentally on the continuing growth of output, which makes it feasible ultimately to close and then reverse the gap between domestic saving and investment.

The process can be depicted by a simplified model adapted from the difference-equation model presented by Avramovic and his associates.(7) In the model below, growth proceeds as the result of increasing investment and a fixed incremental capital-output ratio. All external debt is assumed to finance the gap between investment and domestic saving; changes in reserves and capital inflows other than interest-bearing debt are ignored and all prices are assumed to be constant. Amortization of past loans is also ignored on the plausible assumption that, as long as the gap exists, scheduled loan repayments will be offset by new borrowing. Thus debt accumulates as the result of the gap between investment and saving and of the interest on the growing debt.

Investment and saving are related to income as follows:

$$I(n) = krY(n) = krY_0e^{rn};$$
$$S(n) = sY(n) = sY_0e^{rn},$$

where $\underline{I}$ and $\underline{S}$ are investment and saving net of depreciation, $\underline{Y}$ is net national product, $\underline{k}$ is the incremental capital-output ratio, $\underline{r}$ is the growth of real and nominal net national product and income, $\underline{s}$ is the ratio of domestic saving to net national income, $\underline{n}$ represents time, and the subscript zero denotes the year before debt began to be incurred.

Then debt outstanding, $\underline{D}$, at time $\underline{T}$ is the sum of loans taken up to finance the gap between investment and domestic saving from the time the process began, together with the accumulation of interest, $\underline{i}$, at a compound rate on each of these loans from the time at which it was incurred to time $\underline{T}$:

$$\begin{aligned} D(T) &= \int_0^T (I(n) - S(n))e^{i(T-n)}\,dn \\ &= \int_0^T (krY_0e^{rn} - sY_0e^{rn})e^{i(T-n)}\,dn \\ &= (kr - s)Y_0e^{iT}\int_0^T e^{(r-i)n}\,dn, \text{ for } r \neq i. \end{aligned}$$

Therefore,

1) $$D(T) = \frac{kr - s}{r - i} Y_0(e^{rT} - e^{iT}), r \neq i.$$

The ratio of debt to income is

2) $$\frac{D(T)}{Y(T)} = \frac{1}{Y_0 e^{rT}} \left(\frac{kr - s}{r - i}\right) Y_0(e^{rT} - e^{iT}) = \frac{kr - s}{r - i}(1 - e^{T(i-r)})$$

$$\lim_{T \to \infty} \frac{D(T)}{Y(T)} = \frac{kr - s}{r - i}, \text{ if } r > i.$$

Thus if the rate of growth of output exceeds the rate of interest on external borrowing, the debt-income ratio levels off ultimately at (kr - s)/(r - i).

The condition for the debt-income ratio to reach a maximum may be derived:

3) $$\frac{d\frac{D(T)}{Y(T)}}{dT} = \frac{kr - s}{r - i}[-(i - r)e^{T(i-r)}] = (kr - s)e^{T(i-r)}.$$

Setting this expression equal to zero,

$$(kr - s)e^{T(i-r)} = \frac{kr - s}{e^{T(r-i)}} = 0.$$

It is clear from equation 3 that the second derivative is negative if r i. The debt-income ratio is thus asymptotic to (kr - s)/(r - i) since the maximum is reached only when T is at infinity.

Thus with an unchanged (kr - s)/(r - i), the rate of growth of the debt-income ratio will decelerate over time as long as r i, an essential condition. Debt accumulation need not be an explosive process. The question may still be asked whether the limit is a reasonable one in terms of the ability of the borrowing country to service debt. I return to this question below.

If, more realistically, one allows for changes over time in kr and s, it is the closing of the gap between them - that is, between investment and domestic saving - that ends the process of net debt accumulation. The evolution of countries, including the United States in the late nineteenth century, from net capital importers to net capital exporters was presumably the result of such changes in the parameters that are treated as constants in the abstract model.

If world inflation is taken into account, the story changes somewhat. A steady rate of inflation from the beginning of the debt-accumulation process would, of course, lead to higher debt in nominal terms. In equations 1 and 2, the appropriate value of r would include the rate of increase of world prices (expressed in dollars or SDRs) added to the real growth rate.

If this inflation is just fully reflected in the interest rate, i, both the nominal value of debt and the debt-income ratio would be higher than under stable prices. The less the inflation rate is reflected in the interest rate, the lower the limit of debt to income.

What must be analyzed is the effect of the acceleration of inflation in 1972-73. A number of impacts on debt may be identified. Nominal new borrowings had to increase merely to finance an unchanged real gap between investment and domestic saving, but this increase was roughly proportional to the increase in national product that resulted from higher prices. On the other hand, borrowings to refinance maturing debt declined relative to national product and the current gap. Nominal interest rates on new debt, to finance the gap and to replace maturing debt, rose by an inflation premium and thus enlarged the amount of subsequent new borrowing that was required; but interest rates on the borrowings by developing countries rose by less than the increase in the inflation rate, since the latter was generally expected to subside. Thus the greater the proportion of debt to national product and the longer the maturity on the debt a country had incurred before the inflation began - inflation that was unanticipated and therefore not reflected in interest rates before 1972-73 - the more it stood to gain.

It seems clear that the net effect of the unanticipated inflation has been to lighten the burden of debt. Even though the nonoil developing countries suffered a deterioration in their terms of trade, as did all oil-importing countries, the increase in world prices reduced the real value of outstanding debt in 1973-74, as shown in Table 2.2, where the deflator is an index of the export prices of developing countries, excluding petroleum. Even when deflated debt did not fall, it rose less in real than in nominal terms.

MAJOR BORROWERS FROM BANKS AMONG DEVELOPING COUNTRIES

The ten more advanced nonoil developing countries that account for the bulk of recent external borrowing from private sources represented 44 percent of the current deficits of all nonoil developing countries in 1976 (see Table 2.3). From 1973 to 1976, they were responsible for 61 percent of the increase in the aggregate deficit of nonoil developing countries. Furthermore, among the ten countries, Brazil and Mexico loom large in most years.

These ten countries owe a large proportion of the developing countries' debt to private creditors. Table 2.4 shows that, of the total debt to banks of nonoil developing countries

Table 2.3. Current-Account Deficits, Ten Advanced and All Nonoil Developing Countries Selected Years 1968-76(a) (in million of dollars except where noted)

Country	1968	1970	1973	1974	1975	1976
Argentina	47	156	-704	-125	1,281	-617
Brazil	543	569	1,764	7,178	6,744	6,212
Chile	141	95	289	186	578	-25
Colombia	188	330	78	382	126	-320
Mexico	744	1,083	1,423	2,890	4,210	3,417
Peru	53	-146	299	751	1,574	1,231
Philippines	294	69	-439	241	990	1,142
South Korea	561	706	343	2,094	1,955	325
Taiwan	117	-7	-570	1,113	580	-395
Thailand	207	0	-130	-54	503	486
Subtotal	2,895	2,855	2,353	14,656	18,541	11,456
Subtotal as proportion of total	0.43	0.33	0.22	0.50	0.49	0.44
Total, all nonoil developing countries	6,800	8,700	10,900	29,500	38,200	25,800

(a) Goods, services, and private transfers; minus sign denotes surplus.

Sources: Country data, IMF, International Financial Statistics, vol. 29 (August 1976), vol. 30 (September 1977); total, row 5, table 2, above; and IMF, Annual Report, 1976, p. 20.

Table 2.4. External Bank Debt and Increase of Reserves, Ten Advanced and All Nonoil Developing Countries, 1975 and 1976 (in billions of dollars)

	Bank Debt(a)		Increase of Reserves
Country	1975	1976	1976
Argentina	3.2	3.4	1.2
Brazil	14.8	21.2	2.5
Chile	0.8	1.1	0.3
Colombia	1.6	1.6	0.6
Mexico	13.5	17.9	n.a.
Peru	2.3	2.8	-0.1
Philippines	2.0	2.6	0.3
South Korea	3.3	3.9	1.4
Taiwan	2.1	2.6	0.4
Thailand	1.2	1.4	0.1
Subtotal	44.8	58.5	6.7
Subtotal as proportion of total	0.71	0.72	0.58
Total, all nonoil developing countries	63.0	80.9	11.6

(a) End of year.
n.a. Not available.

Sources: Bank debt - Bank for International Settlements, Forty-sixth Annual Report: 1st April 1975-31st March 1976, pp. 86-87, 1977, pp. 112-14 (includes debt with maturity of one year and less); reserves - IFM, International Financial Statistics, 30 (September 1977):25, converted from special drawing rights.

(including short-term debts, which is excluded from the debt totals in Table 2.2), the ten countries owe almost three-fourths, and Brazil and Mexico alone almost half. Bank debt in turn is the major form of debt from private sources. These countries have issued a relatively small amount of securities in foreign markets.

The more advanced developing countries were already borrowing from private lenders before the sharp increase in their current-account deficits in 1974. A number of them - notably, Brazil and Mexico - had established their access to the Eurocurrency markets and other banks in the late 1960s and early 1970s.

Borrowing from private sources accelerated after 1973. The external debt of 46 middle-income nonoil developing countries to private creditors increased from $34 billion at the end of 1973 to almost $69 billion at the end of 1976. For these countries, total debt in relation to exports of goods and services increased from 77 percent in 1967 to 105 percent in 1976.(8)

The changes from 1967 to 1975 in the ratio of external public and publicly guaranteed debt to gross national product and to exports are shown in Table 2.5 for the ten major borrowers.

Except for Chile, Peru, and Mexico, the ratios of debt to exports decreased, increased moderately, or remained relatively low (Philippines) from 1967 to 1975. I shall consider the ratios to GNP below.

The debt-service ratio - annual interest plus amortization relative to exports - is often used as a measure of creditworthiness. But it is a defective measure, as Avramovic and his colleagues point out,(9) principally because maturities are bunched. Thus, for example, almost 60 percent of Brazil's public and publicly guaranteed debt outstanding at the end of 1974 was repayable over the following five years. For most of the ten countries, a large proportion of debt outstanding to private creditors comes to final maturity in the next five years.(10)

There will thus be need for rollovers or for new loans to replace maturing loans. This is hardly a novel predicament for bankers. If the basic economic prospects for the debtors are satisfactory - a question examined below - the bunching of maturities represents a short-run liquidity problem, not a fundamental inability to carry debt.

In some cases, high debt-service ratios may not require formal debt refinancing, for private capital will be attracted by satisfactory economic performance. Such was the experience of Japan in the early 1960s and of Mexico in the mid-1960s.(11)

Whether or not private lenders will be willing and able to refinance maturing debt while continuing to increase outstanding debt as required to finance deficits is not predictable. If

Table 2.5. Ratio of External Public and Publicly Guaranted Debt to GNP and to Exports of Goods and Nonfactor Services, Ten Advanced Nonoil Developing Countries, 1967 and 1975

	Ratio			
	Debt to GNP		Debt to Exports	
Country	1967	1975	1967	1975
Argentina(a)	0.11	0.08	1.04	0.84
Brazil	0.08	0.12	1.43	1.24
Chile	0.19	0.44	1.22	2.14
Colombia	0.14	0.18	1.15	1.22
Mexico(a)	0.09	0.15	1.01	1.89
Peru	0.13	0.21	0.72	1.52
Philippines(a)	0.03	0.08	0.19	0.41
South Korea	0.13	0.28	1.00	0.90
Taiwan	0.08	0.12	0.36	0.28
Thailand(a)	0.05	0.04	0.25	0.22

(a) Total debt is substantially higher than public and publicly guaranteed debt.

Sources: Data from the World Bank, except 1975 ratios for Chile, which are computed from World Debt Tables, vol. 2 (September 2, 1977), World Bank Atlas: Population, Per Capita Product, and Growth Rates (World Bank, 1976), and IMF, International Financial Statistics, vol. 30 (September 1977).

the improved current-account positions of 1976 are maintained, the amount of net new bank loans needed by nonoil developing countries will be rather small. Even so, some of the banks that have been heavy lenders may feel incapable of increasing their exposure, or may choose not to do so even if they can. To throw light on this question would require a separate study. But the banks' eagerness to expand their lending will continue to depend on the underlying economic performance of the debtor countries.

THE ECONOMIC PERFORMANCE OF THE ADVANCED NONOIL DEVELOPING COUNTRIES

This section examines first the broad indicators of economic performance of the ten advanced developing countries in recent years. It then attempts to assign plausible values to the parameters of the growth-debt model in order to determine how far these countries are from the limit of the ratio of debt to income. Finally, it explores whether the service on debt at the limit would be an unbearable burden.

Real growth rates for the ten countries are shown in Table 2.6. Except for Argentina, even in the 1960s, their growth rates were higher than the average of industrial countries. Five of the ten showed a significant acceleration in output growth in 1970-73. In 1974-75, output was affected

Table 2.6. Growth Rates, Ten Advanced Nonoil Developing Countries, Selected Periods, 1960-75(a)
(percent per year)

Country	1960-70	1970-73	1973-75(a)
Argentina	4.4	3.8	2.7
Brazil	6.2(b)	11.4	6.8
Chile	4.9	1.2	-4.8
Colombia	5.2	6.9	5.3
Mexico	7.0	6.1	5.1
Peru	5.5	5.7	5.2
Philippines	5.4	6.8	6.0
South Korea	8.7	11.1	10.7
Taiwan	9.0	11.8	4.8
Thailand	7.9	7.5	5.5

(a) Compound annual rates of growth of gross domestic product at 1970 prices.
(b) 1973-76 for Philippines, South Korea, Taiwan, and Thailand.
(c) 1963-70.

Sources: Computed from country data in IFM, International Financial Statistics, vol. 30 (May 1977 and September 1977).

by the rise of oil prices and the recession in industrial countries but, as noted earlier, developing countries were more successful than industrial countries in maintaining economic expansion. In 1973-75 - or, where the data are available, 1973-76 - growth rates exceeded five percent, except for Argentina, Chile, and Taiwan. (In the last the growth rate averaged 4.8 percent during 1973-76, but from the fourth quarter of 1975 to the fourth quarter of 1976 industrial production increased 20 percent.)

Meanwhile, real interest rates on external debt were quite low. According to the World Bank, interest paid on external public debt outstanding was 4.6, 5.2, and 5.5 percent, respectively, in the three years 1973-75 for all developing countries. On debt to private creditors, the rates were 7.0, 8.6, and 8.4 percent, respectively, for the three years.(12) If the rate of world inflation, in terms of dollars, is approximated at seven percent, real interest rates on debt to private creditors could not be said to exceed one percent.

Data on the volume of total exports are available for only six of the ten countries. They are shown in Table 2.7 for 1973-76 on a base of 1970 = 100. In some cases, notably South

Table 2.7. Indexes of Volume of Exports, Selected Nonoil Developing Countries, 1973-76 (1970=100)

Country	1973	1974	1975	1976
Brazil(a)	173	195	203	206
Peru	72	72	66	67
Philippines	145	111	132	177
South Korea	305	333	410	557
Taiwan	221	211	209	322
Thailand	139	152	147	199

(a) Excluding coffee, including coffee, the volume indexes are 155, 158, 165, 167. Coffee constituted 20 percent of the value of exports in 1973 and 21 percent in 1976.

Source: IMF, International Financial Statistics, vol. 30 (September 1977), country pages.

Korea and Taiwan, the performance is phenomenal. Except for Peru, which was affected by recession-induced decreases in demand for mineral products in industrial countries and by the fall in the fishmeal catch, the countries for which a measure of export volume is available outperformed most industrial countries by a considerable margin. In Japan, probably the industrial country with the largest export expansion, the volume of exports almost doubled from 1970 to 1976; for Germany, exports increased 53 percent and for the United States, 48 percent.

In assigning values to the parameters of the limit of debt to net national product, $(\underline{kr} - \underline{s})/(\underline{r} - \underline{i})$, the major problem is that estimates of saving rates derived independently of investment rates are not available. The alternative is an attempt to measure directly $\underline{kr} - \underline{s}$, the gap between net investment and net saving as a proportion of net national product.

I measure the gap by subtracting net payments of interest and dividends from the deficit on goods and services. The resulting figure should represent the absorption into domestic use of goods and services from abroad. When divided by net national product, it provides an estimate of $\underline{kr} - \underline{s}$. The year 1974 is chosen for calculations because national-accounts data are not available for 1976 for many countries and because, in 1975, the trade deficits of developing countries were temporarily enlarged by the world recession. The results are presented in Table 2.8. The gap shown in column 1 is larger than it appears it will be for 1976, given that the current-account deficits fell from 1974 to 1976 while net interest payments increased. On the other hand, the 1976 deficits may be abnormally low as the result of import restrictions and rates of growth that, for most countries, had not yet returned to the rates of 1970-73. For these reasons, it seems sensible to use the ratio of the gap to net product in 1974 as more or less normal.

Table 2.9 applies the debt-income model presented earlier but in nominal prices. The gaps of Table 2.8 are divided by estimates of $\underline{r} - \underline{i}$, to offer, in column 3, a measure, country by country, of the limit of the debt-income ratio. For an estimate of $\underline{r}$, I add a world-inflation factor of seven percent to the real growth rates of 1970-73, which are assumed to represent long-term rates. I assume an interest rate, $\underline{i}$, of eight percent even though, as noted earlier, outstanding debt - a mix of loans from official and private sources - carried an interest rate in 1975 between 5.5 and 8.4 percent.

Comparison of column 3 with Table 2.5 reveals that in 1975 all ten countries were substantially below their debt-income limit. But that observation may have little significance if the limit of the debt-income ratio is so high that it would involve an intolerable interest burden on the country.

Table 2.8. Calculation of Gap Between Investment and Saving as a Proportion of Net National Product, Ten Advanced Nonoil Developing Countries, 1974
(in billions of dollars, except where noted)

Country	Gap (Deficit on Goods and Services Other Than Net Interest and Dividends Paid (1)	Net National Product (2)	Ratio, Gap to Net National Product (3)
Argentina	-0.441	50.44(a)	-0.01
Brazil	6.278	88.53(a)	0.07
Chile	0.233	7.81(a)	0.03
Colombia	0.210	10.18	0.02
Mexico	1.860	58.59(a)	0.03
Peru	0.601	10.90	0.06
Philippines	0.429	13.23	0.03
South Korea	2.006	15.14	0.13
Taiwan	1.123	12.81	0.09
Thailand	0.283	12.38	0.02

(a) Net national product is assumed to equal 0.9 times gross domestic product.

Sources: Column 1 - IMF, Balance of Payments Yearbook, 1967-74, vol. 27 (IMF, 1976), converted from SDRs to dollars; column 2 - IMF, International Financial Statistics, vol 30 (September 1977, converted to dollars, for all countries but Chile, for which the source is World Bank Atlas: Population, Per Capita Product, and Growth Rates (1976), p. 19.

Column 5 therefore shows the ratio of debt to exports of goods and services at the limit on the assumption that the ratio of exports to net national product remains what it was in 1974 (column 4). And column 6 presents the ratio of interest payments to exports of goods and services that would prevail at the limit, still assuming an 8 percent nominal interest rate.

Several anomalies are evident in Table 2.9. Argentina was in surplus in 1974 on current account. Over the ten

Table 2.9. Debt-Income Limits and Interest Burdens, Ten Advanced Nonoil Developing Countries, 1974

	Ratio					
Country	Nominal Growth Rate Minus Interest (1)	Gap to Net National Product (2)	Debt-to-Income Limit (3)	Exports to Net National Product (4)	Debt to Exports at Limit (5)	Interest to Exports at Limit (6)
Argentina	0.03	-0.01	-0.33	0.10	...	...
Brazil	0.10	0.07	0.70	0.11	6.36	0.51
Chile	0.002	0.03	15.00	0.28	53.57	4.29
Colombia	0.06	0.02	0.33	0.19	1.74	0.14
Mexico	0.05	0.03	0.60	0.11	5.45	0.44
Peru	0.05	0.06	1.20	0.17	7.06	0.56
Philippines	0.06	0.03	0.50	0.27	1.85	0.15
South Korea	0.10	0.13	1.30	0.35	3.71	0.30
Taiwan	0.11	0.09	0.82	0.51	1.61	0.13
Thailand	0.07	0.02	0.29	0.26	1.12	0.29

Sources: Column 1 - real growth rate in 1970-73 from Table 2.6 above (divided by 100) plus 0.07 (a measure of world inflation) minus 0.08 (nominal rate of interest on debt); column 2 - from column 3, Table 2.8, above; column 3 - column 2 ÷ column 1; column 4 - exports of goods and servies in 1974 from IMF, *International Financial Statistics*, vol. 29 (August 1976), net national product from Table 2.8 above; column 5 - column 3 ÷ column 4; column 6 - column 5 x 0.08.

years 1967-76, Argentina's balance of payments fluctuated between surplus and deficit; on average there was a current-account deficit of about $75 million. Even that figure would yield a surplus on goods and services less interest and dividends. Thus it is difficult to come up with a gap between investment and saving for Argentina. In any event, the ratios of debt to GNP and to exports are relatively low; in 1976 and the first half of 1977, reserves increased substantially. Argentina, then, can be left aside in considering whether the group of ten countries is headed for difficulties because of overborrowing.

In the case of Chile, an extremely low growth rate in 1970-73 (1.2 percent per year) produced a very high and unrealistic limit of debt to income. Assuming the growth rate of the 1960s (4.9 percent), and using the other ratios shown in Table 2.9, the last column would come out at 0.22, a not intolerable interest burden.

Chile's ratios of debt to GNP and to exports were high in 1975, as Table 2.5 shows, but partly because of low levels of exports and GNP. Real GDP fell 13 percent in 1975. Copper exports, which constitute a varying but high proportion of total exports, fell eight percent in volume and 40 percent in price in 1975. In addition, the "chronic limitations on the economic system were aggravated during 1971-73 as the result of the drastic reorientation in economic policy and the reorganization of the country's productive structure, which have caused serious difficulties in recent years for the restoration of the economy's internal and external equilibrium."(13)

If, in the other countries, debt were to rise to its maximum ratio to income, the interest burden would be high, as a proportion of export proceeds, in the cases of Brazil, Mexico, Peru, and possibly South Korea. The remaining countries - Colombia, the Philippines, Taiwan, and Thailand - would, at the debt limit, have annual interest payments equal to 15 percent or less of their exports of goods and services.

In 1975, Brazil's ratio of public debt to GNP was 0.12, as shown in Table 2.5. In 1976, the ratio of <u>total</u> debt - amounting to $26 billion - to GNP was about 0.20.(14) Applying the interest rates estimated by the World Bank for 1975 to the distribution of this debt between official and private creditors yields total interest payments in 1976 of $1.9 billion. This comes to 17 percent of Brazil's exports of goods and services in 1976.

It appears that Brazil does not have unlimited leeway for further increases in external debt <u>relative to its exports</u>. On the other hand, in a growing world economy, that country has considerable scope to increase its debt without raising the ratio of interest payments to exports.

If Brazil's real GNP were to expand nine percent per year in the future (compared with 11 percent in 1970-73); if its exports keep up with the growth of its GNP (in the years 1971-75, Brazil's exports in real terms rose faster than its real GDP); and if world prices continue to rise at seven percent per year, Brazil's debt could increase more than $4 billion a year in the next few years without raising the ratio of debts to GNP or to exports. A higher rate of growth of GNP and exports would permit larger annual increases in debt without raising the debt burden.

How fast would the debt-income ratio creep up if Brazil continued to maintain a gap equal to seven percent of its net national product, as is assumed in Table 2.9? Equation 3 of the model helps to answer this question. After 20 years of debt-financed growth, the ratio increases by 0.01 a year; after 30 years, by 0.003. By now, therefore, the ratio is likely to rise rather slowly. Still, the ultimate limit is too high.

Plainly, Brazil cannot go on indefinitely with a gap as large as that assumed in Table 2.9. In fact, the gap has decreased since 1974, both absolutely and in relation to GNP. Brazil grew at a real rate of 8.8 percent in 1976,(15) while the gap was about four percent of net national product. A gradual narrowing of the gap, relative to GNP, should be possible without interfering with a rapid rate of growth. What it requires is an increase in the saving rate, public or private. Given the rapid growth of real per capita income in recent years (6.3 percent a year in 1965-74), Brazil should be able to adopt policies to accomplish this increase.

For Mexico, too, the ultimate ratio of debt to income appears too high, though not as high as that of Brazil. Mexico's total debt at the end of 1976 was about $20 billion. If its growth rate returns to six percent and world inflation continues at seven percent, Mexico's debt could rise by $2.6 billion a year without increasing the ratio. In any event, the discovery of large oil reserves bodes well for Mexico's exports. Mexico is unlikely to become a problem case.

Peru's export difficulties have already been alluded to. It is a "problem" country and negotiations with the International Monetary Fund and with private creditors are currently under way.

South Korea is the only other country among the ten with a high limit of debt to income and, at the limit, a relatively high ratio of interest payments to exports. Korea is now far from those limits. Total debt at the end of 1976 is estimated by the World Bank at $7.5 billion, which amounts to 30 percent of Korea's net national product. Equation 3 indicates that, after ten years of debt-financed growth, the debt-income ratio rises by 0.05 a year; after twenty years by less than 0.02.

With the same method as for Brazil, Korea's interest payments in 1976 may be estimated at $473 million, which amounted to only five percent of its exports of goods and services in that year. South Korea thus will have ample time before it must narrow the gap because the interest burden of debt has become oppressive.

Thus, from the viewpoint of the growth-cum-debt process, the countries considered here fall into three categories: 1) those that can go on indefinitely borrowing abroad to finance an excess of investment over domestic saving; 2) those that may have to curtail their borrowing somewhat but appear to be in a position to do that without too much sacrifice of domestic consumption; and 3) two mineral-exporting countries that have been strongly affected by the recession and slow recovery in the industrial nations. These two countries account for only 7.5 percent of the total debt of the ten countries.

In general, therefore, the performance and prospects of the major borrowers permit an optimistic judgment about their creditworthiness.

WHAT COULD GO WRONG?

One of the dangers often cited by those who are concerned about the heavy buildup of debt by developing countries since 1973 is that the borrowers may be using the external resources to finance consumption rather than investment. Table 2.10 presents data for the ten countries on the ratio of gross fixed capital formation to gross domestic availabilities - domestic product plus net imports of goods and services.(16) Except those for Brazil, the data are in current prices and a question arises about what results would be shown by deflated accounts. Nevertheless, it it striking that only two of the countries, Chile and Colombia, exhibit a decline in the ratio of gross fixed investment to available resources after 1973, and in the case of Colombia the decline was slight. From this evidence, no basis exists for the fears that heavy borrowers among developing countries are not maintaining their rates of investment.

Another concern relates to the ability of the debtor countries to export in the future. The analysis of the growth process here has focused only on the investment-saving gap. The so-called foreign-exchange gap, or trade limit,(17) was ignored. In other words, it was assumed implicitly that this group of advanced developing countries could expand its exports, if necessary, to compensate for a reduction in net capital inflow. This in turn requires that the industrial countries keep their markets open to the exports - particularly exports of manufactures - of the developing countries. Quite apart from the usual arguments against import restrictions, in this case they would create a transfer problem for developing

Table 2.10. Gross Fixed Capital Formation as a Percentage of Total Absorption, Ten Advanced Nonoil Developing Countries, 1970-76(a)

Country	1970	1971	1972	1973	1974	1975	1976
Argentina	20.0	19.2	20.1	19.9	20.2	20.8	n.a.
Brazil(b)	n.a.	20.7	22.6	24.2	27.6	28.4	n.a.
Chile	13.8	12.9	11.5	13.1	13.9	11.7	n.a.
Colombia	20.0	20.0	18.4	17.7	19.1	18.2	n.a.
Mexico	19.1	17.8	19.4	20.7	21.6	22.6	n.a.
Peru	13.4	14.7	14.1	15.1	17.3	17.6	16.6
Philippines	15.7	16.2	15.6	15.8	17.9	22.3	22.9
South Korea	22.6	20.9	19.1	22.9	23.3	23.5	22.6
Taiwan	21.8	23.5	26.0	27.7	26.7	29.2	30.4
Thailand	22.8	21.7	21.4	21.0	22.2	22.2	22.3

(a) Total absorption = GDP - exports + imports of goods and services = consumption + gross fixed investment + increase in stocks + government consumption.
(b) Computed from data expressed in 1973 prices.
n.a. Not available.

Sources: Except for Brazil, computed from IMF, International Financial Statistics, vol. 30 (September 1977), country pages; for Brazil, Inter-American Development Bank, Economic and Social Progress in Latin America: 1976 Report, p. 397.

countries and force them to rely more on external borrowing.

Another recession in the industrial nations would be a problem for the debtor countries. As in 1975, their exports would decline and their current-account deficits would swell. Unless they too fell into recession, their borrowing needs would increase. One can only hope that banks would act rationally and exhibit even greater willingness to extend maturities or in other ways refinance debt while meeting the additional borrowing requirements. From past experience, banks have every reason to act sympathetically. Their loss experience on foreign loans in recent years has been only one-fifth of their chargeoffs on domestic loans.(18)

There is no concrete evidence that lenders perceive increasing risk on international loans to developing countries. For example, two Eurobond issues by the government of Brazil with similar terms in other respects sold to yield 10.00 percent in May 1976 and 8.92 percent in July 1977. Over this same interval the average yield on long-term international bond issues of governments fell from 9.31 percent to 8.36 percent.(19) Even if the perception of risk has changed, the question of concern is whether the change will be reflected in a reduced willingness to lend to developing countries.(20)

Finally, it can be predicted with a fair degree of confidence that even if external conditions do not create problems for developing countries, some of them will encounter balance-of-payments problems of their own making. Economic policy formulation has been less than fully successful even in the industrial countries in recent years. In the developing countries policy mistakes, if not earthquakes, droughts, blights, and other natural disasters, can be expected to occur from time to time and the consequences will have to be dealt with. These consequences could involve public and formal debt renegotiations, as in the case of Zaire recently. Such isolated instances do not invalidate the major thrust of this paper - that the advanced developing countries look to be good credit risks worthy of a continued flow of new loans as well as refinancing of maturing loans.

It is also a fair judgment that, while other developments in the world economy could make it more difficult for the advanced developing countries to service their debts, the generation of debt in itself is unlikely to cause serious general problems for the world economy or its financial system.

One justification for the establishment of a new supplementary facility in the IMF is that it will calm the disquietude of bankers who may worry about the several contingencies discussed here. In fact, the IMF could handle a very large proportion of the intermediation between countries in surplus and countries in deficit that is now being carried by the banks. The fund has the legal authority to borrow not only from governments but also in financial markets. Thus it could absorb funds from OPEC countries and from other surplus countries and pass them on to countries in deficit. In other words, should the private market falter in performing the intermediation function - either by reducing its lending or by exacting excessive rates of interest - there is both a rationale and a means for the substitution of official action. Meanwhile, even if lending by the IMF facility does not mount, the very fact that it exists should strengthen the confidence of private lenders and encourage them to keep the financing process going.

CONCLUDING OBSERVATIONS

The question to which this paper is addressed may soon be a nonproblem; that is, new borrowing from banks could drop off sharply from the levels of the past three years. If the industrial countries resume a healthy rate of expansion, the current-account deficits of developing countries could fall further in 1977. As Table 2.3 shows, in 1976 four of the ten countries considered here were in current surplus, and the deficits of all but one of the others fell.

It seems appropriate to conclude this paper on the theme with which it began - the OPEC surplus. Although much of the analysis has been concerned with the demand for international debt by developing countries, there is also a supply of international claims emanating from OPEC and other surplus countries.

By almost perfect analogy with the Keynesian saving-investment process in a closed economy, one can argue that ex ante deficits on current account must equal ex ante surpluses if a high level of world income is to be maintained. As long as members of OPEC, West Germany, and Japan are unable to reduce their ex ante surpluses, either other countries must incur current-account deficits or world income will fall until ex post surpluses and deficits are equated.

Today, no world body functions analogously to the makers of fiscal and monetary policy within individual countries. In time, that may come. Meanwhile, balance-of-payments deficits and the resultant debt creation should be viewed in macroeconomic terms. The lessons of the 1930s have been learned, albeit imperfectly, regarding domestic policies. It is not evident that the lessons for international policies have yet been adequately appreciated.

NOTES

1. International Monetary Fund (IMF), Annual Report of the Executive Directors for the Fiscal Year Ended April 30, 1977, p. 15.
2. Ibid., p. 21.
3. World Bank, World Debt Tables 1 (September 2, 1977): 47.
4. Robert Solomon, The International Monetary System, 1945-1976: An Insider's View (New York: Harper and Row, 1977), pp. 298-301.
5. IMF Survey 6 (May 16, 1977): 149.
6. See especially Dragoslav Avramovic et al., Economic Growth and External Debt (Baltimore, Md.: Johns Hopkins University Press, 1964); and Goran Ohlin, Aid and Indebtedness: The Relation Between Aid Requirements, Terms of Assistance and Indebtedness of Developing Countries (Paris: Development Center of the Organization for Economic Cooperation and Development, 1966). These analyses are carried

out on the assumption of stable world prices, an assumption relaxed below.

7. Avramovic et al., Economic Growth, pp. 188-92.

8. These data were supplied by the World Bank.

9. Avramovic et al., Economic Growth, p. 42.

10. World Bank, World Debt Tables 1 (September 2, 1977): 210.

11. Reed J. Irvine, Yves Maroni, and Henry F. Lee, "How to Borrow Successfully," Columbia Journal of World Business 5 (January-February 1970): 42-48.

12. World Bank, World Debt Tables 1 (September 2, 1977): 39.

13. Inter-American Development Bank, Economic and Social Progress in Latin America: 1976 Report, p. 186.

14. From data supplied by the World Bank.

15. Inter-American Development Bank, Economic and Social Progress, p. 175.

16. What this amounts to is a measure of I as a percentage of C+I+G, where I is gross domestic investment, C is private consumption, and G is government consumption. If I were measured as a proportion of Y (gross domestic product), the ratio would not go down if a large increase in consumption were matched by increased inports, since Y=C+I+G-X-M, where X is exports, and M imports, of goods and services. Adding M-X to Y and dividing it into I yields a measure of I divided by (C+I+G).

17. Hollis B. Chenery and Alan M. Strout, "Foreign Assistance and Economic Development," American Economic Review 56 (September 1966): 679-733.

18. Robert R. Davies, "Tests Show Banks are Rational, Efficient in Granting LDC Credit," Bond Buyer, Money Manager 6 (August 1, 1977): 9-10.

19. Morgan Guaranty Trust Company of New York, World Financial Markets, various issues.

20. A bit of anecdotal evidence seems pertinent. During the annual meeting of the International Monetary Fund and World Bank in late September 1977, I had a conversation with the minister of finance and the governor of the central bank of one of the ten countries. They told me that because the country's reserves had increased sharply over the past year, they had visited banks in New York seeking to repay debt. None of the banks showed interest in receiving repayment.

3 Debt Escalation: Developing Countries in the Eurocurrency Market

Marilyn J. Seiber

Since the commodities boom came to an end in 1973 and oil prices rose by 400 percent to fuel worldwide inflation and recession in 1974-75, developing countries have borrowed heavily to maintain growth, and, in the process, have changed the face of international finance. In the three years following the oil price hike (1974-76), non-OPEC developing countries registered a cumulative current-account deficit of $109,000 million, and by year-end 1976 their combined disbursed external debt reached an estimated $202.500 million.(1) Of this total, private banks financed $75,000 million. Thus a shift has occurred in the relationships between industrial and developing countries that has not been heralded in bold headlines of the daily newspapers, but has quietly evolved in the panelled chambers of the banking world and on telex wires of the international money market: It is the large-scale entry of the less developed countries into the private international financial - markets the Eurocurrency markets.(2)

Between 1973 and 1977, total publicized Eurocurrency borrowings by nonoil developing countries increased from $4,500 million to $13,400 million - a jump of nearly 200 percent.(3) (This contrasts to the overall increase rate in Eurocurrency net lending of 125 percent in the same period.) As a result, widespread concern has shaken world financial centers over potential defaults by less developed countries (LDCs) on the Euroloans raised on their behalf. As one observer sees it, "Never before in the history of banking has so much been owed by so few to so few."(4) Thus, a rain of warnings has poured down about bank overexposure to risky LDC borrowers and about the possible collapse of weaker banks which would trigger domino effects in the banking system causing heavy financial losses and undermined confidence. On the other hand, the banking optimists contend that "the fear is largely behind us."(5) Citibank Vice Chairman G. A. Constanze has stated, "I know of no developing country today that can't service its private debt. The popular notion that the less developed countries are a disaster area simply doesn't square with the facts."(6) Henry C. Wallich of the Board of Governors of the United States Federal Reserve System concurs and has stated that "to date, these extreme fears have proved unjustified."(7)

Whatever the bankers' points of view, however, they all indicate an increased concern, and possibly an increased role, of official international financial institutions (IFIs) and creditor governments related to private commercial LDC debt. This chapter intends to examine the development and extent of the developing country presence in the Eurocurrency markets, the impact and potential crisis in debt defaults, the role of private banks in the new phenomenon, and the implications for industrial country policies toward LDC debt, international banking and the official international financing institutions.

THE LDC PHENOMENON: ENTRANCE TO THE EUROMARKET

Factors Behind the Phenomenon

In 1973 an IMF staff paper declared, "From available data it appears that a surge in gross Eurocurrency borrowing by developing countries is underway."(8) See Appendix 3A for an explanation of the origin and operations of the Eurocurrency market. From 1970 to 1974, medium- and long-term borrowings by nonoil developing countries in the Eurocurrency market jumped from $300 million to $6,252 million - and continued climbing: 1974 - $8,199 million; 1976 - $11,019 million; 1977 - $13,427 million.(9)(See Table 3.1.)

Table 3.1. Publicly Announced Eurocurrency Credits (in billions US$)

	1973	1974	1975	1976	1977
Industrial countries	13.8	20.7	7.2	11.3	17.2
Non-OPEC LDCs	4.5	6.3	8.2	11.0	13.4
OPEC countries	2.7	1.1	2.9	4.0	7.4
Communist countries	0.8	1.2	2.6	2.5	3.4
Total	21.8	29.3	21.0	28.8	41.6

Note: Figures have been rounded.
Source: Morgan Guaranty Trust Company, World Financial Markets, March 1978, p. 4.

This marked rise in borrowing in the Eurocurrency markets - which have provided a large and relatively accessible source of funds on favorable terms and fairly long maturities - does not owe as much to improved conditions and economic performance in the borrowing countries as it does to developments and change in the Eurocurrency markets themselves. First, new operational techniques in the Eurocurrency market facilitated increased risk-taking by Eurobanks that otherwise would be hesitant to loan to developing countries - namely, syndications and consortia methods, the rollover credit approach, and floating interest rates reduced the potential default risk borne by a single bank. Second, the rapid increase in the number of banks active in the Euromarkets led to intensified interbank competition and a search for new borrowers. Third, the dramatic rise in Eurocurrency deposits from $20 billion in 1967 to $200 billion in 1975 due to placements by central banks during the boom era of the early 1970s and petrodollar deposits later, made it possible to lend to borrowers that previously may have been assessed as marginal. Fourth, Eurobanks sought to geographically diversify their portfolios (and thereby spread risk) and thus looked for new borrowers in the direction of the developing countries. Finally, the rising tolerance level of Eurobanks toward developing countries was spurred, in addition to the above, by 1) a less stringent view of performance indicators at the time of extremely high rates of increase for commodity prices, and 2) increased familiarity with lending to developing countries.

The supply side was not the only stimulus to LDC borrowing in the Euromarket, however. Increased demand was also a factor. First, with rising commodity export prices and general international economic health, developing countries were pushing their economic development programs which required capital outlays and heavy external borrowing. Second, the relative stagnation in the flow of official development assistance resulted in greater demand for other means of financing. In some countries, reliance on foreign equity capital was reduced as developing countries sought to exploit their resources via contractor or agency arrangements with foreign companies, raising in the process the demand for foreign funds. Finally, in the advanced developing countries that could use domestically produced capital goods to implement projects, Eurocurrency borrowing provided funds at a lower cost than would have been paid to raise these resources internally.(10)

With these basic factors working, the period of rising LDC participation in Eurocurrency borrowing, 1970 to the present, can be examined in two phases: 1) the boom years of the early 1970s through 1973 caused by rising commodity prices and an expanding international economy, and 2) the post-oil price rise years and petrodollar recycling from 1974 to present.

The Boom Years: No Limits to Growth

Prior to 1970, Eurocurrency markets did not greatly affect developing countries and were primarily the domains of multinational corporations and public borrowers of the industrial countries. But with the economic boom of high-priced commodities and investment opportunities in the early seventies, bankers viewed developing countries in a different light and eagerly flocked South to new nesting grounds. The economic stars of the Third World, e.g., Mexico, Brazil, South Korea, were on the rise and were increasing their private borrowing rate faster than their official loans. According to Emma Rothschild, "The most ecstatic increase came in Euro-borrowing."(11) For United States and foreign banks the period was a time of euphoric expansion. Developing countries were classified into two categories of promise - those with fast growing exports of manufactures and those with "new rich commodity exports."

The dream of riches applied to bankers and borrowers alike. There was a delirious feeling in 1973 that the world boom was forever - and the rare air of perpetually rising expectations was universal.(12) Bankers breathed profits and, against the background of increasing competitive pressures and money to lend, offered Euroloans at a price that was not refused. By 1973 developing country customers could not borrow fast enough for enthusiastic Eurolenders - it was a borrower's paradise for developing countries.(13)

Although developing countries borrowed externally prior to 1970, most credits were obtained from official sources. During and after the commodities price boom from 1970-73, LDC borrowing intensified so that in the 1970s developing countries borrowed more than in their previous history.(14) From 1971 to 1973 developing countries borrowed $45 billion - 20 percent of which was from private banks.(15) According to Jo W. Saxe, Chief of the International Finance Division of the World Bank: "There is reason to believe that all or almost all of the borrowing of developing countries from private banks abroad has been directly or indirectly from the Eurocurrency markets."(16)

In 1971 publicized Eurocurrency credits to developing countries were nearly $1 billion, up from $300 million in 1970. (Approximately 8 percent of public debt was to banks.) Although exact figures vary by source, in 1974 Morgan Guaranty Trust Company reported that nonoil developing countries' borrowings in the Eurocurrency markets increased substantially in the next three years. (See Table 3.2.) Strong credit demand continued through the first half of 1974 in which non-OPEC developing country credits reached $4.26 billion, or 21.5 percent of the $19.8 billion. It is estimated however, that several billion more in credits were extended to

Table 3.2. Publicized Eurocurrency Credits by Country Category, 1970-1977
(in billions of US$)

Category	1970	Percent	1971	Percent	1972	Percent	1973	Percent	1974	Percent	1975	Percent	1976	Percent	1977	Percent
Industrial countries	4.24	90	2.60	60	4.09	60	13.78	63	20.68	70	7.23	34	11.25	39	17.2	41
Nonoil LDCs	0.30	6	0.94	24	1.48	22	4.53	21	6.25	21	8.20	39	11.01	38	13.42	32
OPEC LDCs	0.15	3	0.35	9	0.93	14	2.75	13	1.06	4	2.90	13	3.99	14	7.42	18
Communist countries	0.04	1	0.06	2	0.29	4	0.78	4	1.23	4	2.59	12	2.50	9	3.39	8
Total	4.73	100	3.96	100	6.79	100	21.85	100	29.26	100	20.99	100	28.84	100	41.63	100

Note: Percentage figures have been rounded and may not add to 100.

Source: Morgan Guaranty Trust Company, World Financial Markets, March 1978, p. 4.

developing countries during this 1974 period but were unannounced.(17) Additionally, Eurocurrency borrowing by developing countries was limited to a small number of countries. (See section on "Eurocredit Distribution among Developing Countries.") Furthermore, during the early boom years before confidence in the Eurocurrency market began to erode in the second half of 1974, maturities on loans to developing countries were quite favorable.(18)

Following the strong growth through the first half of 1974, concern rose about the ability of the international financial structure to cope with payments imbalances caused by the large increase in oil prices. (This concern was heightened by disclosures of individual institutional difficulties and failures.) Eurolending fell off - only to rise again as banks stepped in to fill the financing breach caused by massive LDC current-account deficits, largely due to oil prices and the lowered availability of official financing. In short, private banks and the Eurocurrency markets became the financial intermediaries for recycling pyramiding petrodollars.

LDC Deficits and Petrodollar Glut: Eurocycling

After mid-1974, boom turned to gloom as developing and industrial countries alike struggled to cope with burgeoning deficits, rising inflation, and deepening recession. Phase two of the Eurocurrency market and developing countries began.

Since the oil price hikes in the winter of 1973-74, developing countries were faced with an increased oil import bill of $15 billion per annum.(19) More than just direct oil imports forced them to the wall, however. Developing countries also paid more for food, fertilizer, and manufactured imports while prices of their own exports dropped. Further, prices of many "poor country commodities," e.g., copper, tin, jute, collapsed in 1975. In the first half of 1975 the commodity price index dropped 18 percent.(20) In addition, worldwide recession caused industrial countries to reduce their developing country imports while inflation in the price of manufactured goods contributed about equally with the oil price increases to LDC deficits in 1974-75.

Rather than cut back on national development programs, however, developing countries chose to borrow externally to finance spiraling deficits. It was necessary not only to meet normal domestic needs of expanding economies, but also to make restructuring adjustments in the economies. As a result, until 1976 the rate of growth of LDC imports was not reduced significantly. And as Shaw Sin-ming reports in Far Eastern Economic Review, "Probably the most undiscussed issue...is the embarrassing fact that had the developing countries not maintained a steady level of imports, the 1974-75 recession in the North - the South's main supplier - would have become more severe."(21)

Hence, developing countries bore nearly the full brunt of OPEC surpluses and recession and accrued massive current-account deficits. From a deficit range of $9-11 billion in the early 1970s, nonoil developing countries' combined current-account deficit soared to about $29 billion in 1974, continued climbing to $37 billion in 1975, and dropped to $26 billion in 1976.(22) (See Table 3.3.) As a consequence, net new

Table 3.3. Global Current-Account Balances (in billions of US$)

	1974	1975	1976	1977 (est.)
Industrial countries (OECD)	-22	+ 7	-14	-19
OPEC oil exporters	+70	+38	+41.5	+41
Nonoil LDCs	-29	-37	-26	-23

Source: U.S. Department of the Treasury, Report on the External Debt of Developing Countries and on Debt Relief Provided by the United States, January 1978, p. 8.

financing requirements of these countries totaled an estimated $109 billion in 1974-76 which represents nearly a 140 percent increase from the previous three-year period.(23) In 1976 alone, financing requirements reached $49 billion - $30 billion for current-account deficits, $2 billion for amortizations, and $7 billion to increase reserves.(24) For 1977, preliminary figures suggest a further reduction of the LDC aggregate deficit to $22-23 billion. However, the OECD Secretariat has predicted this improvement to be short-lived, and 1978 may show an $11 billion increase in the developing countries' current account deficit to about $34 billion.(25)

The mirror image of the developing countries' deficits, of course, has been the mounting OPEC current-account surpluses. In the three years, 1974-76, thirteen oil exporters amassed payments surpluses of $150 billion and in 1977 were taking in about $45 billion more a year than they could spend on imports.(26) In 1974 the OPEC surplus surged from $5 billion in 1973 to a current-account surplus of $70 billion. This surplus was cut nearly in half in 1975 to about $38 billion as OPEC imports increased rapidly and the combination of recession, warm weather, and conservation in the oil-importing countries curbed demand. In 1976 the trend reversed, and the OPEC current-account surplus rose to $41.5 billion as OPEC countries met physical limitations (i.e., labor and infrastructural bottlenecks) on imports, world petroleum demand increased with recovery of the international economy, and petroleum inventories were raised by several importing countries in anticipation of a further petroleum price increase. For 1977, Morgan Guaranty Trust Company has estimated an OPEC surplus of $35 billion, and a $10 billion decline to $25 billion has been projected for 1978.(27) In 1977 four members of OPEC - Saudi Arabia, Kuwait, Qatar, and United Arab Emirates - had more than 80 percent of the total OPEC surplus.(28)

With excess oil funds rapidly accruing, the OPEC surplus countries needed safe investment opportunities and turned primarily to the banking systems of the stronger Western countries and private financial markets to deposit their funds in short- and long-term assets. Thus, the private financial markets have served as a substantial investment vehicle and flow-through intermediary for excess petrodollars needed to finance deficit countries - a process called "recycling." In 1974 OPEC countries invested an estimated $22.5 billion in the European banking system.(29) However, deposits fell off in the second half of 1974 due to declining confidence related to growing world payments imbalances and bank failures (i.e., the Bankhaus I.D. Herstatt) which caused OPEC depositors to reassess the quality of bank intermediaries and become increasingly selective. As a result, depositors preferred investing only in the "bluest chip" Eurobanks in order to minimize risk. OPEC investors also preferred short-term, overnight and call deposits which eroded the banks' matching procedures with medium-term loans. By 1975 a marked drop in Eurocurrency deposits to $8 billion occurred due to declining OPEC surpluses and increased investor interest in Eurobonds.

The tide again turned in 1976, however, and Eurocurrency placements by OPEC nations began rising. By the end of June 1977 OPEC countries' holdings of bank deposits in major market centers totaled about $72 billion of which $58 billion was in Eurocurrencies.(30) The Bank for International Settlements estimates that roughly 25 percent of the net deposits of the European offshore market come from oil-producing countries. (The figure was less than 10 percent in 1974 at the time of Herstatt's failure.) Of the $162 billion OPEC cumulated total between 1974 and 1977, 39.4 percent has gone to Eurocurrency and other bank deposits.(31)

The changing trends in OPEC Eurocurrency deposits is reflected in the market's ease or stringency on Euroloan conditions, particularly for developing country borrowers. In the last half of 1974 under "alarmist" warnings of impending chaos and breakdown in the Euromarkets, strains and pressures increased on credit stringency and reduced the ease by which developing countries could obtain credit on favorable terms in the Euromarket. Eurobanks began to scrutinize the purpose of loans, debt service abilities, and creditworthiness factors. Average maturities declined from the seven- to ten-year range to five years; spreads over the London Inter-Bank Offer Rate (LIBOR) increased from 1 to 1 3/8 points through 1975; front-end fees increased; and syndication became more difficult. Even the most prosperous developing countries faced difficulties with more expensive and uncertain credit as banks evaluated potential borrowers with more case-by-case scrutiny.

By mid- and late-1975, however Eurobankers were feeling pressures from the recession and consequent drop-off in industrial country borrowing. Hence, competition for loan outlets increased. In the first nine months of 1976, the Eurocurrency market expanded at a fairly modest pace, and with improved LDC deficit positions, Euroborrowing conditions for developing countries eased slightly. Interest rates declined modestly, although pressures on spreads remained and bankers were trying to hold margins at one percentage point and raise management and facility fees.(32) In general, most effective rates for LDC borrowers with "well-established" links were two percentage points while those with less than prime ratings paid over three percentage points. Toward the end of 1976, however, the creditors' market turned to a debtors' market.

The pace of Eurocurrency activity "increased strikingly" in the first months of 1977, although the expected boom for the year did not materialize. The remarkable feature, however, was the incidence of "jumbo loans." During 1975 and early 1976 syndicated markets arranged several $500 million loans and one $600 millon loan, but in late 1976 and early 1977, several $1 billion loans were credited. Venezuela was the first to break the billion dollar barrier in September 1976 and did so again in January 1977.(33)

Along with the marked tendency to larger syndicated Eurocurrency credits were the further squeeze on lending margins (see Table 3.4) and lengthened maturities beyond five to seven years. The one percent LIBOR margin was breached, and a number of developing countries came to the international credit markets for the first time (e.g., India, Mauritius) or for the first time on a large scale (e.g., Jordan, Trinidad and Tobago).(34) Overall, however, gross Eurocurrency lending to non-OPEC developing countries increased at a slower pace than in the previous two years - a reflection of reduced financing needs of major borrowers (Brazil, Philippines) and reduced credit standing of others (Turkey, Peru).

The considerable international liquidity conditions are continuing in 1978, and many developing countries have

Table 3.4. How They Shrink: Average Interest Spreads (basis points*)

	1973	1975	1976	1977	1978
Nonoil LDCs	121	165	187	177	158
OPEC	129	167	133	159	104
Small OECD countries	94	158	137	109	83

*Basis point = 1/100 of one percent in the yield of an investment.
Note: Figures are for the fourth quarter of each year except for 1978 which shows first quarter spreads.
Source: Euromoney, June 1978, p. 183.

renegotiated past loans at lower spreads and longer maturities, or are borrowing to prepay older, costlier loans and thereby restructure their debt profiles. Since 1976, countries also have borrowed to replenish their reserves. As a group nonoil developing countries have increased reserves by 80 percent since 1973. In 1976 reserves increased by $10 billion (see Table 3.5), and in the first three-quarters of 1977, they increased by $6 billion.

Table 3.5. Whose Reserves Went Up? (in millions of US$)

	Reserves End-1976	Change Over Year
Brazil	6,477	+2,443
India	3,074	+1,701
South Korea	2,960	+1,410
Argentina	1,608	+1,156
Malaysia	2,420	+ 942
Indonesia	1,499	+ 913
Colombia	1,158	+ 637
Taiwan	1,607	+ 438
Singapore	3,353	+ 386

Source: Economist, April 16, 1977, p. 91.

To some optimists, the performance of the Eurocurrency market during the throes of the last few years attests to the flexibility, resiliency, and capacity of the market to serve needs in the face of abrupt developments. The Euromarket not only survived the worst recession since the 1930s, but expanded, prospered, and exhibited its "exceptional buoyancy and ease of adjustment to world situations."(35) Nonetheless, fears remain among the pessimists about Eurobank exposure to developing countries, the large build-up of LDC debt, and future trends in current-account deficits. Robert Solomon of the Brookings Institution has warned that "so long as oil exporting countries and others earn more than they spend on imports, the rest of the world faces an irreducible deficit which must be financed by borrowing."(36) As long as there are large surpluses in the coffers of nations with low import-absorptive capacities, deficits will continue to spring up in one nation as soon as they are suppressed in another.(37) Hence, a closer examination of developing country exposure to the Eurocurrency market and a disaggregated profile are in order.

LDCs FACE DEBT ESCALATION

In 1974-75 nonoil developing countries needed $80 billion to finance deficits and service debts - $36 billion was raised privately. In 1976 developing countries required $42 billion to finance deficits and service debts, and $22 billion was obtained from commercial banks. Hence, for developing countries Euroborrowing increased during the recession as it had during the boom. In fact, probably the most significant feature of the Eurocurrency market in the 1970s - next to the market's overall rapid growth - is the spectacular rise in the LDC share of the total extended Eurocredits. A second changed feature is the extension of Eurocredits to developing countries for general-purpose, balance-of-payments financing. This developing country phenomenon has occurred despite the increased expense of "recession loans" over "boom loans." One reason for the developing countries' turn to Euromarkets, particularly in 1974-75, is their preference for higher private loan rates over the strict conditions attached to official loans, e.g., International Monetary Fund credits, which impose tight standards and economic reforms to comply with stringent monetary and fiscal targets. Moreover, the absence of political strings and tied-aid conditions also has attracted developing countries to the Euromarket.

An Aggregate Overview

In 1970 when nonoil developing countries obtained $300 million in Eurocurrency credits, their market share was a low 6.4 percent of the total $4.73 billion extended. For the next four years, however, their Eurocredit share increased and consistently held at the 21- to 24-percent range reaching $6.25 billion in 1974. (See Table 3.2.) By 1975-76, after the oil price increases had affected financing needs, the share of Eurocredits to nonoil developing countries was pushing the 40 percent mark and credits in 1976 exceeded $11 billion. Although total borrowing increased for nonoil LDCs in 1977, Euromarket emphasis turned to OPEC and industrial country borrowing, and the LDC market share declined.

An aggregate overview of Eurocurrency lending, however, does not provide a clear picture of the developing country phenomenon in the Eurocurrency markets, for as Morgan Guaranty Trust reported for 1977, 81 percent of all Eurocredits to nonoil developing countries went to ten largest borrowers. This skewed extension of loans to developing countries is significant for LDC debt evaluation and industrial country debt policy, and therefore should be examined.

Eurocredit Distribution among Developing Countries

The striking character of Eurocurrency lending to developing countries is its narrow concentration among a few countries. For just as the oil-producing countries have deposited their excess petrodollars in only the bluest chip banks, so too have banks recycled these funds to only the bluest chip developing countries. And although the early 1970s boom years increased LDC participation levels (about 10 to 20 countries) in the Eurocurrency markets, in general, the net international borrowers today are the same groups of countries as before the commodities price rise. According to the IMF's Isham Kapur, "Apart from the few that have borrowed regularly and substantially, other LDC borrowings have been erratic in nature and insubstantial in size."(38) Hence, the ten largest Eurocurrency borrowers in 1977 (see Table 3.6) closely reflect the LDC borrowers during the period 1970-74.

In the boom years when bankers saw manna in the Southern hills, developing countries were viewed as the "new rich" or "fast growing." New borrowers fitting these categories entered the market, and in 1972 several African and Asian countries were able to secure loans. By 1973, an increasing number of countries - including Bolivia, Nicaragua, Zaire, Zambia, and Kenya - were able to raise Euroloans. In 1973 Zaire's debt to banks grew 300 percent and Zambia's

Table 3.6. LDC Eurocurrency Borrowers, 1977
(in millions of US$)

Non-OPEC LDCs	13,427
Brazil	2,814
Mexico	2,700
South Korea	1,265
Argentina	849
Morocco	772
Philippines	698
Chile	591
Taiwan	524
Hong Kong	408
Ivory Coast	265

Source: Morgan Guaranty Trust Company, World Financial Markets, March 1978, p. 4.

increased by more than 600 percent.(39) Yet there was no Eurosyndicates for the Bangladeshes, Burmas, or Chads. When the recession years commenced, LDC Euroborrowing continued to rise but with increased trends toward concentration. This concentration can be examined by individual country borrower, income level, and geographic region.

Country Borrowers

According to Morgan Guaranty Trust, the top ten developing country borrowers in the Eurocurrency markets in 1976 and 1977 secured 86 percent and 81 percent, respectively, of the total Eurocredits extended to nonoil LDCs. As one could expect, the roster of "Big Ten" borrowers largely reflects the fast industrializing, resource rich, or export-led growth economies. Brazil and Mexico, for example, not only have been the largest borrowers but have dominated the LDC market as well, taking 47 percent and 41 percent of all nonoil LDC credits in 1976 and 1977, respectively. Hence, with this record, Emma Rothschild could report in the spring of 1976 that Brazil owed more to foreign banks than all nonoil LDCs in Africa, the Middle East, and South Asia combined.(40) The estimated repayment requirements for these two countries are appropriately boggling; Brazil will have paid \$2.5 billion, \$3.2 billion, and \$5.7 billion in 1976, 1977, and 1980, respectively; Mexico's requirements are estimated at \$1.1 billion, \$1.9 billion, and \$3.0 billion for the same years.(41)

Income Levels

When examining Eurocredit distribution according to income level - based on World Bank categorization by 1975 GNP per capita - the majority has gone to middle-income countries. Whereas high-income developing countries (Argentina, Cyprus, Greece, Jamaica, Malta, Portugal, Singapore, Spain, Uruguay, Yugoslavia) account for nearly one-third of total LDC Eurocredits from 1973 to 1976, middle-income LDCs claim twice as much or 60.6 percent. (See Table 3.7) Only Argentina is

Table 3.7. Eurocurrency Credits by Income Category (in billions of US$)

	1973	1974	1975	1976	Category Total	Percent of Total*
High income	2.57	3.25	3.23	6.41	15.46	32.9
Middle income	4.94	5.80	7.54	10.16	28.44	60.6
Lower income	0.43	0.41	1.68	0.50	3.02	6.4
Total	7.94	9.46	12.45	17.07	46.92	100

*Figures have been rounded.

Note: High income = $1,075 GNP per capita or above.
Middle income = $266-$1,074 GNP per capita.
Lower income = $265 GNP per capita or less.

Source: IFM Survey, Supplement on International Lending, June 6, 1977, p. 188. (Definition of income categories, p. 187).

among the top ten borrowers in 1977 from among the high-income countries. Because of the wide range of economies in the middle-income group, the World Bank has designated subcategories - the upper middle income ($521-$1,074) and middle income ($266-$520). Of the ten largest borrowers in 1977, five countries (Brazil, Chile, Taiwan, Korea, Mexico) are in the upper middle-income category, and three (Ivory Coast, Morocco, Philippines) are in the middle-income group. (The World Bank does not include Hong Kong in the nonoil LDC classification.)

Geographic Region

The Latin American region generally has monopolized the Euroloans to nonoil developing countries both by volume and by number of countries, although Asia stands fairly even when measured by number of countries. In 1977 for example, four Latin American countries (Argentina, Brazil, Chile, Mexico - Peru is usually included) accounted for 69 percent by volume of the Euroloans to the top ten countries or 51 percent of all nonoil LDC Eurocredits. The largest Asian borrowers in 1977 (Hong Kong, South Korea, Philippines, Taiwan) claimed 41 percent of loans to the highest ten borrowers and 28.7 percent of all loans to non-OPEC developing countries.

In summary, two facts emerge from the review of developing country borrowers in the Eurocurrency markets: Only the largest semi-industrial developing countries are able to borrow large amounts in Euroloans (the neediest are virtually excluded), and in 1976 and 1977, over 80 percent of total publicized Eurocredits were granted to only ten nonoil developing countries.

Euroloans and Implications for Debt

Although estimates vary, total outstanding debt owed by developing countries in 1977 reached $200-250 billion - $78 billion of which was owed to private foreign sources. One source estimates that between 1976 and 1976, private debt for developing countries rose by 76 percent.(42) The biggest debt jumps began in 1974 - which also marks the beginning shift to borrowing from private international capital markets. New commitments to LDCs in 1974 totaled $36.33 billion of which private-sourced borrowings accounted for 38 percent or $16.29 billion. This compares to $26.87 billion or 22.1 percent in private debt of the total debt owed in 1973. Private borrowing continued to rise in 1975 and 1976, and in 1975 private banks had financed 40 percent of all nonoil developing countries' capital needs.(43) Net lending to nonoil LDCs by banks tripled from just over $5 billion in 1975 to just under $14 billion by 1976.(44).

The significance of the increased private lending to developing countries has been the substantial shortening of maturities and higher interest rates, particularly in 1974-75. Interest alone on debt is as much as oil importers were paying for debt servicing before 1970.(45) As a result, repayment schedules beginning 1977-78 are heavy, and ballooning amortization is expected in the 1978-80 period. Amortization payments rose from $850 million in 1973 to $10,500 million in 1974, $12,000 million in 1975, and $15,000 million in 1976.(46) The United Nations Conference on Trade and Development

(UNCTAD) has estimated that in 1978, 25 percent of export earnings of the poorest developing countries will go to service debt. Moreover, 27 percent of funds now being raised by the nonoil LDCs is needed to finance maturing debt, and this percentage is expected to increase to 50 percent by 1980 and 65 percent in 1985.(47)

For developing countries, the "intolerable proportions" of the level of debt and servicing requirements are magnified by worries of reduced export earnings through unstable commodity prices and rising import costs. This could signal possible abandonment of development programs, needed dams, agricultural projects - as well as possible political unrest. While it is clear what the debt future and Euroborrowing will be, it is clear that even if new LDC borrowing declines significantly, debt repayment requirements will continue to be a heavy burden for most LDCs.

Future Trends in LDC Eurocurrency Borrowing

It is unlikely that nonoil developing countries will be in a position to continue borrowing on the same scale as in the 1974-76 period, although LDC Euroloan activity is picking up in 1978 after a lull in 1977 due to declining current-account deficits and increased reserve positions. While it is difficult to predict market conditions and continued liquidity, for the near-term in 1978 while slow growth and weak capital spending in industrial countries continues, banks will be awash in funds and looking to developing countries for lending opportunities. The highly competitive conditions now existing among banks will enable most developing country Euroborrowers to renegotiate old loans on more favorable terms and borrow to prepay older, costlier debts - a process which has had a strong start in 1978. While this factor may ease repayment burdens and "bunching," developing country demand for credit will be spurred by sizable current-account deficits (possibly increasing by $11 billion in 1978),(48) balance-of-payments financing needs, and maturing external debt. Dampening Euroborrowing needs and credit demand will be the developing countries' continued policies of domestic economic stringency, strict demand management, import restrictions, inflation control, and reserves buildup. With this combination of factors - international liquidity, LDC financing needs, and improved LDC economic policies - banks will continue lending to creditworthy developing countries. Moreover, bankers realize that cutting back would only restrict the means of earning funds to repay existing debt. In fact, Robert Z. Aliber of the University of Chicago believes that developing countries are better credit risks than industrial countries and have not borrowed enough.(49)

Future Eurocurrency borrowing trends by nonoil developing countries depend greatly, of course, on the actions and financial situations of OPEC countries including the size of the collective OPEC surplus (dependent on world economic growth, oil demand, and oil price rises), the volume of OPEC expenditures, and future geographic distribution of OPEC investments. OPEC countries probably will show a continued preference for Euromarket deposits - although more direct investments in both developed and developing countries is also likely. This could again raise concern about the long-term ability of the Eurocurrency market to absorb a large volume of investable funds.

Rothschild has observed that "in the months and years ahead, fears will return like monsters."(50) However, some view the prospect of default as unlikely and of minimal impact. This is so because: 1) the markets are prepared for it; 2) default losses on international lending are smaller than on domestic lending; 3) outright default will be uncommon due to reschedulings; and 4) governments and markets will do their best to minimize the impact of defaults.(51)

In short, it appears that the Eurocurrency market will continue to be a dominant channel for the transfer of resources to the Third World. In fact, Morgan Guaranty Trust Company has stated that "the private credit markey will still be called upon to shoulder the bulk of the financial burden,"(52) and in the foreseeable future will be the key factor in stabilizing the developing countries' payments situation. _The Economist_ predicts that "it will continue to be safe for commercial banks to continue to lend to middle-income countries...."(53) However, it is also certain that official and multilateral institutions such as the World Bank, International Monetary Fund, or the United States Federal Reserve System will play a greater role through monitoring, extending credits on strict conditionality, or cofinancing.

There have been warnings on the state of the Eurobanking system's health, however. In 1978 _International Currency Review_ noted that "unfortunately the Eurodollar banking system is in a highly unstable condition. Either liquidity will continue to increase, with the consequent growth of lending to uncreditworthy borrowers; or the rise in bad debts will precipitate a rapid drying up of loanable funds. Ultimately there can be no middle course between the present excess supply of funds and an inadequate availability of loans. In the absence of international efforts to bring the Eurodollar market under control, the situation will remain highly unstable and potentially disastrous."(54)

In sum, although the future path of the developing countries in the Eurocurrency markets is not clear-cut, it appears that continued borrowing will be substantial based on available funds and LDC needs. The state of the Eurobanking system and OPEC actions are important considerations; however, the market will likely continue to exhibit a high degree of flexibility and bankers will consider loans to developing countries on a case-by-case basis.

THE BANKS' ROLE IN CRISIS CREATION

> A "sound" banker, alas! is not one who foresees danger and avoids it, but one who, when he is ruined, is ruined in a conventional and orthodox way along with his fellows, so that no one can really blame him.
>
> John Maynard Keynes
> August 1931(55)

On Rising to the Occasion

When lending euphoria to developing countries rose to dizzying heights during the boom period on the promise of new frontiers, bankers generally considered sovereign borrowers to be risk-free. Moreover, bankers came to believe they were playing a public spirited function in recycling oil surpluses to deficit nations around the world, and that banks were contributing in a significant way to coping with the problem of recycling. David Rockefeller, for example, has explained the bankers' role as a matter of destiny: "Multinational financial services corporations were called upon not only to expand their more traditional activities, but also to take on important new responsibility as well."(56) In fact, as International Currency Review has commented, "There is nothing wrong with commercial banks rushing to rescue countries experiencing short-term balance-of-payments deficits. Indeed there is a strong case for arguing that bankers are more efficient than the official international financial institutions."(57)

On the other hand, critics of the surge in private lending hold that it has developed too fast, too much, and unwisely - often, according to the New York Times, with lenders "placing millions of dollars in loans [and not] having the most basic first-hand information about the situation."(58) Business Week has stated that "Flush with cash and hungry for profits in a period of low corporate loan demand at home, loans to foreign nations looked good."(59) Combined with what Cheryl Payer calls ignorance and competitive pressures, banks extended loans to borrowers "whose...economic situation alone would not fully justify granting."(60) Payer reports that banks jumped to lending to governments with inadequate information from the borrowing countries on their financial positions and with too little preparation in evaluating national balance of payments and debt-load statistics. In many cases bank decisions to lend appear to have been made on a short-sighted ad hoc basis on the strength of personal contacts. Sometimes the existence of natural resources was considered generally sufficient evidence of creditworthiness. It appears that private creditors often yielded to competitive pressures in seeking larger shares of the foreign markets and thereby made credit easily available and exacerbated LDC debt problems. In Payer's words, any number of banks could play the Eurocurrency game, and when faced with competition and inadequate information, "banks closed their eyes to risk and hoped."(61)

Banks, of course, refute such allegations and contend that lending decisions are based on assessment of economic indicators plus political institutions and past borrowing experience with the applicant sovereign borrower. Euromoney reports, however, that there is a lack of logic and objectivity that characterizes the Euromarkets. Conditions of loans do not exactly reflect the situation of the borrower; and factors of analysis (e.g., debt-service ratio, balance-of-payments condition) do not always appear to be the elements which determine the banks' decisions with regard to credit extensions, spreads, maturities, etc.(62) Becaue of the high competitiveness of the market, banks appear to allocate funds on the basis of quantity rationing with amounts determined by relative creditworthiness of the borrowers. But despite the banks' assurance of selectivity and lending practices toward only those developing countries with "an internal sense of discipline and commitment to import substitution,"(63) fears of overextension and possible defaults hang over many private loans. These are fears, writes Rothschild, "to which many banks have closed their minds, to which governments have also closed their minds."(64)

Confidence Versus Fears...or Whistling in the Dark

There is a widely held view that events of 1974-75 prove the fortitude of the international financial system: "None of the largest banks failed. No countries went broke. The neurotic episodes of 1974 and 1975 did not become a psychosis of the entire system."(65) With the "fear largely behind us," optimists such as Richard Debs of the Federal Reserve Bank of New York, conclude that "the system has not only survived but has come through this period of uncertainty... [toward] ...emergence of an even healthier system."(66) In fact, in congressional testimony the Carter administration has formally rejected the view that banks - particularly United States banks - have become overly committed. Fears of United States bank overexposure have been "greatly exaggerated," reported

United States Treasury Assistant Secretary C. Fred Bergsten. Furthermore, Bergsten is "convinced that the major LDC borrowers, as a group, are in a stronger position today than they were a year ago....Remarkably low spreads on Euro-currency borrowing by these countries are a tribute to their strength...."(67) Finally, Bergsten has denied that United States bank lending to developing countries has posed grave risks to the American economy or banking system. "We find no adverse effect on our own economy, the soundness of our banking system, the availability of credit for domestic purposes, or the entire world economy."(68)

Moreover, David Rockefeller has ascribed the lack of confidence in the banking system to scare stories of the press. Fortune magazine supports this view in an editorial comment: "At a time when banking problems are well on their way to solution, a few over-zealous reporters working with ill-digested statistics have succeeded in conjuring up pictures of a banking system about to collapse and plunge the country into panic."(69) Fortune further alleges that the scare stories are prompted by Congress in an attempt to undercut the Federal Reserve's strict monetary policies - a tactic that "is a hell of a way to try to influence public policy."(70)

Efforts to influence confidence to the contrary, there are also numerous voices attempting to infuse bank prudence and recognition that continuation of banks' functioning to finance LDC current-account deficits cannot go on forever. The underlying fear is the potential for default and overwhelming debt that would undermine confidence of depositors and investors, thus causing large withdrawals of funds and contraction of the credit market. This in turn may require large transfusions from central banks and the International Monetary Fund to bail out the banking system, ultimately fueling inflation and precipitating economic collapse. Among these voices has been that of Arthur Burns, former chairman of the United States Federal Reserve System, who has taken the lead to warn "in strident tones" that banks "will have to cut back on this risky activity." Banks cannot "prudently finance the world's rising oil bill on an indefinite basis."(71) Even the confident Assistant Secretary Bergsten has told reporters that the situation should be watched closely, and regulatory agencies should "watch the banks like hawks."(72)

Bankers themselves are not as confident of the situation as they would like the public - and other bankers - to believe. Some have confessed "a growing sense of unease about the prominence and visibility of commercial banks in the financing of governments,"(73) while others have conceded being "a little nervous about this area."(74) One Senate staffer bluntly summed up the bankers' fears: "The banks are plenty scared. What they're saying is, 'We're in over our heads and we want help from Uncle Sam.'"(75)

Henry C. Wallich of the Federal Reserve contends, however, that the tide has turned for a number of reasons including LDC economic adjustments, a new pattern of orderliness, an improved credit environment with the presence of international financial institutions, and experience of banks and developing countries working together. Moreover, says Wallich, "People are much less concerned about the Brazils and Mexicos - even the Perus and Zaires - than they were a year ago. Largely it is because the crisis has come into focus and fallen into a pattern that by now is becoming familiar.... It also has been made clear that private lenders will have to take their lumps and that governments are not going to bail out the private lender."(76)

Nonetheless, some fears still exist, and the banks' "perilous" situation has been likened to a person astride a tiger: "The dangers of continuing the ride are matched only by fears of what will happen if an attempt is made to get off."(77)

The Bankers' Way Out

With $78 billion in private loans to developing countries and occasional default clouds hanging overhead, it has been observed that some banks would like to "pull in their horns" and "beat a hasty retreat."(78) Others assure that bankers foresee no current danger to the international banking system or no prospect of default of a major borrower. Nonetheless, banks have called for greater cooperative efforts between governments and official international financing institutions to take on the burden of additional loans to developing countries and to direct "massive amounts" of official development assistance to problem nations. They also would like to see governments bearing the main burden of debt rescheduling, and they have pushed for greater cooperation with and reliance on the International Monetary Fund, particularly in providing information and data on countries' economies. Finally, banks would like the IMF to prod developing countries to adopt restrictive monetary and fiscal policies, devalue currencies to restrain imports, and encourage expanded exports. On their own, banks increasingly are conditioning loans - IMF style - on suitable LDC economic strategies or are limiting future loans to the richer, more productive countries or for project and short-term trade financing.

But for the time being, at least, banks will continue to lend to developing countries - if only to ward off a crisis of confidence and to prevent immediate repayment problems. To fail to roll over previously extended loans could easily precipitate the crisis everyone in trying to avoid. The danger of not lending can be as great as that of too much lending.

CONCLUSIONS

In examining the development, conditions, and situation of the developing countries in the Eurocurrency markets, several observations and conclusions can be made.

First, the extent of future difficulties the developing countries may have in repaying Eurocurrency debts cannot be easily predicted or measured. The abilities of LDCs to service their private debt do not depend only on their own economic management policies, progress of development programs, and commitment of leaders to take appropriate and needed courses of economic action. They also depend on: a) the pace of industrial country economic growth; b) general international economic conditions, e.g., recession, commodity prices; c) industrial country policies on trade, industrialization, and technology transfer issues; and d) not least of all, the policies of OPEC countries on oil price increases, accumulation of surpluses, and use and dispersion of those surpluses. Repayment ability also hinges on the willingness of banks to roll over and reschedule loans - a practice that is not unusual, unfamiliar, or infrequent.

Second, it is clear that concern for potential default of developing countries in the Eurocurrency market is limited to a few LDCs with heavy private debt commitments. Those that are heavily indebted, by and large, are the countries with economies that are rapidly expanding and have the capability of repayment, e.g., Brazil, South Korea. There may be questions about a small number of countries that currently are in economic difficulty, e.g., Zaire, Turkey, but their authorities and official and private lenders are working together to iron out the debt problems. And despite the depths of the difficulties sometimes confronted, countries - such as Indonesia and Pertamina - have managed to weather the storm. In fact, it has been observed that LDCs as a group are in less immediate debt trouble than industrial countries, and that "most LDCs have the capability of servicing higher levels of debt than those currently outstanding."(79) In sum, although private debt figures are high in absolute and growth terms, potential problems are limited to a handful of countries.

Third, the banks' exposure and therefore vulnerability to LDC Eurocurrency default is minimal. If defaults occur, it would not be on a scale painful to bank lenders. This is because: a) bank exposure to LDCs is a small proportion of combined bank assets; b) bank portfolios are sufficiently diversified to withstand even a massive rescheduling; and c) government guarantees in lending countries and LDC claims on international agencies diminishes the likelihood of default or rescheduling on bank loans. Hence, although signs of bank nervousness occasionally are apparent, it may be that the bankers' exhibits of confidence are closer to the mark of reason.

Fourth, unless the rise and high prices of oil are diffused, the problems of potential LDC debt default will become more acute. Debt problems will not end if OPEC surpluses and oil prices continue to rise. Hence, debt will mount until oil importers reduce payments deficits either by adjusting to less energy-intensive life-styles and production, or by cutting economic growth, or until OPEC reduces oil prices. Otherwise, with world economic recovery, OPEC oil surpluses will mount higher "year after year, year-in, year-out, until something cracks: the oil price, the world monetary system, the patience of the industrial West, or peace itself."(80) Thus, OPEC policies are probably the most crucial element of the LDC Eurocurrency debt issue. Perhaps, then, instead of seeking the Band-Aid of financing, a cure for OPEC oil prices is in order.

Fifth, industrial country response to developing country private debt appears to be directed only to how the debt can be financed. The massive overhang of credit already extended will quickly multiply if solutions are only viewed in terms of refinancing - and hence piled-on debt.

Sixth, strangely (or understandably - depending on one's perspective) the issue of LDC Eurocurrency debt and the concern it engenders have focused almost entirely on the health of the Eurocurrency markets and the banking system - not on the plight and fate of the developing countries. The ability of developing countries to grow, survive, and break the vicious circle of debt is rarely the primary issue; rather, how to get private banks out of the jam into which they have hurled themselves is the focus of attention. The recent discussions on LDC commercial debt are coming from the banks, not the developing countries. If banks and governments turned their attention to breaking the LDC debt merry-go-round as they have to their own systems, then their own health and well-being might be increased commensurately.

Finally, it may be a propitious time - when confidence is generally high - to explore the possibility of establishing an IMF discount window or similar institution to provide an element of stability if trends turn adversely. As one idea that addresses the private debt problem of developing countries, a secondary market facility is worthy of further consideration. The key is to implement a last resort safety feature before a crisis situation occurs.

In sum, the increased use by the developing countries of Eurocurrency market resources - through both necessity and preference - has escalated the developing countries' debt markedly. However, this escalation is not necessarily an ill omen for the future stability of the Eurocurrency market, the private banking system, or the developing countries themselves. For as most economists respond to queries on specific predictions, the answer is, "It depends."

APPENDIX THE EUROCURRENCY MARKET: WHENCE IT CAME AND WHERE IT'S BEEN

What It Is

The Eurocurrency market is an international banking market specializing in the borrowing and lending of currencies outside their country of issue. Hence, United States dollars, French francs, Japanese yen, or Kuwaiti dinars received and loaned by banks in the United Kingdom would be part of the Euromarket system. The principal depositors of Eurofunds are central banks (which hold large amounts of foreign currencies as reserves), multinational corporations, investment institutions, and the oil exporters. Eurofund borrowers can be commercial banks, official (national) monetary authorities, multinational corporations and other business firms, and semi-government entities, i.e., official international organizations. However, most Eurocurrency transactions are between banks on a short-term basis, and by 1975 the interbank market accounted for approximately 75 percent of foreign currency liabilities and assets of reporting European banks.(81) Moreover, interbank activity contributes to most of the gross increase in the size of the Euromarket. (Gross Eurocurrency statistics include interbank tranactions, whereas net Eurocurrency figures avoid the double-counting of interbank deposits.) In addition to short-term credit, the market can offer medium- and long-term loans, for example, of one, three, five, or even fifteen years. Further, the Eurocurrency system is a wholesale market and the average size of transactions is quite large. Eurobanks do not provide checking facilities (although short maturities of most deposits make close substitutes for liquid assets); rather, banks deal in deposits of a specific time period bearing a stated yield.

The Eurocurrency market is commonly referred to as the Eurodollar market based on the central role of the United States dollar as the major currency. Today about 73 percent of the Eurocurrency market, according to the _Washington Post_, is denominated in United States dollars.(82) _Euromoney_, March 1978, reported that 94 percent of Eurocurrency credits in 1977 were denominated in dollars, although Morgan Guaranty Trust Company reported a 79 percent Eurodollar figure as of September 1977. However, the dollar's position is gradually losing ground to other currencies entering the market, particularly the German mark and recently new Middle East national currencies, e.g., the Kuwaiti dinar. Moreover, the term

"Euromarket" has become a geographical misnomer. Until the mid-1960s, most currency markets have been located in European centers - especially in London - but a significant volume of foreign currency business is now carried out in non-European centers. The Caribbean Islands, Panama, Hong Kong, Singapore, Japan, and Canada have fostered considerable growth in offshore markets. The distribution of Eurobanks by national origin has also shifted. Between 1963 and 1969, the share of United States banks in the London market hovered in the 40 to 50 percent range with the remainder taken up by United Kingdom banks. Since 1973, United States banks accounted for less than 40 percent of the London market, and by the end of 1974, non-United States/United Kingdom banks generated more than 30 percent of the London business. Additionally, multinational consortium banks have increased and in 1974 acounted for seven percent of the Eurocurrency business based in London.

The exact size of the Eurocurrency market is difficult to determine because comprehensive official statistics are lacking. First, redepositing on interbank loans leads to double-counting, and, second, publicity on Eurocurrency credits is voluntary and not all loan transactions are announced. Small direct loans by a Eurobank to a country, for example, are rarely publicized. It has been estimated that only 50 percent of Eurocredits are publicly recorded.(83) To further blur the statistical picture, lack of standardization among banks on terminology, definitions, and procedures contributes to inappropriate comparisons of bank figures.

There is, in Emma Rothschild's words, a kind of ontological obscurity surrounding the Eurocurrency market - it has a kind of viscous, liquid character that seems to be everywhere at once, yet is illusory, and flows to flourish in the most permissive of atmospheres.(84) Eurocurrency transactions are largely free from controls and regulations, are beyond the jurisdictions of central monetary authorities, and operate outside the supervision of governments. Hence, explains Rothschild, "The banks have expanded luxuriantly where they are most free of government restrictions: above all in the Eurocurrency business. Of all the flora of the boom, Eurobanking has been the most fecund."(85)

This lack of restrictions has also made the Eurocurrency business highly competitive which sometimes has led to declines in margins between deposit and loan rates as well as lower rates of return on Eurocurrency assets than those on domestic currency assets in national markets. During periods of increasing competition, the tendency increases for banks to take higher credit risks both in choice of borrowers and acceptance of longer maturities and lower interest rates. Despite the competition, occasionally lowered margins, and sometimes "risky" transactions, however, the Eurocurrency market is in booming health and has been on a sharply upward trend. (See Fig. 3.1.)

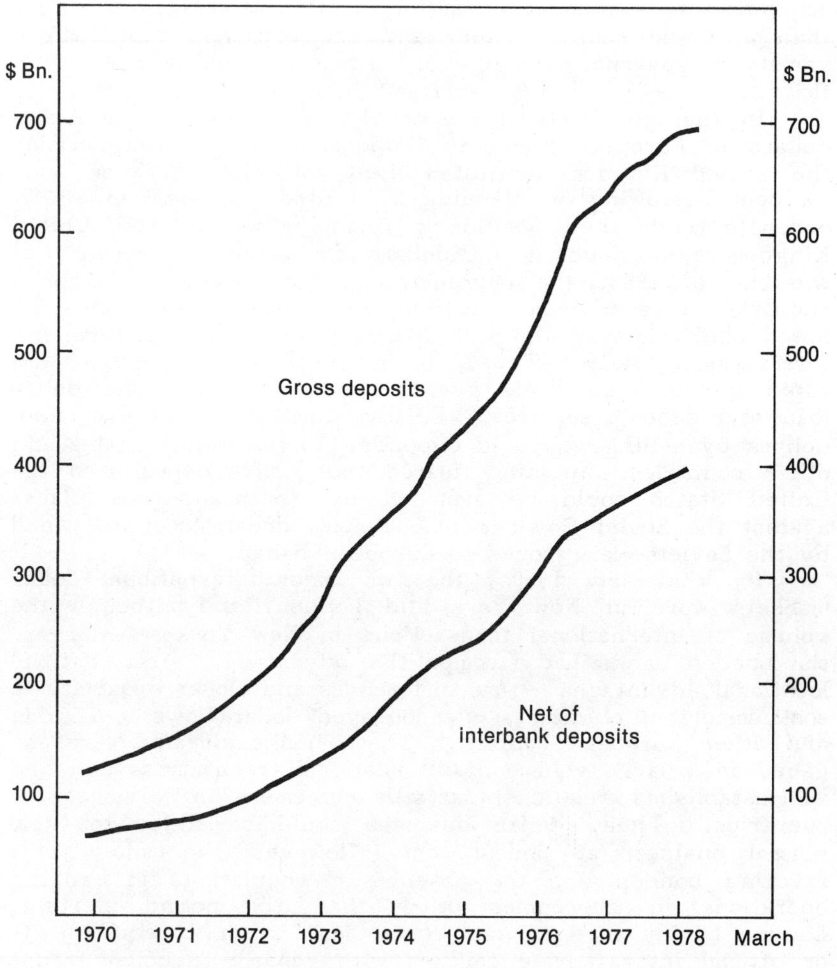

Source: Morgan Guaranty Trust cited in *The Economist*, June 10, 1978, p. 87.

Fig. 3.I. Growth of the Eurocurrency Market, January 1970–March 1978.

Fig. 3.1. Growth of the Eurocurrency Market, January 1970–March 1978.

Source: Morgan Guaranty Trust cited in Economist, June 10, 1978, p. 87.

Origin and Development of the Euromarket

The rise and prominence of the Eurocurrency system are attributed to a number of supply and demand factors rather than a single causal factor, and are primarily rooted in a variety of government regulations affecting banking and capital flows.

In the late 1950s, three developments pushed banks and dollars to Europe. First, in response to the sterling crisis, the United Kingdom instituted tight controls (1957) on nonresident borrowing and lending by United Kingdom banks. In order to retain their position in financing world trade, United Kingdom banks substituted dollars for sterling. Second, at the end of 1958, the currencies of major Western European countries were made convertible for nonresidents. This allowed banks to buy and sell dollars freely to use in financing international trade. Thus, foreign exchange conversion and rapid international trade growth created the need for dollar loan and deposit services. Finally, the Soviets were earning dollars by selling gold and exporting to the United States and other countries, but they feared that dollar deposits in the United States could be attached by Americans with claims against the Soviet Government. Hence, dollar accounts owned by the Soviets were moved to European banks.

By the early 1960s, the two major international dollar markets were in New York and London, and although the volume of international transactions in New York was larger, the London banks had a competitive advantage. First, natural locational advantages - time differences and closer proximity to some important customers - encouraged dollar flows to London and other European centers. These banks already were engaged in a large volume of international transactions and had well-established relationships with customers in a variety of countries. Thus, dollar business could be added to their normal business at modest cost. However, the major factor favoring London was the absence of regulations in banking operations in currencies other than the pound sterling. London banks were not subject to legal reserve requirements or official interest rate ceilings with respect to dollar transactions as in the United States. Therefore, London banks could pay higher interest rates and operate with narrower margins.

Another major factor of Eurocurrency growth was the imposition by United States authorities of capital restrictions and regulations beginning in the early 1960s. In 1963 an interest equalization tax was introduced which effectively closed New York capital markets to many foreign borrowers. By 1965 the Voluntary Foreign Credit Restraint Guidelines were instituted to control nonresident lending by banks and other financial institutions in order to cope with the United

States balance-of-payments deficit. Hence, beyond certain limits banks could only lend abroad with funds borrowed abroad. The credit restraint program was strengthened and made mandatory in 1968. These two sets of controls had two important effects on the growth and structure of the Eurocurrency market. First, United States companies wanting to finance new or additional foreign investment outlays had to rely more on funds outside the United States. Second, in order to avoid losing out in the growing international loan business, United States banks - which were constrained in lending to foreign residents including foreign branches of United States companies - had to raise funds outside the United States. They therefore shifted a large part of their international business from New York to offshore centers by establishing branches in London and elsewhere.

Another United States restriction in 1969, Regulation Q, prohibited banks from increasing interest rates on time deposits, including certificates of deposit, which resulted in a substantial drain of funds attracted to London rates. In the process, interest rates rose sharply in Europe which further increased the outflow of deposits from the United States to the Eurodollar market. When the United States Federal Reserve eased monetary restrictions in 1970 and United States banks could compete again for time deposits domestically and repay outstanding debts to their London branches, the Eurobanks were left with liquid funds. But since major European countries were following tight monetary policies at the time, there was ample demand for funds by Euroborrowers.

Growth of the Eurocurrency market continued rapidly throughout the early 1970s even after United States restrictions on capital outflows were eased. However, by mid-1974 concern for the viability of some bank and uncertainty about the future of the market caused growth to be checked sharply, and in mid-1975 when growth resumed, it was at a reduced rate. (See Table 3.8.)

The rise to prominence of the Euromarket in the late 1960s and early 1970s should not be viewed only in terms of supply factors and regulation avoidance, however. The growth of increased currency funds outside domestic markets also coincided with the growth of multinational corporations and the need for a more sophisticated international capital market. Combined with the general expansion of world trade and the increase in direct foreign investment, the Eurocurrency market had ample demand factors to encourage its growth. Additionally, tacit approval and assistance of governments in the main Eurocurrency system also has facilitated the Euromarket's development.

Table 3.8. Eurocurrency Market, 1970-Sept. 1977
(in billions of US$)

	1970	1971	1972	1973	1974	1975	1976	Sept. 1977
Gross size	111.3	145.4	200.2	303.1	369.9	456.6	558.8	616.2
Net size	65.0	85.0	110.0	160.0	215.0	250.0	310.0	360.0

Note: Based on foreign currency liabilities of banks in major European countries, the Bahamas, Cayman Islands, Panama, Canada, Japan, Hong Kong, Singapore, and Bahrain.

Source: Morgan Guaranty Trust Company, World Financial Markets, March 1978, p. 6.

The Market in Operation

The Eurocurrency market has been termed a "highly efficient system for allocating credit among lenders and borrowers."(86) Although Euroloans extended outside the interbank market can be arranged directly between the bank and borrower, medium-term loans exceeding the $10-20 million range rely increasingly on syndication or consortia techniques in order to spread the risk of large-scale loans and reduce the individual Eurobank's vulnerability to default potentials. A syndicated credit is an international loan shared by a number of Eurobanks, sometimes as many as 50 or more, which is arranged by a lead bank (often the bank approached for the loan). This system has allowed many small and medium-sized banks to operate in the Eurocurrency market. Consortia lending is organized by a specialized institution set up to provide international loans and consists of a subsidiary bank owned by a multinational group of banks.

When a sovereign borrower, for example, approaches a bank to obtain a Euroloan, the bank may either commit the full amount of the loan (and may sell participation certificates, that is, shares of the loan which are sold to other banks), or the bank may initiate syndication. One of two procedures may be used. The first is the "broadcast system" whereby the managing bank arranges a syndication by advertising worldwide via telex or telephone for participation of banks. The second method is "straight syndication" whereby the loan is committed from the beginning by a group of banks selected by the managing bank. The second method was more commonly used in the past, but the broadcast system is now more frequent. Benefits of the syndication procedures to the Euromarket system have been in the facilitation of larger Euroloans, enabling small and medium-sized banks to participate, and accepting the more risky borrowers that would otherwise be unable to contract loans in the market. The prime beneficiaries have been Third World governments.(87)

The negotiable items of a Eurocurrency loan contract (e.g., terms, maturity, currency, fees) are determined primarily by market conditions and the borrower's creditworthiness. Historically, these terms have varied more over time than across borrowers - although in tight money periods discrimination among borrowing countries is evident. (Nonnegotiable items specify legislation to which the contract is subject, tax liabilities of each party, etc.) Medium-term Euroloans increasingly feature use of rollover and floating interest rate credit arrangements to further minimize risk for both borrower and lender. Thus, a revolving credit typically allows interest rate adjustment every three to six months until final maturity on the basis of prevailing interest rates. Most loan contracts specify lending rates as a margin over deposit rates of "reference banks," usually taken to represent the London Inter-Bank Offer Rate, or LIBOR. The size of the interest rate "spread" over LIBOR, or margin, is a nominal expression of risk held by the lending bank. (Eurobanks can operate on small margins and still obtain a good return on capital due to lack of interest risks, reserve requirements, and the level of efficiency achieved in handling large volumes of funds.) Other fees include a commitment fee charged on the unused portion of funds (e.g., annual 0.5 percent) plus a nominal management fee. In some cases, loan agreements include a multicurrency clause which offers a choice of currencies in which the loan can be drawn in whole or in part, thus providing flexibility under conditions of exchange rate uncertainty which can alter the effective rate of borrowing.

Traditional medium-term maturities, or "commitment periods," on Euroloans are three to five years. In a survey by Giddy and Ray,(88) it was found that the most significant determinant of a loan maturity (for developing countries) is the country's debt-service ratio, which, if the current and projected ratio is high, suggests impairment on ability to repay. A frequent practice for banks it to avoid "uneven maturities" for deposits and loans by matching deposit maturities with those of their loans. (The floating interest rate reduces risk when maturities of assets and liabilities are not matched.) However, in recent years, Carl H. Stem has found in interviews with Eurobankers a "considerable movement away from loans matched by deposits, especially during periods of heightened competition such as 1972-73."(89)

Repayment schedules of Euroloans vary and can be paid in one sum or installments, usually with a large "balloon" payment at the end when the loan becomes due.(90) For some developing countries with a high degree of creditworthiness, repayment at the borrower's discretion is sometimes permitted. A prepayment option often specifies a penalty fee.

Eurocontracts do not always specify the purpose for which the loan is to be used and often depends on the perceived creditworthiness of the borrower. (In 1974 almost half of all publicized Eurocredits were obtained for nonspecific purposes by governments and public financing institutions. The majority of the other half went to public utilities, transportation, and fuel projects.) Euroloans increasingly have been extended to sovereign borrowers for balance-of-payments purposes.

Creditworthiness evaluation has become an increasing concern to Eurobanks. Credit risk analysis is usually done by the lead bank in a syndication arrangement. (Creditworthiness is defined as the market's perception of the borrowing country's ability and willingness to meet future interest and principal payments on the loan.) Creditworthiness is determined by a variety of factors including the borrowing country's balance-of-payments position, economic growth potential, debt-service ratio, management and government, and "gut feel" by those who deal in loans. However, Walter Wriston, Chairman of Citibank, has cautioned that "in the last analysis, credit is not numbers. It's people. So in the management of a country - as in that of a company - the determinative force is the ability of a government to react to circumstances."(91) In sum, based on findings of Giddy and Ray when 52 medium-term Eurocurrency loans to LDCs in 1974 were examined, the closer a country comes to meeting the criteria of a developed country, the higher the credit evaluation and the more favorable the terms.(92)

NOTES

1. "World Bank is Extending Debt Reporting to Cover Private, Non-Guaranteed Loans," IMF Survey 7:172.
2. Ian H. Giddy and Russ Ray, "The Eurodollar Market and the Third World," University of Michigan Business Review 28 (March 1976): 11.
3. Morgan Guaranty Trust Company, "Eurocurrency Bank Credit," World Financial Markets, March 1978, p. 4.
4. "Lender of Last Resort to Topsy," Economist, June 10, 1978, p. 87.
5. Emma Rothschild, "Banks: The Coming Crisis," New York

Review of Books 23 (May 27, 1976): 16.

6. Lee Lescaze and Don Oberdorfer, "Foreign Lender Citibank's Big Stakes, Hedged Bets," Washington Post, April 24, 1977, p. A-10.

7. Henry C. Wallich, "The Role of Banks in the North-South Dialogue" (Remarks before the Conference on International Economic Cooperation, Bonn/Bad Godesberg, Germany, April 12, 1978), p. 2.

8. Azizali F. Mohammed and Fabrizio Saccomanni, "Short-Term Banking and Eurocurrency Credits to Developing Countries," IMF Staff Papers 20 (November 1973): 628.

9. Morgan Guaranty Trust Company, "Eurocurrency Bank Credit," p. 4.

10. Mohammed and Saccomanni, "Short-Term Banking," p. 617.

11. Rothschild, Banks, p. 18.

12. Ibid.

13. Ibid.

14. Ibid. p. 16.

15. "The Quality of International Credit," Euromoney, March 1977, p. 7.

16. Ishan Kapur, "An Analysis of the Supply of Eurocurrency Finance to Developing Countries," Oxford Bulletin of Economics and Statistics 39, (August 1977): 173.

17. Morgan Guaranty Trust Company, "Eurocurrency Market Developments," World Financial Markets, July 16, 1974, p. 5.

18. As a percent of total Eurocredits extended to developing countries in 1973-74, 17.5% were for 1-6 years; 62.5% were for 7-10 years; and 13.9% for over 10 years. See "Reasons for Discrimination, Not Alarm," Banker, Euromarket Survey, January 1977, p. 52.

19. "Developing Country Prospects and Issues, 1977," Development Issues, Draft Report, Agency for International Development, April 1977, p. 15.

20. Ibid., p. 17.

21. Shaw Sin-ming, "Massive Defaults Ahead?" Far Eastern Economic Review, April 8, 1977, p. 42.

22. U.S. Department of the Treasury, Report on External Debt of Developing Countries and on Debt Relief Provided by the United States, Report to Congress, January 1978, p. 8.

23. Morgan Guaranty Trust Company, "Coping with the Imbalance in International Payments," World Financial Markets, January 1977, p. 4.

24. Alena Wels, "Banks Loans to LDC's Seen Losing Steam," Journal of Commerce, March 10, 1977.

25. Chase Manhattan Bank, "The Payments Outlook for the LDC's," International Finance, February 6, 1978, p. 1.

26. "A Safety Net for Tumbling Allies" (editorial), New York Times, April 22, 1977, p. A-26.

27. Morgan Guaranty Trust Company, "The 1978 OPEC Surplus Revised Downward," World Financial Markets, February 1978, p. 8.
28. __________. "The OPEC Surplus This Year and Next," World Financial Markets, November 1977, p. 7.
29. "OPEC Surplus Seen as Nearing $145 Billion," Washington Post, May 13, 1977.
30. Morgan Guaranty Trust Company, "OPEC Countries Investments," World Financial Markets, November 1977, pp. 11, 12.
31. "Lender of Last Resort to Topsy," Economist, June 10, 1978, p. 87.
32. For example, rates for Indonesia dropped 1 7/8% to 1 3/8% over LIBOR (1976); Brazil paid 1 3/4-2% with high participation fees; and Venezuela dropped from 1 1/8 to 1% with a 3/8% management fee and 1/8% facility fee. See "The Quality of International Credit," Euromoney, March 1977, p. 7; and Euromarkets...Activity at Record High in 1976, Borrowings Soar in Last Quarter," IMF Survey 6 (April 1977): 107.
33. "Euromarkets," International Currency Review 9: 27.
34. Morgan Guaranty Trust Company, "International Credit Markets," World Financial Markets, December 1977, p. 7.
35. "Euromarkets," International Currency Review, p. 28.
36. Robert D. Hershey, Jr., "Banks Loans Abroad Called Successful by Officials of U.S.," New York Times, April 6, 1977, p. 53.
37. "Disaggregating Loans to LDC's," Journal of Commerce, March 15, 1977, p. 4.
38. Kapur, "Analysis of the Supply," p. 174.
39. Rothschild, "Banks," p. 18.
40. Ibid.
41. Charles N. Stabler, "Poorer Countries Face Test of their Ability to Repay Bank Loans," Wall Street Journal, April 14, 1977, p. 1.
42. Ibid.
43. Reference to private borrowings can include more than Euroloans, but, in effect, Euroloans are the bulk of private borrowings. See Isham Kapur, p. 173.
44. Bruce Nussbaum, "OPEC's War, or When the U.S. Lending Has to Stop," Far Eastern Economic Review, April 8, 1977, p. 35.
45. "A Safety Net for Tumbling Allies" (editorial), New York Times.
46. Nussbaum, "OPEC's War," p. 35.
47. Mohammed and Saccomanni, "Short Term Banking," p. 617.
48. M. van den Adel, "A Burst of Credits," Euromoney, March 1978, p. 54.
49. Robert Z. Aliber (Remarks at a U.S. Export-Import Bank Symposium on Developing Country Debt, Washington, D.C., April 21, 1977).

50. Rothschild, "Banks," p. 22.
51. Giddy and Ray, "The Eurodollar," p. 15.
52. Ann Crittenden, "Loan Growth Down for Poor Countries," New York Times, March 28, 1977, p. 45.
53. "The Clouds Clear Over Poor Country Debt," Economist, April 16, 1977, p. 91.
54. "Euromarket Report," International Currency Review 10 (May 12, 1978): 51.
55. John Maynard Keynes, cited in Rothschild, "Banks," p. 18.
56. Rothschild, "Banks," p. 16.
57. "Euromarkets," International Currency Review, p. 31.
58. Cheryl Payer, "Will the Government Have to Bail Out the Banks?" Bankers Magazine 160 (Spring 1977): 84.
59. "The IMF Wields Sudden New Power," Business Week, March 28, 1977, p. 86.
60. Helmut Haeusgen, "Why Today's Yields on Eurocredits are not Enough," Euromoney, March 1977, p. 14.
61. Cheryl Payer, "Third World Debt Problems: New Waves of Defaults," Monthly Review, September 1976, p. 4.
62. "Quality of International Credit," p. 7.
63. Wels, "Bank Loans to LDCs."
64. Rothschild, "Banks," p. 22.
65. Ibid., p. 16.
66. Ibid.
67. C. Fred Bergsten, Letter to the Editor, Euromoney, June 1978, p. 13.
68. Hobart Rowen, "Administration Supports IMF Loan Increase," Washington Post, April 6, 1977, p. E-5.
69. "The False Alarm Bank Scare," (editorial), Fortune 93 (March 1976): 103.
70. Ibid., p. 104.
71. Hershey, "Bank Loans Abroad," p. 53.
72. "Approving Witteveen's Proposal" (editorial), Journal of Commerce, April 20, 1977, p. 4.
73. Payer, "Third World Debt Problems," p. 1.
74. Stabler, "Poorer Countries Face Debt," p. 29.
75. William J. Holstein, "Concern is Voiced over Global Lending," Washington Post, March 13, 1977, p. K-2.
76. "The Sick Men of the Euromarkets," Euromoney, March 1978, p. 13.
77. Payer, "Will Government Have to Bail Out Banks?" p. 83.
78. "Billion Dollar Banks Go on the 'Watch List,'" Business Week, March 28, 1977, p. 23.
79. "Burns Finds Business Nervous Over Deficits; Wants IMF to Watch Banks' Loans to Poor Lands," Washington Post, February 28, 1977, p. 57.
80. Leonard Silk, "The IMF and Debt of Poor Nations," New York Times, March 28, 1977, p. C-45.

81. Paul de Grauwe, "The Development of the Eurocurrency Market," Finance and Development 12 (September 1975): 16.
82. Larry Kramer, "Global System Hyperventilating," Washington Post, April 22, 1979, p. G-1; and "Alternatives to the dollar," Euromoney, March 1978, p. 129.
83. Payer, "Will Government Have to Bail Out Banks?" p. 84.
84. Rothschild, "Banks," p. 18.
85. Ibid., p. 17.
86. Some Questions and Brief Answers about the Eurodollar Market, staff study, prepared for use of Joint Economic Committee (Wahington, D.C.: U.S. Government Printing Office, 1977), p. 3.
87. Giddy and Ray, "The Eurodollar Market," p. 12.
88. Ibid., p. 14.
89. Carl H. Stem, John H. Makin, and Dennis E. Logue, eds., Eurocurrencies and the International Monetary System (Washington, D.C.: American Enterprise Institute for Public Policy Research, 1976), p. 338.
90. Little is known about the prospect of repayment of Euroloans as scheduled - even by national authorities. No single examinations authority has an overview of the repayment situation in the Eurocurrency system.
91. Giddy and Ray, "The Eurodollar Market," p. 14.
92. Ibid.

BIBLIOGRAPHY

Books and Journals

"Are Banks Letting Countries Off the Hook?" Euromoney, March 1978, pp. 44-45.

"Asian LDCs Get Favorable Financing: Impact on Companies." Business Asia 9 (April 8, 1977): 105-08.

"Better Mood, but High Tension Continues." International Currency Review 7 (January-February 1975): 11-15.

"Billion Dollar Banks Go on the 'Watch List.'" Business Week, March 28, 1977, pp. 23-24.

"The Clouds Clear Over Poor-Country Debt." Economist, April 16, 1977, p. 91.

Davis, Steven I. "How Risky is International Lending?" Harvard Business Review 55 (January-February 1977): 133-43.

Economics Group of Chase Manhattan Bank. "The Payments Outlook for LDCs." International Finance, February 6, 1978, p. 1.

"Eurobond Market Complacency Irritates Nervous Medium-Term Sector." International Currency Review 7: 16-19.

"The Eurocurrency Markets." Barclay's Review 51 (February 1976): center spread.

"Euromarkets." International Currency Review 9: 27-31.
"Euromarkets Weigh International Credit Risks." International Currency Review 9: 20-24.
Falon, Padraic. "Liberia - Profile of an African Borrower Entering the Eurodollar Market." Euromoney, February 1977, pp. 57-62.
"The False Alarm Bank Scare." Editorial. Fortune, no. 3 March 1976, pp. 103-04.
Far Eastern Economic Review, April 8, 1977, pp. 33-120.
"Financing Developing Countries' Soaring Deficits." International Currency Review 7 (September-October 1975): 11-14.
Friedman, Irving S. "Most Eurocurrency Borrowers Remain Good Risks." Euromoney, March 1977, pp. 16, 18, 21.
Giddy, Ian H., and Ray Russ. "The Eurodollar Market and the Third World." University of Michigan Business Review 28, (March 1976): 11-15.
Haeusgen, Helmut. "Why Today's Yields on Eurocredits are not Enough." Euromoney, March 1977, pp. 13, 14.
"Industrialized Countries Edge Out 'Other Borrowers' as Credit Doubts Increase." International Currency Review 8: 27-31.
"It is difficult to believe that this eagerness to lend, sometimes on unprofitable margins and frequently without adequate credit appraisal, is any more advisable today than it ever has been." International Currency Review 8: 11-15.
Kapur, Ishan. "An Analysis of the Supply of Eurocurrency Finance to Developing Countries." Oxford Bulletin of Economics and Statistics 39 (August 1977): 171-88.
"Lender Of Last Resort to Topsy." Economist, June 10, 1978, p. 87.
Morgan Guaranty Trust Company. "Coping with Imbalance in International Payments." World Financial Markets, January 1977, 19 pp.
________. "Euro-currency Bank Credits." "Euro-currency Market." World Financial Markets, March 1978, pp. 4, 6.
________. "Eurocurrency Market Developments." World Financial Markets, July 16, 1974, pp. 4-9.
________. "Financial Markets and Economic Development." World Financial Markets, mimeographed. September 16, 1975, 7 pp.
________. "International Credit Developments." World Financial Markets, mimeographed. March 1977, 19 pp.
________. "International Credit Markets." World Financial Markets, December 1977, pp. 3-9.
________. "OPEC Countries Investment." World Financial Markets, November 1977, pp. 10-13.
________. "The 1978 OPEC Surplus Revised Downward." World Financial Markets, February 1978, pp. 7-8.
________. "The OPEC Surplus This Year and Next." World Financial Markets, November 1977, pp. 4-10.

"LDCs May Lose, But Not Yet." Euromoney, February 1977, p. 125.
O'Brien, Lord. "The Prospects for the Euromarkets." Euromoney, September 1975, pp. 66-69.
Payer, Cheryl. "Third World Debt Problems: New Wave of Defaults." Monthly Review 8 (September 1976): 1-22.
________. "Will the Government Have to Bail Out the Banks?" Bankers' Magazine 160 (Spring 1977): 83-86.
"The Quality of Interntional Credit." Euromoney, March 1977, p. 7.
"Reasons for Discrimination, Not Alarm." Banker, January 1977, pp. 51-55.
Rothschild, Emma. "Banks: The Coming Crisis." New York Review of Books 23 (May 27, 1976): 16-22.
"The Sick Men of the Euromarkets." Euromoney, March 1978, pp. 10-15.
Stem, Carl H.; Makin, John H.; and Logue, Dennis E.; eds. Eurocurrencies and the International Monetary System. Washington, D.C.: American Enterprise Institute for Public Policy Research, 1976. 413 pp.
"Talking to West Germany's Finance Minister, Hans Apel." Euromoney, March 1977, pp. 45-47.
Van den Adel, M. "A Burst of Credits." Euromoney, March 1978, pp. 54-61.
________. "The Jumbos and the Mammoths Confront More Choosey Bankers." Euromoney, March 1977, pp. 23-32.
"Wanted: A Central Eurodollar Information Agency." International Currency Review 8: 13-15.
"Why the Banks Bailed Out Peru." Business Week, March 21, 1977, pp. 117-18.

Newspaper

"Banking Business Booms in Bahamas." New York Times, March 3, 1977, pp. 47, 51.
Bennett, Robert A. "Less Developed Country Loans Pose Questions for Regulators." New York Times, May 15, 1977, pp. F-1, 14.
"Burns Finds Business Nervous over Deficits: Wants IMF to Watch Banks' Loans to Poor Lands." Washington Post, February 28, 1977, pp. 51, 57.
Crittenden, Ann. "Loan Growth Down for Poor Countries." New York Times, March 28, 1977, pp. 43, 45.
"Disaggregating Loans to LDCs." Editorial. Journal of Commerce, March 15, 1977, p. 4.
Hershey, Robert D., Jr. "Banks Loans Abroad Called Successful by Officials of U.S." New York Times, April 6, 1977, p. 53.
Holstein, William J. "Concern is Voiced over Global Lending." Washington Post, March 13, 1977, p. K-2.

Lescaze, Lee, and Oberdorfer, Don. "Foreign Lender Citibank: Big Stakes, Hedged Bets." Washington Post, April 24, 1977, pp. A-1, 10.
Oberdorfer, Don. "Banks, not U.S., Now Give Brazil its Foreign Aid." Washington Post, March 20, 1977, pp. A-1, 5.
Rowen, Hobart. "Administration Supports IMF Loan Fund Increases." Washington Post, April 6, 1977, pp. F-1, 5.
________. "A Turning Point in Global Lending." Washington Post, March 27, 1977, pp. L-1, 12.
"A Safety Net for Tumbling Allies." Editorial. New York Times, April 22, 1977, p. A-26.
Silk, Leonard. "The IMF and Debts of Poor Nations." New York Times, March 28, 1977, pp. 43, 45.
Stabler, Charles N. "Poorer Countries Face Test of Their Ability to Repay Bank Loans." Wall Street Journal, April 14, 1977, pp. 1, 21.
"Treasury Aid Says Bank Loans Abroad Aren't Worrisome." Wall Street Journal, April 6, 1977.
Wels, Alena. "Bank Loans to LDCs Seen Losing Steam." Journal of Commerce, March 10, 1977.

Government and International Organizations: Documents and Publications

Bank for International Settlements. Forty-Sixth Annual Report. April 1, 1975 - March 31, 1976. Basle, Switzerland, June 14, 1976, 138 pp.
Bergsten, C. Fred. Statement before the Subcommittee on Financial Institutions Supervision, Regulators and Insurance of the Committee on Banking, Finance, and Urban Affairs. House of Representatives. Department of the Treasury. Press Release #B-153, April 5, 1977. 12 pp.
De Grauwe, Paul. "The Development of the Eurocurrency Market." Finance and Development 12 (International Monetary Fund: September 1975): 14-16.
International Monetary Fund. "Euromarkets...Activity at Record High in 1976, Borrowings Soar in Last Quarter." IFM Survey 6 (April 4, 1977): 97, 105-07.
________. "Growth of International Lending Near 20% for Second Year." IMF Survey 6 (February 21, 1977): 49, 53-55.
________. "Interim Committee Supports New Facility." IMF Survey 6 (May 2, 1977): 129, 136.
________. "Moderate Euromarket Activity Increase This Year Forecast by OECD." IMF Survey 6 (April 4, 1977): 103-05.
________. "Slowing Rate of Growth in Capital Market Lending is Shown by Data for 1977." IMF Survey, April 17, 1978, pp. 113, 115.
________. "World Bank Extending Debt Reporting to Cover Private, Non-Guaranteed Loans." IMF Survey, June 5, 1978, pp. 10-15.

Mohammed, Azizali F., and Saccromanni, Fabrizio. "Short-Term Banking and Eurocurrency Credits to Developing Countries." IMF Staff Papers 20 (International Monetary Fund: November 1973): 612-37.

Some Questions and Brief Answers about the Eurodollar Market. A Staff Study. Prepared for Use of the Joint Economic Committee. Washington, D.C.: U.S. Government Printing Office, February 7, 1977. 17 pp.

4 Loans to LDCs: Five Myths*

Charles S. Ganoe

More than three years ago, it became fashionable in the press and among politicians to point to bank loans to less developed countries as the next real estate investment trust credit disaster. Stories suggesting the debt problems of LDCs might lead to the failure of major banks with heavy exposure in faraway countries crept from the financial sections to the front pages. Security analysts began to write ominously of the potential loan losses of banks with active international departments.

The attack on international lending put many banks on the defensive. In the past several years, almost every annual report of the 50 largest banks in the United States included a lengthy and detailed explanation of loans to less developed countries.

Some rationality is now beginning to creep into the argument, in part because a number of studies by government agencies and private foundations have put the debt problem of LDCs into better perspective. Moreover, international bankers themselves have managed to sort out the facts. While conceding that many LDCs do have a debt service problem, they are now able to demonstrate that the stories predicting heavy losses, even bank failures, were greatly overstated. Seen in retrospect, it is now clear that many of the scare stories and political diatribes on bank lending to LDCs were based on a number of popular myths. Five such myths stand out.

---

*This chapter is reprinted, with permission, from the November 1977 issue of Journal of Commercial Bank Lending. Copyright © 1977 by Robert Morris Associates, the national association of bank loan and credit officers.

MYTH NUMBER 1: There will be massive defaults by the LDCs.

Many critics of international lending have seen the widespread failure of real estate investment trusts in the early 1970s as the forerunner to similar cross-the-board default by LDCs. This analogy is highly dubious.

Real estate investment trusts are characterized by a common function and purpose, common financial resources, and, most important, common economic bases. The collapse of real estate markets in our country following overexpansion in the 1960s led directly to the financial distress of the real estate investment trusts.

In contrast to real estate investment trusts, each LDC is a separate entity, and the similarities between countries are relatively limited. Upon analysis, each of the 86 LDCs can be seen as highly divergent. Geography alone results in vast differences between countries in terms of natural resources, export markets, import requirements, industrial development, and all the other economic factors which contribute to the financial strength or weakness of a given country.

The differences go beyond the geographic and economic. The institutional framework of each country differs: The structure of government, political system, external relations and foreign policy, the human resources and the energy and work ethic of the people, and a whole host of other factors make every country unique in terms of its credit standing and its ability to service debt.

To be sure, there are a few countries tied by geography or a heavy dependence on one or two commodities, such as coffee and copper, for their international economic survival. Failure of one could have a domino effect on those which are linked. These tend to be smaller countries to which United States banks have relatively modest exposure, however, and even those countries which have the most similar economic characteristics tend to differ significantly in their costs of production, alternate financial resources, political strengths, and general ability to tide themselves over periods of adversity.

In the final analysis, unless there is a war or an act of God on a scale not foreseen, the likelihood of widespread default on the part of a significant number of countries, especially important debtor countries, is quite unlikely. Each country's credit stands on its own and the default by one has very little impact on the debt service capacity of another.

MYTH NUMBER 2: Loans to default-prone, low-income LDCs are sizable.

Press articles and political speeches invariably include vivid descriptions of the problems of Bangladesh and Zaire, often with pictures of starving masses in the streets of Calcutta or some other forlorn city. The implication: United States bank loans have gone to a bottomless poverty pit for which the day of reckoning is inevitable.

The fact is that a very high portion of United States bank loans to LDCs are concentrated in approximately one dozen so-called "higher income" countries, whereas the credits to the impoverished countries of the Asian subcontinent and tropical Africa are very modest in volume. Moreover, as will be explained later, United States bank loans to the low-income, lesser developed countries are usually limited to a few select borrowers (such as the government of the largest, most established banks) on relatively short maturities.

The Federal Reserve put this issue in perspective when it published a survey of United States bank claims on foreigners as of December 31, 1977. Covering more than 124 reporting banks with total assets of $1 billion and more than $50 million of foreign credits, the study showed that, of the $45,831,000 owed by nonoil exporting LDCs, 68 percent represented debts of only five countries: Mexico, Brazil, Korea, the Philippines, and Taiwan. All of these countries are categorized as higher- or middle-income LDCs by the World Bank and are characterized by growing economies with a broadening industrial base and by close economic and political ties to the United States.

Table 4.1 lists the United States bank claims on LDCs broken down by per capita income plus the oil-exporting and Eastern European countries as reported by the Federal Reserve. A review of the annual reports of the largest United States banks indicated a remarkable similarity from bank to bank; very few banks depart significantly from the exposure pattern revealed in Table 4.1, and what variances there are can be explained by geographical or historical factors.

MYTH NUMBER 3: Since the debt can never be paid, default will surely occur.

This is a favorite of politicans. Bankers don't have to be told that debt-service ability, not the ability to repay the principal and interest in full at maturity, is the critical question. There is an irony to the argument of the politicians because they know full well that the debt of the United States Government will never be fully repaid, nor will the debt be

Table 4.1. Foreign Claims of United States Banks as of December 31, 1977 (in millions of US$)

1. Higher-Income LDCs (per capita $2,000 - $500)	
Brazil	$11,992
Mexico	11,213
Taiwan	2,805
Argentina	2,639
Peru	1,831
Colombia	1,293
Chile	821
Israel	667
Nicaragua	562
Malaysia	511
Costa Rica	424
Dominican Republic	283
Jamaica	247
Guatemala	226
Uruguay	203
Zambia	182
Trinidad and Tobago	44
Paraguay	33
Total	35,982

Table continued

Source: The data in this table were extracted from a Federal Reserve, Press Release, June 8, 1978.

Table 4.1. (Continued)

2. Middle-Income LDCs (per capita $500-$200)	
Korea	3,072
Philippines	2,049
Syria	856
Thailand	555
Morocco	462
Bolivia	446
Egypt	427
Ivory Coast	347
Honduras	253
El Salvador	188
Jordan	101
Tunisia	95
Ghana	78
Cameroon	60
Kenya	39
Senegal	25
Total	9,059
3. Lower-Income LDCs (per capita less than $200)	
Zaire	252
Sudan	219
India	187
Malawi	70
Pakistan	59
Total	790
3. Oil-Exporting Countries	
Venezuela	5,378
Iran	2,202
Indonesia	2,199
Algeria	1,540
Ecuador	1,040
United Arab Emirates	664
Saudi Arabia	591
Kuwait	536
Gabon	184
Nigeria	128
Iraq	92
Qatar	72
Libya	58
Total	14,685

(Table continued)

Table 4.1. (Continued)

5. Eastern Europe

U.S.S.R.	1,551
Poland	1,313
Yugoslavia	1,149
East Germany	979
Hungary	896
Bulgaria	527
Romania	226
Czechoslovakia	192
Total	8,163

repaid of the 50 states, most municipalities, school districts, authorities, and public utilities.

To be sure, loans to private corporations in lesser developed countries may be at greater risk because local economic conditions could be particularly harsh, adversely affecting the ability of even a going business from refinancing its maturing obligations. But only a small percentage of United States bank loans to LDCs are directed to private companies, and almost no such loans are made in the weakest LDCs.

The vast portion of LDC debt is owed by the governments themselves, government-owned companies and agencies, or by banks of national importance. Space does not permit an analysis of the factors upon which the solvency of these borrowers is dependent. However, it is fair to argue that they are, in every sense, no different than a government body or a public utility in the United States; that is, their liabilities will not have to be liquidated as long as they can service their debts, maintain the confidence of creditors, and keep open sources of refinancing.

For the larger and important countries, the sources of refinancing are manifold. Even if they lose the confidence of their usual creditors, there is still a very good chance that assistance will be forthcoming from international agencies, such as the International Monetary Fund, or from friendly foreign governments with a political, military, or economic interest in their stability and solvency.

MYTH NUMBER 4: If default occurs, bank losses will be heavy.

This argument - and the rebuttal - is akin to Myth Number 3. No one can deny that individual countries might find themselves insolvent and, as a consequence, bank loan maturities could go unmet. At the same time, the major banks in these countries could find themselves in trouble.

Except for private companies or smaller banks which would comprise a small minority of the total loans for United States banks, none of the debtors will go out of business or dissolve. When a country finds itself insolvent, the course will be to renegotiate the payment schedule on term loans; that is, there will be a stretchout. Short-term financing for trade needs may be totally unaffected. Most governments realize that creditor confidence is imperative to restore solvency, and, even in the worst situations, they strive to keep current the short-term trade debts incurred by the government or the major banks in the country.

This certainly has been the experience in the post-World War II era. A half dozen or more countries have found themselves unable to meet their maturing obligations. Negotiations were undertaken on a government-to-government basis, and refinancing or stretchout programs were developed which left the foreign bank creditors largely unaffected. Some term loans from foreign banks were extended, but the short-term financing continued to roll over in normal course.

Losses, if any, were sustained by foreign lenders only on credits to small, unimportant banks which were allowed to fail or to local companies which could not weather the economic crisis. This has never been a serious problem because, as already indicated, the amount of United States bank loans to smaller bank or to private corporations in the weaker LDCs has been very low. These corporations would not include those of international standing such as airlines and mining and petroleum companies, however.

MYTH NUMBER 5: Loans to LDCs are improper.

While not stated explicitly, press and political criticism has often been pervaded by a self-righteous inference that lending to LDCs is wrong, representing a misuse of bank assets and forming a kind of conspiracy between greedy bankers and profligate hottentots. Until such lending ends in a disasterous worldwide bankruptcy, critics suggests that American customers who would otherwise use the loan funds for better purposes are the ultimate losers.

Statistical data on United States bank lending in recent years clearly indicate that the growth in international loans has paralleled the decline in domestic loan demand. The larger banks searched for earning assets overseas when business was slack and the growth of alternative loan sources for domestic borrowers, such as commercial paper, left the banks with surplus capital and a dearth of borrowing customers.

It should also be noted that a sizable portion of the deposit funds used to grant these foreign loans were generated from overseas. With excess capital, internationally minded banks opened overseas branches to leverage themselves further by taking Eurocurrency deposits to relend to suitable borrowers.

The critics fail to recognize that these lending activities have had a profound impact on the ability of the LDCs to survive the OPEC-induced oil price increases and the resulting world recession. Those banks which have been increasing their loans to LDCs have, in effect, been recycling the oil surpluses of the OPEC countries back to the deficit-ridden LDCs.

Few critics appreciate that these countries would not have had a deficit if financing were not available. The only alternative to them would have been a drastic cutback on imports so that their foreign exchange outgo would not exceed foreign exchange income. To cut back rapidly could have had catastrophic consequences. The sudden reduction in the standard of living in these LDCs might well have produced riots and revolution. Even without political turmoil, the severe economic recession certainly would have badly hurt United States export sales and undoubtedly would have spread like a cancer to all of the industrial countries.

PUTTING THE FUTURE IN PERSPECTIVE

If seen in terms of facilitating the adjustment process, the future of United States bank loans to LDCs takes on a different picture. That picture also looks different if it is recognized that a high percentage of the total loans are extended to a dozen or so higher-income LDCs which enjoy growing and increasingly diversified economies and, in most cases, close ties to the United States.

LDCs Doing Better Than the Figures Indicate

A number of recent studies have shown that the major borrowing LDCs are doing better than might be indicated by the figures. Exports, which generate the foreign exchange to service external debt, have been expanding nicely for many countries. Inflation, the great savior for all debtors, both domestic and foreign, is playing its role, and the debt burden of LDCs expressed in real terms is not nearly as bad as the figures suggest.

Tables 4.2 and 4.3 show this phenomena and how the ratio of exports to the debt of the LDCs has actually improved.

Table 4.2. What Inflation Does for Debtors: Developing Country Debt

Year	Disbursed Debt Outstanding (current prices in billions of dollars)	Increase in Export Prices (percent)	Debt Relief Through Inflation (in billions of dollars)	Real Value Disbursed Debt Outstanding (1970 prices in billions of dollars)
1971	58	2	1	57
1972	65	6	4	60
1973	72	29	21	52
1974	90	44	40	45
1975	116	0	0	58
1976	142	9	13	65

Source: Stephen H. Goodman, vice president, Export-Import Bank, Euromoney, June, 1977.

Table 4.3. How the Ratio Has Improved

Year	Exports (in billions of dollars)	Relation of Exports to Debt (percent)
1971	38	66
1972	46	71
1973	67	93
1974	97	108
1975	90	78
1976	115	81

Source: Stephen H. Goodman, vice president, Export-Import Bank, Euromoney, June 1977.

Assistance to LDCs: Political and Economic Necessities

There are other hopeful signs. One happy by-product of the press and political attention given to the problem has been the increased awareness on the part of United States Government officials and the international lending agencies of the need to take measures to assist the LDCs. Helping them achieve an orderly adjustment to the oil price increases, meet temporary liquidity needs, stretchout and fund external debt, and have available a safety net in the case of unforeseen crises are not perceived as schemes to bail out the banks. Rather, these government measures are increasingly recognized as political and economic necessities undertaken for reasons of self-interest and to promote worldwide economic prosperity.

Judging LDCs on Their Individual Merits

No one can deny that there is an overall LDC debt problem or that individual countries may well find themselves confronted with a genuine crisis in which their maturing debt obligations go unpaid. It is important to see the problem in rational terms, however, and not with frantic fears of worldwide default leaving United States banks with large amounts of LDC loans they will never collect. Indeed, the solution to the problem depends on recognizing that United States bank loans to LDCs must be seen on a country-by-country basis and that, for the most part, they are limited to better-grade countries, to borrowers of good standing, and to transactions which are sound and sensible. Each individual LDC credit stands on its merits, and any grand, lump-sum default is next to impossible.

If banks continue this business, the borrowing countries will have the leeway, with the help of official institutions and government-to-government assistance, to work out programs designed to keep their debt service abilities on an even keel. Banks must feel free to offer their assistance, however, without political attack or fear that wary security analysts will issue ominous reports causing bank stocks to tumble. Perhaps we should not forget that our own country was once an LDC, and without the understanding and forebearance of our European creditors, the many crises which confronted our nation in the nineteenth century could well have reshaped our economic history as well as that of our creditors, leaving us today an LDC debtor rather than a developed creditor.

II

Narrowing the Focus: A Case Studies Perspective

5 A Banker's View: Country Analysis*

Charles S. Ganoe

Although it was not widely recognized and clearly understood, the art of country analysis has been practiced by a small cadre of international-minded academics, government officials, bankers, and businessmen for many decades. With the growth of business schools and the attendant need to justify their existence, the proliferation of computers with their ability to manipulate vast quantities of data, and the enshrinement of inspired research as the source of obsolete answers, country analysis has come to be viewed in some quarters as a science rather than an art.

Those who have attempted to reduce this art to a science have equipped themselves with the ability to assimilate vast quantities of statistical data and have developed a great variety of ratios and other analytical tools to evaluate the present standing and future prospects of given countries. While statistical analysis employing modern techniques of our computer world are certainly of great importance in undertaking an analysis of the economic prospects of a country, they clearly do not tell the whole story and there is a serious risk in drawing firm conclusions from them.

Indeed, an argument can be made that a good country analyst should leave the processing of the financial data and statistical ratios to others. Instead, he should buy a good history book on the given country. After he has finished the history book, he should purchase a book on economic geography which treats such factors as raw material availability,

---

*This chapter was originally presented at a meeting of the Association of Reserve City Bankers, Boca Raton, Florida, April 4, 1978.

agricultural production and so forth. Then he should buy a book on politicosociology which describes the ethnic makeup of the population and the needs and aspirations of the people.

After these books have been read, perhaps the analyst can make some sense out of the figures and ratios. But if he really wants to round out the country analysis, he should take about six month off to make an extended visit to the country, wearing T-shirts and jeans and traveling the back roads as well as the main highways. He should ride the buses, walk the beaches, and drink in the workers' bars. At the conclusion of the visit, he should put his bankers' clothes on for a few days to call on the central bank, the finance ministry and the major commercial banks, making sure he talks with the middle-level technicians who prepare the figures he analyzes.

After he has completed all of this, he will realize that the figures and statistics may be fun to play with, and perhaps useful to get things started, but they are not "where the babies are made."

THE PROBLEMS WITH COUNTRY DATA

The inadequacy of statistical analysis alone to determine country risk is based on four basic problems:

1. The lack of accounting and informational standards;
2. The serious difficulties in gathering reliable data;
3. The problems arising from imaginative accounting, wishful thinking, window dressing and downright dishonesty in the preparation of data; and
4. The fact that statistics can only measure the past history of a country, whereas the real need is to look forward and not backward.

The Absence of Standards

Accounting is not an absolute science. The problem is compounded with respect to country data, since there are absolutely no agreed standards, criteria or definitions. During the 1960s and early 1970s, the United States measured its balance of payments in three different ways, none of which were entirely logical. Under these methods, if a suspicious oil sheik sold petroleum to the United States demanding currency in return and, being distrustful of banks, buried the dollar bills in the desert, it would show as a credit item in the United States balance of payments! Even today in the United

States we have two consumer price indexes and there is considerable debate whether either one properly measures inflation.

In addition to the absence of accounting standards, the manner in which given transactions are recorded differs from country to country and under different circumstances. For example, when the United States sells wheat to India under an aid program, it is booked as an export by the United States at market prices, but it is recorded in India as an import at their subsidized cost.

Then there are basic accounting dilemmas. Should one value gold at $42.50 per ounce or at the current market? If one treats gold at market, is it politically possible for the country to sell it, or even pledge it? In short, international accounting for country analysis is a very inexact science and there is plenty of room for different points of view and different ways to book data.

There is a growing call for the establishment of some kind of agreed standards for country analysis. This is not likely to come in our lifetime, however, because there are just too many practical problems and too many differences in systems. For example, socialist countries record transactions quite differently than free-market economies. There are even attitudinal differences in basic accounting principles: the less developed countries argue, for example, that the standards applied by the IMF and most United States and European banks are based on the postwar conditions in the western industrial countries and do not recognize that the same standards are not always suitable for developing countries in other parts of the world.

Lack of Reliability

It is not difficult to appreciate the problems of reliability of data when one recognizes that the United States, with the largest computers in the world and by far the largest armies of statisticians and data collectors, has difficulty in preparing accurate figures on its own status and performance. The Census Bureau has miscalculated our population by at least five million and perhaps 10 million people. The Bureau of Budget has misestimated the United States Government spending by as much as ten billion dollars even one or two months before the end of a fiscal year.

Many less developed countries have no idea of their true population, since major segments live outside the money economy. They use the crudest kind of sampling techniques to measure such figures as gross national product, exports and imports. International trade figures, in particular, can be grossly inaccurate in many LDCs because of the large volume of smuggling which occurs over land borders, especially where the tariff barriers to legitimate trade are very high. Many countries have no idea of the amount of their external debt. Even the United States does not record the amount of its private external debt.

Imaginative Accounting

As to imaginative accounting, one can only say the "governments will be governments." If this seems unusual or irregular, I need only point out that John Lindsay, one of Yale's finest products, permitted New York City to engage in these practices for eight years.

It should not be forgotten that the disclosure of adverse data can have political implications in almost any country. In the vast majority of the less developed countries, the central banks are not independent of the government but, rather, are controlled by the political party in power. It is not at all unusual, therefore, for even central banks to issue misleading and incorrect data. Before we criticize them, we should remember that J. Edgar Hoover, L. B. Johnson and Richard Nixon, among others, did exactly the same thing in this country.

The pressure brought by the IMF and the commercial banks on these countries to provide more data could even increase the credibility gap. If the IMF tells certain LDCs that more data is necessary in order to obtain credits, the attitude of these countries could well be, "If it is figures they want, it is figures that we will give them." The opportunities for imaginative accounting to run wild are unbounded.

In early 1978, we had a shocking case of outright dishonesty when it was disclosed that Peru, with the cooperation of one of the world's largest banks, engaged in window-dressing exercise over the New Year's weekend designed to show their reserves at forty million dollars more than actually existed. This bizarre episode prompted the IMF to publicly disclose the situation and issue a memorandum questioning the accounting practices of the Peruvian government.

The Past Versus the Future

As to the fourth deficiency, it is true that trends can be ascertained, and sometimes early warnings can be foreseen, in preparing a statistical analysis of a given country. Furthermore, these statistics do suggest additional questions and can be very valuable in developing lines of investigation to be pursued in the search for qualitative information about a given country and/or borrower.

One must be extremely careful about jumping to conclusions, however. The past does not forecast the future, especially in the international scene. The international economy is so immensely complex and subject to so many variables that no amount of figures can accurately predict the future solvency of a given country. Most importantly, political, economic and social events can dramatically affect the future of any country, whether they be wars, revolutions, elections, oil price increases, or whatever.

SOME FORWARD PROGRESS

This is not to suggest figures have no meaning or value. Nor is this to question the wisdom and utility of country analysis. On the contrary, there have been some very positive developments with respect to information received from foreign countries in recent years which markedly improve the validity and reliability of country analysis techniques.

First of all, we are now receiving much more country information than we received in the past. This is particularly important because in this field the whole is likely to be greater than sum of the parts. The more information which is available, the better the qualitative judgments on a given country are likely to be. By evaluating all available information in combination, and by applying various analytical techniques which are still being refined, there is no question we can make better country risk decisions today because the information is more complete and accurate than, say, ten years ago.

Secondly, and this is very important, the country data received today is much more timely. Timeliness is of the essence. As an example, the 1971 balance-of-payments figures published by the IMF were not available until 1974. This is because the IMF delayed publications until it received figures from all of its member countries. Today it no longer waits for this information; it publishes the data as it is received, and this is all to the good.

Thirdly, there is much more cooperation and coordination between the sources of this information. This includes:

1. International Agencies -International Monetary Fund (IMF), World Bank, Bank for International Settlements, Organization for Economic Cooperation and Development (OECD), and the United Nations;
2. United States Government Agencies - Federal Reserve, Treasury Department, Export-Import Bank and, now, even the CIA which is cooperating with qualified inquirers;
3. Foreign governments and foreign central banks;

and

4. Commercial banks, particularly those which issue newsletters.

SOME DISTURBING DEVELOPMENTS

While all of this is positive, there are disturbing developments as well, especially with respect to the attitude of the regulatory agencies in appraising the credit standing of foreign countries. These disturbing developments include:

1. The growing use of models and indicators;
2. The overuse of computers with the danger of fixed modes;
3. Politicians and the press trying to get in the act; and
4. Danger that a fraternity of insiders is being cultivated.

Models have become a Washington fad. The Export-Import Bank spent a lot of time and money developing models of foreign countries, but they missed completely the current financial difficulties of Turkey.

The Comptroller of the Currency has been working on two models. One of these models uses a statistical analysis of the four past years to predict the status of a given country for the forthcoming year. The Comptroller hopes to develop a second model using the same four-year data but predicting ahead for four years, recognizing that a projection of this length involves a high degree of judgment.

The Federal Reserve has been trying to develop international indicators. According to reports, they are considering five indicators to be used as a screening device for the purpose of categorizing countries into two groups, "Class A" and "Class B" will be countries which report negative ratios with respect to two of the five indicators. If a country is placed in the second category, presumably the examiners will be predisposed to classify all loans extended to them.

The problem with all models and indicators is that they are no good if the input data is no good. Garbage in means garbage out. More importantly, there is a serious danger that bank examiners in the field will misunderstand and misuse the output of these models and indicators. They will oversimplify. They will classify all loans to "Class B" countries mechanically in a highly arbitrary fashion. No matter how sophisticated the senior personnel in Washington might be, it is impossible for them to make sure that the field examiners will use the output of these models intelligently.

In the end, their misuse can result in these models and indicators being self-fulfilling. If bank examiners arbitrarily classify loans to given countries because the models and indicators draw adverse conclusions, credits to these countries will dry up and the outstanding debts will not be paid.

The Curse of Computers

All of this will be acerbated by the inflexibility of computers and their failure to take into account extraneous variables and qualitative considerations. These inadequacies are built into any computerized system. Moreover, a tremendous investment is required in the programming of these computers and, once a model is decided upon, there is a natural resistance to change it. As a consequence, the programs that are being written today by the regulatory authorities are likely to be in place for ten years, no matter how bad they prove to be.

Congressional Pressures

One of the reasons the Comptroller and Federal Reserve are developing models and indicators is pressure on them from Congress. Congress has been on the backs of the regulatory agencies to make sure that country evaluations are made on the basis of independent judgments. Congress has criticized the regulatory agencies in the past on the grounds that they get all of their information from the bankers they regulate. The development of their own models and indicators is their response to these changes.

There will be increased pressures in this area. Furthermore, it will be picked up by the press with the usual misleading headlines, all of which is bound to have adverse repercussions for the banking industry.

The Growing Fraternity

These developments will also encourage an existing trend, i.e., the development of a closed fraternity of bankers "in the know." There are today international credit officers and country specialists who associate with each other and with the technocrats in the government agencies in much the same way bond traders and foreign exchange traders fraternize. Up to a point this is healthy; it can solve some touchy problems, e.g., the conflict of interest in publicly disclosing adverse information known to government agencies. However, it can be overreached if the fraternity becomes to strong. Eventually privileged bankers get privileged information while others are shut out. This raises the problem of inside information in a new context. Furthermore, it has implications for regional banks which do not have the financial resources to hire the staff to cultivate these inside contacts.

CONCLUSION

In conclusion, it should be re-emphasized that the usual information, especially statistical data, is not the key to the country analysis. It is what one does with the information which counts.

Because of problems of reliability - and because of the limited value of past data in predicting the future - this statistical information is only truly useful if it is interrelated with a firsthand knowledge of the country.

It is necessary to see a country to make an evaluation. A bank must have traveling officers visiting foreign countries frequently who have the ability to develop wide sources of information, not just the conventional contacts. For countries of heavy credit exposure, a bank must have its people reporting continously, preferably through its own office in the country staffed with trained United States bankers and with local nationals. It also helps to send the bank's economists to these countries regularly for their analysis and special point of view.

A firsthand knowledge of a country provides a bank with the wherewithal to screen, analyze, interpret, weigh and evaluate the country information available from all of the various sources. All of the know factors which measure country risk can be taken into account to make intelligent, sensible judgments. When there is a firsthand knowledge of a country, the statistical data can have some meaning.

This requires manpower - trained manpower - expensive manpower. It is necessary to have people in the field to develop reliable sources of information. It is also necessary to be kept up-to-date. Finally, a bank must have the wherewithal to go through information which continuously become available to glean from it the keys, to know what information is important, and what questions still need to be asked. And it must be recognized, as we go forward, the increase in available information will make it harder, not easier, because it will require an even greater investment in people and knowledge.

6 The Philippines: Land of the Morning, Child of Debt*

Marilyn J. Seiber

The Philippines - unlike Peru or Korea - is neither a country in trouble nor a developing country superstar. Rather it is a middle-income, average growth, financially pragmatic developing country - one that official and private creditors alike rank at the top of their creditworthiness scales. By September 1978, the Philippines had amassed a total outstanding debt of $7.57 billion - a figure more than three times the $2.2 billion of 1972.(1) In 1976 it was the third largest nonoil developing country borrower ($1,337 million) in the private international credit markets. That year the United States Treasury Department listed the Philippines as a potential problem country that "should be watched very closely."(2) The following year, the Philippines dropped to fifth place among developing country private market borrowers, but was the second highest borrower in Asia. Despite this high growth record of the country's external debt, industrial country bankers and investors have not lost their nerve for casting their credits to the Philippines. In the spring of 1978, bankers and investors oversubscribed for a $500 million "jumbo" syndicated loan and a 100 million deutsch marks (DM) bond issue. Moreover, the Philippines Central Bank has announced intentions to add $1 billion annually to its foreign debt bill.

In a short time, the Philippines has become a major developing country borrower, has taken advantage of market conditions and official assistance, and has broken ground for developing countries in international financial circles. In the

---

*The Philippines National Anthem begins, "Land of the morning, /Child of the sun returning...."

process it also has established a sound record of pragmatic borrowing and has earned a reputation for responsible financial management. Hence, with the warnings of recent years against impending developing country debt disasters, it would seem useful to examine one middle-level developing country which has borrowed heavily from official and private sources, yet has been able to hold its own and keep its debt-servicing capacity above water.

This chapter therefore will tell the Philippine debt story, how the country has compiled its debt record and what is expected in the future. This review will include the Philippines' economic profile, its record of official and private external borrowing, its debt history, justifications for its high-level borrowing, and comments on its future debt path.

THE PHILIPPINE ECONOMIC PROFILE

> Statistically, the Philippines is among the more successful, but not most successful, developing nations.
>
> Philip Bowring
> Far Eastern Economic Review
> October 8, 1976

The Philippines is an archipelago of 7,100 islands and 44 million people. It is well endowed with mineral and agricultural resources relative to its size and population, has an educated, trained labor force, and maintains reasonable access to investment and capital flows. In the words of a 1977 World Bank report, "...the Philippines have the physical and human resources required for sustained economic improvement..."(3) The economy continues to rely heavily on agriculture, fishery, and forestry, although industrial production is gaining rapidly, and in 1977 manufacturing accounted for 24.2 percent of gross domestic product.(4) Over 50 percent of Phillipine exports are basic commodities, while over 90 percent of the country's imports are capital goods and industrial raw materials. This leaves the Philippines extremely vulnerable to world commodity conditions - a fact witnessed in the 1974-75 worldwide economic downturn. At that time, the Philippines faced adverse external terms of trade, recession in export markets, significantly higher costs for all imports, and domestic inflation. On the whole, however, the Philippines has done well, and its commendable performance reflects the country's underlying strength and resilience. As D. F. Amerman of the Journal of Commerce recently observed, "One inarguable truth emerges - the economy of this nation...is growing and growing at a healthy pace."(5)

Economic Growth

Considering the extreme conditions with which the Philippines has had to cope - tremendous oil import bills, higher costs for imported raw materials, machinery, and equipment, and a fall-off in demand for traditional and non-traditional exports - the Philippine growth performance has been quite impressive. (See Table 6.1.) Gross national product (GNP) increased by 6.3 percent in 1977 to $2.06 billion, although this growth rate fell short of the 7 percent

Table 6.1. Annual Philippine GNP Growth, 1972-1977*
(percent)

Year	Growth
1972	4.9
1973	9.6
1974	6.0
1975	5.9
1976	6.7
1977	6.3
1978	7.0 (est.)

*Growth rates are in real terms, adjusted for inflation.

Source: Far Eastern Economic Review, October 8, 1976, p. 51 (for 1972-75); D. F. Amerman, "Philippine Economy Grows at Healthy Rate," Journal of Commerce, May 31, 1978, p. 1 (for 1976-78).

target due to slowed export growth and sluggish investment. Real growth of the economy averaged 5.1 percent per annum in 1968-72 and 6.9 percent annually during 1973-1977.(6) Philippine officials estimate a 7 percent real increase in GNP for 1978 (although preliminary figures at mid-year were in the 6 percent range) and are targeting for an annual 8 percent real growth for the period 1978-82.

Philippine growth strategy has emphasized industrialization with a focus on infrastructure and export-oriented products. Two distinct phases are evident. In the first phase, 1950 to mid-1960s, large-scale capital and import-intensive enterprise dominated in the Manila region with import substitution policies for consumer imports in the latter years of the period. But little stimulus for domestic production of raw materials, intermediate goods, and new exports was generated. In the late

1960s, the beginning of the next phase, officials redirected the import substitution strategy and gave increased impetus to exports while emphasizing a more balanced regional program. Industrial structure has not changed substantially from the 1950s, however, and production continues to be capital-intensive. New directions for growth in labor intensive, nontraditional exports are planned for 1978-82, and President Marcos has cited four policies for future industrial development: export-oriented industries, labor-intensive production, backward integration, and regional dispersion.(7)

For 1977, manufacturing and mining led the economy's growth while agriculture and construction growth slowed. The record in 1977(8) shows:

Manufacturing	+ 7.5% (1976 - + 5.7%)
Mining/Quarrying	+16.8% (1976 - + 3.2%)
Agriculture	+ 4.9% (1976 - + 7.9%)
Construction	+ 6.0% (1976 - +28.0%)

It is notable that in 1977 the Philippines exported rice (about 40,000 metric tons to Indonesia and Malaysia) for the first time in this decade.

External Accounts

The Philippines' external accounts have been a source of concern to officials, with a large negative trade balance causing the greatest worry. The overall balance of payments for 1977 registered a surplus ($164 million) for the first time in three years (see Table 6.2) but is expected to deteriorate slightly in 1978 due to short-term loan repayments.

Table 6.2. Philippine Balance of Payments, 1973-1977
(in millions of US$)

1973	+ 664.0
1974	+ 110.0
1975	- 520.8
1976	- 163.7
1977	+ 164.0
1978	- 50.0 (est.)

Sources: Asian Development Bank; U.S. Embassy (Manila) Economic Trends Report, March 17, 1978. p. 2.

The country's balance of trade has not fared nearly as well, however, and in December 1976 it was observed that "one of the most serious problems...President Marcos faces is how on earth to fund the huge trade deficit which has become a worrying feature of the Philippine economy in recent years."(9) The balance of trade has registered -$1,164.7 million (1975), -$1,059.8 million (1976), -$763.9 million (1977),(10) and may exceed $1 billion in 1978. In 1977 exports grew 22.2 percent compared to 11 percent in 1976, and for the first time reached the $3 billion level. Imports increased by 7.7 percent to $3.92 billion but declined in real terms. The Philippine trade deficit is largely a result of its "appalling terms of trade"(11) which between 1974 and 1976 collapsed by 25 percent due to oil price increases and the recessionary fall in export prices. (See Table 6.3.) Export prices moved up

Table 6.3. Philippine Terms of Trade Index, 1970-1980

1970	101.4
1971	93.2
1972	82.0
1973	97.9
1974	97.9
1975	74.0
1976	75.0
1980	78.0 (est.)

Source: Philip Bowring, "Anatomy of a Debt Burden," Far Eastern Economic Review, October 8, 1976, p. 51.

94 percent in 1973-74 but dropped sharply in 1976. During that same period, 1974-1976, the Philippines' oil bill shot up from $190 million to $800 million. In 1977 imported petroleum cost the Philippines $1.1 billion, or one-third of its total import bill.(12) The country consumes about 200,000 barrels of oil per day, and in 1977, 73 percent or 37.5 million barrels came from the Middle East. Recent offshore oil discoveries in the Palawan region are planned to come on-stream in 1979, however, and the Philippines hopes that these discoveries will supply ten percent of domestic needs and a foreign exchange savings of $100 million annually. The United States Embassy in Manila reports current optimistic projections at 40,000 barrels or 15 percent of consumption by mid-1980.

To counter its terms of trade trends, the Philippines is attempting to diversify its export products and markets which until now have made the country a price-taker. Exports largely have been concentrated in a few traditional products - coconuts, sugar, logs, minerals - which in 1976 accounted for 67 percent of commodity export earnings. Nontraditional exports, which totaled 2 percent of exports in 1968, reached a 33 percent share in 1977 and hopefully will be 50 percent of the export total by 1980. These products include garments, electronic and electrical goods, chemicals, cement, and wood manufactures. In 1977 manufactured exports grew 31 percent to 25 percent of the export total. This year the Philippines signed agreements with fourteen countries for better market access of nontraditional export products and to secure more favorable terms of trade.(13)

Diversification of markets also is part of the country's trade turnaround strategy. The United States and Japan have - and still do - claimed the largest portion of Philippine exports,(14) to wit:

	1972	1977
United States and Japan	74.4%	58.1%
European Community	13.7%	18.4%
Association of Southeast Asian Nations	1.6%	4.0%

Buttressing the Philippine export efforts are the new Philippine Export Council to coordinate industrial export strategies; the Philippine International Trading Company formed in January 1977 to deal with state trading firms in the socialist countries; and three planned export processing zones in addition to the zone now operating in Bataan.

In addition to boosting trade receipts, the Philippines is working to stimulate domestic and foreign investment to increase capital inflows. Investment sagged in 1977 with new approvals down by 45 percent to $105 million from the $191 million level in 1976. Foreign investors accounted for $45.7 million of the total approvals in 1977.(15) The 1977 decline is attributed to the cutbacks in the agro-based, mining, and minerals processing sectors. According to the Philippine Central Bank, the Philippines received $801 million in direct foreign equity investment from February 1970 to December 1977.(16) (This does not include $103 million invested through stock exchanges.) Leading foreign investors are the United States ($370.1 million or 46 percent), Japan ($178.5 million or 22 percent), and Canada (52.21 million or 7 percent).(17)

Challenges Ahead

Despite the Philippines' considerable economic efforts, its economy is not out of the woods yet and faces considerable obstacles and challenges. Inflation rose slightly above the 7 percent target to 7.9 percent in 1977 for metropolitan Manila, but the inflation rate for the country as a whole was higher at 9.9 percent. Moreover, unemployment is above the 10 percent mark (the exact rate is undetermined), and 500,000 jobs must be created annually to keep up with the 2.7 percent population growth rate and prevent the unemployment rate from rising. Economic dualism is striking, and while Manila's metropolitan middle class is growing and vigorous, the rural malnourished and underemployed have their economic gains largely cancelled by population growth. Finally, income and growth benefits are badly distributed within the economy, and the lot of the poor has improved slowly if at all.(18)

To help combat these ills, the Philippine Government recently adopted the most comprehensive fixed-term development plan for the period 1978-1982 which is part of a 5-, 10-, and 20-year planning cycle. The plan calls for annual real GNP growth of 8 percent; increased export and import rates of 19 percent and 17 percent, respectively; and a cut in the current-account deficit to $790 by 1982. Other goals include a strengthened balance-of-payments position, greater food and energy self-sufficiency, reduced income inequality, and accelerated domestic resource mobilization.(19) In President Marcos' words, "The critical problem is how to finance the massive national development effort. It is in the area of capital building where national development programs face their greatest test."(20) Hence, for the Philippines' economic problems, development financing is key -- and herein lies the basis for Philippine debt.

DEBT FOR DEVELOPMENT

The Overview

> The soaring of Philippine foreign debts will be the crux of the nation's monetary problems in 1978.

Thus predicted Keith Lorenz of the Journal of Commerce in January 1978, but it does not appear that the Philippines' financial managers are quite so pessimistic, nor are inventors in the international capital markets. For despite a 19 percent increase in external debt outstanding in 1977 - an increase of $1.05 billion over the 1976 level of $5.52 billion(21) - the

Philippine Central Bank intends to borrow $1 billion annually to finance development, consolidate and prepay existing debt, and meet debt-servicing requirements. According to Finance Secretary Cesar Virata, of the total $6.57 billion debt by end-1977, $5.5 billion was in fixed-term loans, and the balance is in revolving trade credits.(22) (See Table 6.4.) Of the

Table 6.4. Philippine External Debt Outstanding, March 31, 1978
(in millions of US$)

Type	Private Sector	Public Sector	Sub-total
Revolving	632.3	357.7	990.0
Fixed-term	2,310.4	3,623.3	5,933.7
Total			6,923.7

Source: Central Bank of the Philippines, Bondline, First Quarter 1978, vol. 22, no. 1, p. 9.

foreign obligations outstanding at the end of 1977, $5.63 billion, or 86 percent, had been used to finance establishment of manufacturing plants, purchases of capital goods, and construction of infrastructure projects. Fourteen percent, or $958 million, was paid for oil imports.(23)

Since 1972, the annual average increase of Philippine external debt has been 40 percent. It has tripled since end-1972 ($2.2 billion) and doubled since end-1974 ($2.907 billion). (See Tables 6.5 and 6.6.)

Among official creditors, the largest is the United States with $2 billion or 35 percent of total claims. The ranking of creditors(24) shows:

United States	$ 2 billion or 35 percent
Japan	$903 million or 16 percent
International Monetary Fund	$551 million or 10 percent
World Bank	$375 million or 7 percent
United Kingdom	$322 million or 6 percent
Asian Development Bank	$148 million or 2 percent

Not only has the gross volume of external borrowing increased significantly, but the pace of incremental borrowing

Table 6.5. Philippine External Debt Outstanding, 1970-1979 (in billions of US$)

1970	1.83
1971	.95
1972	2.20
1973	2.35
1974	3.24
1975	3.96
1976	5.52
1977	6.57
1978	7.57 (third quarter)

Sources: Asian Wall Street Journal, March 30, 1978, p. 3, and other issues; Asia 1978 Yearbook (Hong Kong: Far Eastern Economic Review Ltd.), p. 295.

Table 6.6. Main Features of Philippine Loan Commitments, 1970-72 and 1973-75

	Official Creditors		Private Creditors	
	1970-72	1973-75	1970-72	1973-75
Average amount (US$m)	212.4	376.5	34.6	236.0
Average interest (percent)	5.4	6.1	8.1	8.7
Average maturity (years)	17.8	23.4	5.1	10.2
Grant element (percent)	29.0	27.0	5.0	6.0

Source: Asian Development Bank, Key Indicators 9, no. 1 (April 1978), p. 42.

has accelerated as well, particularly since 1974. With international commodities prices plummeting and oil prices gushing up, the Philippines was faced with the choice of either continuing development programs and thus import levels, or tightening the economic belt to restrain foreign exchange outflows. The Philippines opted for the former alternative. Hence, heavy external borrowing has occurred - 83 percent of total net capital inflows since 1974 - to support its current-account deficits. (See Table 6.7.)

Table 6.7. Net Official and Private Capital Flows, 1970-1976 (in millions of US$)

	1970	1971	1972	1973	1974	1975	1976
Multilateral	17.5	26.3	21.9	42.3	78.8	140.2	143.8
Official, Development Assistance Committee (of the OECD) countries	128.4	110.7	173.4	230.5	134.0	152.7	236.5
Private, Development Assistance Committee (of the OECD) countries	170.4	-7.1	31.4	2.9	163.2	108.4	689.4

Source: Asian Development Bank, Key Indicators, vol. IX, no. 1, (April 1978), pp. 32. 34, 35.

The growing rate of new borrowing also has been related to rising debt service obligations. Hence, increased borrowing has translated into higher debt payments and debt-service ratios (DSRs) as Table 6.8 indicates:

Despite the worsening burden of debt payments, the debt-service ratio has stayed well under the Philippines' legal ceiling of 20 percent.(25) Also, a lid on new borrowing has been imposed by the International Monetary Fund related to an IMF three-year Extended Fund Facility Loan of $330 million.(26)

The borrowing limit is set for loans of 1- to 15-year maturities with subcategories of 5 and 10 years. The 1977 total limit was $860 million which the Philippines barely met with a loan level of $854.7 million.(27) For 1978 the ceiling is placed at $1,145 million. As of August 1978, Central Bank approvals in the 1-to-15-year maturity range totaled $834 million.

Table 6.8. Philippine Debt Payments and Debt-Service Ratios, 1970-1978

Year	Payments (in millions of US$)	DSR (percent)
1970	621.0	34.0
1971	96.6	6.6
1972	404.0	29.0
1973	214.5	8.8
1974	187.7	5.1
1975	230.2	7.6
1976	222.7	6.8
1977	727.0	14.0
1978	963.0	17.0

Note: Years are already cited in footnote, i.e., 1971, 1973-76.

Sources: Asian Development Bank, Key Indicators vol. IX, no. 1, (April, 1978), pp. 40, 41 (for years 1971, 1973-1976); Asian Wall Street Journal, March 30, 1978, p. 3 (for years 1972, 1977); and Far Eastern Economic Review, October 8, 1976, p. 51.

Thus, with the Philippines' debt regulatory policies and an International Monetary Fund payments adjustment program, creditors - particularly private lenders - have been more than willing to lend to the Philippines. Their confidence in Philippine creditworthiness lies in its financial vigilance - a fact which stems from the country's debt crisis in the sixties.

The Debt Crisis of the Sixties

Actually, the crisis occurred in 1970 and 1971, but 1969 marked the low point for the Philippines' current-account deficit, foreign assets, and reserves and the high point of short-term credit expansion during the period 1967-73.(28) By the late 1960s, short-term borrowing ranged from two-fifths to three-eighths of the total external public debt and was continuously rolled over every 120 to 180 days. But by June 1971, the Central Bank's exposed position and the condition of the economy made foreign banks unwilling to roll over loans. At the same time, local borrowers were unable to repay credits due to the peso devaluation with the effect that the Development Bank of the Philippines, which had guaranteed their debt, became liable.

The crisis, according to P.A. Wellons, is attributed to two events. First was the public sector's reliance on foreign banks. In the mid-1960s, the government's interference in foreign exchange transactions was minimal, and authorities did not monitor the terms of foreign borrowing. They therefore "could not analyze the maturity structure of the country's entire debt, nor could they consider the size of the debt and its impact on the balance of payments."(29) Thus, a persistent balance of payments resulted from 1967-69 which depleted foreign reserves and forced authorities to borrow abroad. This led to the build-up of short-term payables in 1970-71.

The second factor leading to crisis was private sector short-term debt which overlapped with public debt in two ways. First, the government-owned Philippine National Bank was the largest commercial bank and a conduit for private external debt. Second, the Development Bank of the Philippines, also a government institution, had guaranteed substantial private foreign debt - almost one-third of the country's total external debt in 1970.

To deal with the crisis, the government instituted "a wrenching program of debt readjustment and regulation..."(30) First, monetary authorities floated the peso (for a nearly 65 percent devaluation), restructured Central Bank loans by consolidating loans and lengthening maturities, regulated long-term debt, and discouraged short-term credits. For the regulation of future debt and prevention of similar crises, the Philippine Congress amended the Foreign Borrowing Act in 1970 which, inter alia, placed a 20 percent debt service ceiling on loan repayments, limited the permissible resources, set minimum maturities and maximum interest rates, and provided for allocation of external debt receipts among sectors of the economy.(31)

This comprehensive regulatory system, which is directed by the External Debt Management Office of the Central Bank, not only pulled the Philippines out of crisis (aided by the commodities boom), but also laid the foundation for future borrowing and created a basis for the Philippines' reputation for creditworthiness and reliability. In 1973 the Central Bank set out to establish its credit in the Euromarkets. At the end of that year it had estimated the oil price impact and trebled its foreign exchange cushion to $3 billion. In 1974 it was able to secure loans from international banks when other countries were being shut out. And in 1975, bankers said their books were not yet filled with Philippine paper.(32)

Hence, the sixties does much to explain the Philippine authorities' approach to external borrowing - described as "sober even dour and certainly cautious"(33) - and their intent to anticipate and meet contingencies to forestall future liquidity crises. It also explains foreign creditors' response to Philippine external financing needs. The Philippine Government's policy of rigorous debt management and financial integrity has earned it high credit ratings and confidence. It also made the Philippines the fifth largest developing country borrower in international credit markets in 1977.

The Philippines in Private Markets

Like God, investors and bankers
help those who help themselves.

Philip Bowring
Far Eastern Economic Review,
October 8, 1976

In 1976 Philip Bowring of the Far Eastern Economic Review observed that "The Philippines is among the poorest of the non-oil producing countries to have borrowed in a major way in international markets."(34) Indeed, in 1977 it was the second largest borrower ($689 million) in the Asian syndicated loan market, and 1978 appears to be another big year. Of the non-OPEC developing countries, total Philippine borrowing in the international capital markets in 1977 is surpassed only by Mexico ($3.86 billion), Brazil ($3.55 billion), Korea ($1.33 billion), and Argentina ($942 million). (See Table 6.9.)

Table 6.9. Philippine Eurocurrency Credits and International Bond Issues, 1970-1977 (in millions of US$)

	1970	1971	1972	1973	1974	1975	1976	1977
Eurocurrency bank credits	5	-0-	50	187	843	363	970	698
International bond issues	-0-	-0-	-0-	25	17	30	367	118
Total	5	-0-	50	212	861	393	1337	816

Source: Morgan Guaranty Trust Company, World Financial Markets, March 1978, pp. 3-5.

So far in 1978, foreign bankers are flocking to the islands, and Philippine corporations are lining up at loan windows. The first major coup was accomplished by the Central Bank, however. In May 1978 a consortium of 60 banks led by Manufacturers Hanover Trust, Ltd., announced a "jumbo" loan - a $500 million, 10-year (3-year grace), at 1 percent over the London Inter-Bank Offer Rate (LIBOR). This financing is the largest commercial loan to the Philippines, and its terms and pricing are among the most favorable ever.(35) It also makes the Philippines the first Southeast Asian country recipient of "jumbo" syndicated financing. The loan is part of the Central Bank's new consolidated borrowing program and is expected to cover the Central Bank's borrowing requirements for the remainder of 1978.

The jumbo loan has been hailed as a breakthrough for developing countries in international capital markets. Originally the Central Bank intended to borrow the $500 million in two parts - $250 million in the first half of 1978 and $250 million in the second half. But by April 1978 a rush of subscriptions pushed up the loan to $450 million, and by May the total climbed to $500 million. A clause is included in the loan terms, however, that stipulates that one-half must be used for purposes other than refinancing existing debt.(36) The $500 million jumbo loan is considered a reflection of the Philippines' high credit rating in the international financial community.

Philippine authorities hardly had time to bask in the glories of their "jumbo" accomplishment, however. The next day it was announced that another consortium of banks led by Citibank had agreed to adjust the terms of a $256.6 million loan extended to the state-owned National Power Corporation which is to help finance a $1 billion nuclear power plant project. The original agreement was for seven years at 1.75 percent over LIBOR. After four months of negotiations, the consortium converted the loan to 11 years (1976-1987) with four and one-half years grace, and divided the loan into two tranches for adjustment purposes. On the $107 million already drawn, interest of 1.75 percent over LIBOR will apply until 1983 and thereafter will be 1.125 percent until maturity. On the remaining undrawn portion, $149.6 million, interest will be 1.125 percent over LIBOR. The new agreement does not include a prepayment provision.

The Central Bank also has obtained other loans under its new Consolidated Foreign Borrowing Program which is centralizing foreign borrowing for the government and its agencies. Central Bank borrowing is for relending the government agencies and to private firms in which the government has substantial exposure. The purpose is to prepay higher-cost old loans and to relend to local borrowers who can not secure terms as good as those of the Central Bank. Under this program, the Central Bank secured a $100 million syndicated loan in March 1978 from a consortium led by Bankers Trust of New York (seven years, 1 percent over LIBOR), and a $43 million solo credit from the Bank of Tokyo (ten years, 1 percent over LIBOR) in April 1978. As of March 1978 the Central Bank was trying for loans of $150 million for Marinduque Mining and Industrial Corporation and of $57 million for the Development Bank of the Philippines.

In competing for loans that will fit under the $1,145 million loan ceiling for 1978, Philippine companies have scrambled to secure their needed credits and have found money easily in the now highly liquid international capital market. For example, the following loans(37) have been secured:

$250.0 million, Philippine Sugar Commission
$130.5 million, San Miguel Corporation
$105.0 million, Philippine Long Distance Telephone Company
$ 43.0 million, Benguet Consolidated
$ 22.7 million, Republic Telephone Company
$ 20.0 million, Construction and Development Corporation of the Philippines
$ 75.0 million, Philippine Airlines
$ 64.0 million, Philippine National Oil Company
$ 70.0 million, National Power Corporation

Philippine authorities also have sought new methods and sources of loan monies. In 1977 the Philippines turned to Kuwait and Bahrain for petrodollar denominated bond floats and raised, in dinars, $17.5 million and $23 million from the two countries respectively. In addition, the Philippines secured direct loans from Kuwait ($12.28 million) and Saudi Arabia ($19.5 million).(38) In another venture in the international bond market, a German issue of ten-year, yen-denominated bonds was oversubscribed and raised $50.2 million. In Japan a first public offering of seven-year mark-denominated bonds raised $68.2 million at 6.75 percent and will be important in developing the market for Philippine securities in Japan. The switch to yen in Germany and marks in Japan is due to regulations in the two countries requiring that proceeds from bonds be converted before being taken out of either country in order to avoid speculation in their appreciating currencies.(39) These bond issues may be breaking new ground for other Asian developing countries which are expected to follow suit. According to Finance Secretary Virata, the Philippines is "probably the lowest per capita income country that has had a bond issue."(40)

Another source of funding has been the Philippines' new offshore banking system which opened for business in April 1977. One year later, 17 foreign banks had been authorized to open Offshore Banking Units (OBUs). This along with expansion of foreign currency deposit units (FCDUs) has widened access to overseas sources of capital. Most foreign banks involved in loan syndications have offshore banking units, local branches, or representative offices, and this has been a plus for the Philippines in providing greater familiarity and assessments of risk.

In surveying the magnitude and acceleration of Philippine external borrowing, one could either be skeptical of its ability to carry further debt or be confident of its record and creditworthiness. Whichever the observer's position, however, Philippine authorities at least are confident of continued external support, and their plans for the future reflect this.

1978 AND BEYOND

Finance Secretary Cesar Virata has announced that the Philippines will borrow $1.7-1.8 million in 1978. One billion dollars will be net borrowing and the remaining for debt servicing. The $1 billion figure appears to be the minimum requirement if existing development plans are to be met. (As noted earlier, not all external borrowing comes under the IMF new debt ceiling.) Of the total, official sources will provide $800 million, commercial and export credits will equal $860 million, and revolving credits will account for $100 million. Official credits are expected to break down(41) as follows:

World Bank/International Development Association	$350-400 million
Asian Development Bank	$150-175 million
Overseas Economic Corporation Fund of Japan	$120-150 million
United States Agency for International Development	$ 50- 60 million
Australia	$ 40 million
Others - Organization of Petroleum Exporting Countries (OPEC) Special Fund, Saudi Fund, United Nations Development Program (UNDP), International Fund for Agricultural Development (IFAD)	Balance

The Central Bank's consolidated borrowing program will play a key role in borrowing plans. The $800 million official borrowings will be rechanneled to the private sector, particularly to small- and medium-scale industries, agricultural loans to small farmers, and to shipbuilding for interisland and fishing vessels. Commercial credit will go to private sector projects, capital goods imports not financed by foreign export credit institutions (e.g., the United States Export-Import Bank), and for joint projects with the private sector.(42) The consolidated borrowing should account for $703 million of the IMF $1,145 million limitation for 1978.(43) The consolidation procedure does not preclude government financial institutions, e.g., the Philippine National Bank, the Development Bank of the Philippines, from borrowing directly from international financial institutions, however.

Continued heavy borrowing, of course, brings into question the future requirements for debt servicing and the increased burden this entails. For 1978 Central Bank Governor Gregorio Licaros forecast payments of $963 million, or 17 percent of 1977 foreign exchange earnings. Future debt-servicing accounting for existing debt through December 31, 1976 and new approvals through 1981(44) are as follows:

	1979	1980	1981
Existing debt	$866 million	$924 million	$871 million
New approvals	222 million	437 million	655 million
Total	$1,088 million	$1,361 million	$1,526 million

The Philippine Central Bank expects that beyond 1981, debt service payments will reach $3,405.4 million, but Governor Licaros expects the debt-service ratio to drop:(45)

1978	17 percent
1979	16 percent
1980	14 percent
1981	10 percent
1982	7 percent

(It should be noted that these debt-service ratios reflect service on debts currently on the books only; that is, the figures assume there will be no borrowing in the future. There have not yet been attempts to develop ratios which include projections of future borrowings.)

One method of lowering future debt service ratios and lightening the burden of expected repayments is the Central Bank's strategy for retiring older, high-cost loans for new loans at better terms. Public loans are not the only targets of renegotiations, however. Finance Secretary Virata has publicly urged Philippine borrowers to renegotiate loans - and seek government support if needed. Other Asian governments are renegotiating loans as well, and the rush to do so has commercial banks digging in their heels against refinancing old loans at lower rates. But market conditions of high liquidity and therefore intense competition among commercial banks has given Asian borrowers the upper hand. The situation in Manila may be more extreme due to the 17 new offshore banking units for which the Central Bank is almost their sole customer. Bankers are distressed ("gnashing teeth" as one observer put it) by the trends of borrowing in a highly liquid market at easier rates for early repayment of costlier loans. Most loan contracts in the post-oil-crisis period did not have prepayment penalty clauses, and, now being awash with loanable funds, bankers have little choice but to comply for fear of business going elsewhere. Banks fear major losses on earnings from the high interest, balance-of-payments loans made two to three years ago. As one American banker understated their case, "No one is happy about repayments." However, one remedy for easing the bankers' pain - as with the $500 million Philippine jumbo loan - has been the restriction on use of easier term loans to project rather than refinancing. Still it is a borrower's market.

IN DEFENSE OF BORROWING

Not all debt observers are comfortable with the Philippines' accelerated borrowing record. It was reported in January 1978 that "banking circles are alarmed by the continuing trade and fiscal deficits and high government expenditures which characterize the economy."(46) In a letter to President Marcos, however, Central Bank Governor Licaros pointed out that the debt burden has not grown nearly as fast as the amounts the country has borrowed. In the period 1972-77, outstanding debt has tripled while debt service has not even doubled ($404 million to $727 million). According to official statements, the debt service load is well within Philippine repayment capabilities (and the Philippine legal limit) and moreover will be on a decelerating scale. (However, the caveat should be added that the Philippines' steadily increasing debt service load in the face of current account deficits, flagging growth in export earnings, and increasing protectionist pressures in the industrial countries, makes the Philippine debt burden subject to possible difficulties in servicing.) "The low debt service ratio," defends Licaros, "reflects validity and prudence in the Government's debt management policies."(47) Further, he has pledged continued prudence in external debt management. Future borrowings will be based strictly on repayment capability, loans will be used in accordance with set priorities, and borrowing terms will be as favorable as possible to the Philippines.(48)

The Phillipines has borrowed heavily to finance its foreign trade deficit and to support a large program of capital expenditure on infrastructure and industrial development. External borrowing has been necessary to supplement internal savings to meet the goals and targets of development, explains Virata. "We therefore must borrow judiciously and invest resources in productive industries, specifically in export and labor-intensive industries."(49) Licaros has added that foreign borrowings should be viewed against the perspective of economic benefits derived from the projects financed by such borrowings.

The final justification comes from President Marcos who contends that debt grows as a result of development needs, and "efforts to tap external sources are based on the soundness of economic programs....Foreign institutions and banks lend only to those with a capacity to pay. And a test of soundness is the continuing confidence that our efforts receive in the field of international development finance."(50)

WHITHER PHILIPPINE DEBT?

The future of Philippine debt, the country's capacity to service growing payments, and therefore its continued creditworthiness, will be affected not only by economic and policy factors which the Philippines can to an extent control, but also by international economic conditions over which it has little impact. Foremost of course is the performance of the Philippine economy - the outlook of which one observer has described as cloudy at best. The Philippines' ambitious five-year plan for the period 1978-82 will require external borrowing to support, but in turn will have to succeed in its targets to support continued borrowing. Critical to the ease of new borrowing will be the Philippines' current-account performance. The plan calls for an appreciable decline by 1982 despite the worsening situation in 1978. Exports are projected to grow at a faster rate than import growth, and although traditional commodity exports will rise, nontraditional exports will carry the burden of growth performance. To the extent that exports fall short of targets, it will be more difficult to finance imports needed for development programs. Thus, an eye to selectivity of development projects will be important in minimizing external debt servicing burdens.

Aside from domestic factors affecting the economy's performance, - e.g., weather and agriculture conditions, structural constraints - the Philippines also must contend with crucial external factors. Among these are its terms of trade, new export opportunities and open markets, competition from other countries or from substitutes, growing protectionism from importing countries, and continued access to official and private capital on reasonable terms. Strong and continuing economic recovery of key industrial nations will be critical to generate increased demand for Philippine exports. Further oil price rises also will be an important factor to Philippine borrowing needs and servicing capacities.

Equally important will be the international banking community itself. Thus far, heavy Philippine external borrowing has been acceptable to bankers partly because of the country's debt reform laws of 1970 and partly because of its improved reputation for orderly government since martial law. The bankers' continued vote of creditworthiness for the Philippines depends on their perception of how the country is using - or wasting - its resources. Also important will be the availability of longer-term lending, e.g., from the World Bank, to influence bankers' evaluations by keeping debt service low.

Another factor is world liquidity, and although this is not easily predictable, its continuation would ease the Philippines' future debt service payments. It has been said that current liquidity conditions will not last long - perhaps a year - and interest rates are likely to rise as corporate demand for credit picks up in the United States and Europe.(51) If liquidity tightens, the Philippines might encounter a drop in bankers' interest - although not necessarily by all banks. Those with offshore units in the Philippines and those with significant loan investments are likely to continue their support. At any rate, the current aggressive drive by Philippine credit managers to renegotiate old loans bodes well for the country's future borrowing abilities and debt limits.

In the end, the burden of continued accessibility of the Philippines to external capital falls on the shoulders of its debt managers. The Philippines has a corps of influential, internationally respected, and highly competent financial and economic leaders: Gregorio Licaros, Governor of the Central Bank; Cesar Virata, Finance Secretary; Girardo Sicat, Chairman of the National Economic Development Authority; Vincente Paterno, Industry Secretary. Their reputations and performance as economic managers have provided the Philippines with much of its high international credit standing.

In sum, it appears that although the level of Philippine external debt has taken quantum leaps and is expected to continue rising, the Philippines has its debt servicing well in hand. This is due to the far-sighted financial planning of its managers, its external borrowing laws, and the use to which external resources are put. The Philippines performs creditably in its external economic management. But what it can not control are the international economic conditions to which the country is subject and so vulnerable. These are the factors that one must watch to gauge the future of Philippine debt - the ones that the Philippines is working so vigorously to overcome.

NOTES

1. Michael T. Malloy, "Philippines Cites Strong Signs for Investment," Asian Wall Street Journal, October 10, 1978, p. 3.
2. U.S. Department of Treasury, Report on Developing Countries' External Debt and Debt Relief Provided by the United States, Executive Communication 2433 (Washington, D.C.: U.S. Government Printing Office, 1976), p. 12.
3. "The Philippines: Asia's Dynamic New Society," Business Week (Special Advertising Section), June 12, 1978, p. 23.
4. Asian Development Bank, Key Indicators of Developing Member Countries of ADB 9 (April 1978): 9.
5. D. F. Amerman, Jr., "Philippine Economy Grows at Healthy Pace," Journal of Commerce, May 31, 1978, p. 1.
6. Swiss-Philippine Society, "RP to Repay $96 Billion Foreign Debts," Newsletter 1: 9.
7. "Interview with President Ferdinand E. Marcos," Business Week (Special Advertising Section), June 12, 1978, p. 26.
8. U.S. Embassy (Manila), Economic Trends Report, Philippines, Airgram A-52, March 17, 1978, pp. 3-4.
9. "Philippine Peso," International Currency Review 8 (November/December 1976): 143.
10. U.S. Embassy (Manila), Economic Trends Report, p. 2; see also Economic Trend Report, September 7, 1978, p. 5.
11. Philip Bowring, "Anatomy of a Debt Burden," Far Eastern Economic Review, October 8, 1976, p. 48.
12. "Philippine Peso," International Currency Review 9 (May 12, 1978): 154.
13. Amerman, "Philippine Economy Grows," p. 15.
14. D. F. Amerman, Jr., "Philippines Seeks to Expand Markets," Journal of Commerce, June 1, 1978, p. 1.
15. Amerman, "Philippine Economy Grows," p. 15.
16. "Foreign Investment in Philippines Totaled $801 Million in 1970-77," Asian Wall Street Journal, April 25, 1978, p. 3.
17. Ibid.
18. Parvaz Hasan, "Growth and Equity in East Asia," Finance and Development 15 (June 1978): 30.
19. "Philippine Economy is Healthy but Growing Only Moderately," Commerce America 3 (June 5, 1978): 14.
20. "Interview with President Ferdinand E. Marcos," p. 26.
21. "Philippine Foreign Debt Increased 19% in 1977 to Over $6.5 Billion," Asian Wall Street Journal, April 28, 1978, p. 3.
22. Cesar Virata, "How the Philippines Will Borrow in 1978," Euromoney, April 1978, p. 87.
23. Leo Gonzaga, "Manila Doubles Its Money," Far Eastern Economic Review, June 2, 1978, p. 52.
24. "Philippine Foreign Debt Increased 19%," p. 3.
25. The United States Embassy in Manila has pointed out that

Philippine calculations of DSR differ from, say, those of the World Bank. By the latter's definition, the DSR figure will be close to 20 percent and probably will be higher in 1979.
26. The IMF Extended Fund Facility provides balance-of-payments assistance to allow for structural change in the economy which is necessary for correcting the payments imbalance. So far (October 1978), only the Philippines, Haiti, Kenya, Mexico, and Jamaica have used the facility.
27. The ceiling does not include loans for use by the Central Bank. When this bank relends to other government institutions, only a portion is counted against the IMF ceiling. If the bank loan increases the indebtedness of the institutions, it would count against the ceiling. If it is used to prepay outstanding loans, it would not.
28. P.A. Wellons, Borrowing by Developing Countries in the Eurocurrency Market, Development Center Studies (Paris: Organization for Economic Cooperation and Development, 1977), pp. 161-85.
29. Ibid., p. 162.
30. Ibid., p. 161.
31. Ibid., p. 168.
32. Ibid.
33. Bowring, "Anatomy of a Debt Burden," p. 47.
34. Ibid., p. 51.
35. "Philippines Inks $500 Million Loan," Journal of Commerce, May 30, 1978, p. 33.
36. "Big Loan Package to Philippines Gets $400 Million in Bids," Asian Wall Street Journal, April 6, 1978, p. 3.
37. Leo Gonzaga, "Ceiling Hangs Over Manila," Far Eastern Economic Review, March 31, 1978, pp. 48-49.
38. "Philippines, Economy," Asia 1978 Yearbook, p. 295.
39. Michael T. Malloy, "The Region," Asian Wall Street Journal, April 5, 1978, p. 1.
40. Ibid.
41. Virata, "How the Philippines Will Borrow," p. 87.
42. Ibid.
43. Leo Gonzaga, "Banking, No Less for the Locals," Far Eastern Economic Review, April 14, 1978, p. 62.
44. Seth Lipsky, "IMF Report Shows Concerns About Parts of Philippine Economy," Asian Wall Street Journal, April 4, 1978, p. 6.
45. Gonzaga, "Manila Doubles Its Money," p. 52.
46. Keith Lorenz, "Philippine Dilemma Worries Business," Journal of Commerce, January 19, 1978, p. 17.
47. Swiss-Philippine Society, "RP to Repay," p. 10.
48. Gonzaga, "Manila Doubles Its Money," p. 52.
49. Swiss-Philippine Society, "Total Foreign Borrowings in 1977 $6.5 Billion," Newsletter 1: 9.
50. "Interview with President Ferdinand E. Marcos," p. 26.
51. Gonzaga, "Ceiling Hangs Over Manila," p. 49.

BIBLIOGRAPHY

Amerman, D. F., Jr. "Philippine Economy Grows at Healthy Pace." *Journal of Commerce*, May 31, 1978, pp. 1, 15.

_________. "Philippines Seeks to Expand Markets." *Journal of Commerce*, June 1, 1978, pp. 1, 15.

Asia 1978 Yearbook. Hong Kong: Far Eastern Economic Review, pp. 294-97.

Asian Development Bank. *Key Indicators of Developing Member Countries of ADB* 9 (April 1978). 204 pp.

"Asian Loan Tactics Upset Bankers." *Far Eastern Economic Review*, February 17, 1978, pp. 38-39.

"Banks in U.S., Tokyo Give Philippine Agency Credit of $250 Million." *Wall Street Journal*, June 2, 1978, p. 25.

"Big Loan Package to Philippines Gets $400 Million in Bids." *Asian Wall Street Journal*, April 6, 1978, p. 3.

Bowring, Philip. "Anatomy of a Debt Burden." *Far Eastern Economic Review*, October 8, 1976, pp. 47-52.

"The Business Outlook, Philippines." *Business Asia*, February 17, 1978, p. 56.

Caouette, John B. "Overdue Boom in Euromarket Loans Begins," *Euromoney*, April 1978, pp. 153, 155.

"Foreign Investment in Philippines Totaled $801 Million in 1970-77." *Asian Wall Street Journal*, April 25, 1978, p. 3.

Gonzaga, Leo. "Banking, No Less for the Locals." *Far Eastern Economic Review*, April 14, 1978, pp. 60, 62.

_________. "Ceilings Hangs Over Manila." *Far Eastern Economic Review*, March 31, 1978, pp. 48-49.

_________. "Manila Doubles Its Money." *Far Eastern Economic Review*, June 2, 1978, pp. 51-52.

Lipsky, Seth. "IMF Report Shows Concerns About Parts of Philippine Economy." *Asian Wall Street Journal*, April 4, 1978, pp. 1, 6.

"Loan Refinancing by Philippines is Restricted." *Asian Wall Street Journal*, March 31, 1978, pp. 1, 5.

Lorenz, Keith. "Philippine Dilemma Worries Business." *Journal of Commerce*, January 19, 1978, pp. 1, 17.

_________. "Philippines to Join Producing Nations." *Journal of Commerce*, June 1, 1978, p. 31.

_________. "Rise in Philippine Debt Seen Crux of '78 Monetary Problems." *Journal of Commerce*, January 20, 1978, pp. 1, 27.

_________. "Tensions Building in the Philippines." *Journal of Commerce*, April 7, 1978, pp. 1, 19.

Malloy, Michael T. "Manila, Banks Agree to Ease '76 Loan Terms." *Asian Wall Street Journal*, May 22, 1978, p. 6.

_________. "Philippines Cites Strong Signs for Investment." *Asian Wall Street Journal*, October 10, 1978, p. 3.

_________. "The Region." *Asian Wall Street Journal*, April 5,

1978, pp. 1, 10.

________. "Wide Trade Gap for Philippines Forecast by U.S." Asian Wall Street Journal, March 28, 1978, p. 3.

"Marcos Wants Access to World Markets for Philippine Goods." Asian Wall Street Journal, March 30, 1978, p. 2.

Morgan Guaranty Trust Company. "International Bond Issues and Eurocurrency Bank Credits." World Financial Markets, March 1978, p. 5.

"Philippine Agency to Get 10-Year $79 Million Loan." Wall Street Journal, May 18, 1978, p. 34.

"Philippine Economy is Healthy but Growing Only Moderately." Commerce America 3 (June 5, 1978): 14-15.

"Philippine Oil a Step Closer." Far Eastern Economic Review, November 4, 1977, pp. 49-51.

"Philippine Peso." International Currency Review 10 (May 12, 1978): 152-56.

"Philippine Power Firm Gets $70 Million Loan." Asian Wall Street Journal, May 18, 1978, p. 6.

"The Philippines, Asia's Dynamic New Society." Business Week. Special Advertising Section, June 12, 1978, pp. 23-49.

"Philippines, Banks Set Accord to East Terms of $256.6 Million Loan." Wall Street Journal, May 22, 1978, p. 6.

"Philippines Counts Its Blessings." Far Eastern Economic Review, November 18, 1977, pp. 58-59.

"Philippines Inks $500 Million Loan." Journal of Commerce, May 30, 1978, p. 33.

"Philippines Loan." Washington Post, May 31, 1978, p. E-3.

"Philippines Sees Foreign Debt Payments Climbing to Record $963 Million in 1978." Asian Wall Street Journal, March 30, 1978, p. 3.

"Philippines Sees Small '78 Deficit for Payments." Asian Wall Street Journal, May 6, 1978, p. 3.

Swiss-Philippine Society. Newsletter 1 (May 1978). "RP Bond Float in Tokyo Successful; Issue in Germany Oversubscribed," pp. 8-9; "Total Foreign Borrowings in 1977 $6.5 Billion," p. 9; "IMF Loan Ceiling $950 Million," p. 9; "RP to Repay $96 Billion Foreign Debts," pp. 9-10.

U.S. Department of the Treasury. Report on Developing Countries' External Debt and Debt Relief Provided by the United States. Washington, D.C.: U.S. Government Printing Office, 1976. Executive Communication 2433. 91 pp.

U.S. Embassy, Manila. Economic Trends Report Philippines. Airgram A-52. Unclassified, March 17, 1978. 11 pp. September 7, 1978, 7 pp.

________. "Press Release of IBRD Consultative Group Meeting." Unclassified, December 1977. 5 pp.

Virata, Cesar. "How the Philippines Will Borrow in 1978." Euromoney, April 1978, p. 87.

Wellons, P.A. Borrowing by Developing Countries in the Eurocurrency Market. Developing Center Studies. Paris: Organization for Economic Cooperation and Development, 1977. 449 pp.

7 Finding Jamaica's Way*

J. Daniel O'Flaherty

For those who still believe that Western-style pluralistic democracy is compatible with the prevailing economic situation in the developing world, Jamaica is an important country. In 16 years of independence it has maintained the spirit and the institutions of the democratic tradition it inherited from the British. At the same time the Jamaicans have a severe case of nearly every current LDC economic disease: high unemployment and inflation, profound international payments imbalance, foreign debt, fluctuating commodity prices, black markets, dislocated populations and scarce capital.

The question for Jamaica, as for so many other countries, is not whether democracy is compatible with stagflation and underdevelopment, but what the popular role should and can be in a government which needs above all to increase economic discipline. The dilemma of the Jamaican Government is a deep and, as yet, unresolved one. The economics of their situation demand increased productive investment in the public and private sector and the elimination of the trade deficit, both of which require decreased and reoriented consumption. Jamaica's current-account deficit rose from $145 million in 1970 to $248 million in 1976, and debt service, which became the first priority of the Bank of Jamaica, was 4.5 percent of GNP by the end of 1976. The gross foreign liabilities of the Bank of Jamaica had risen from $192 million in 1976 to $241 million by the end of 1977. As of December 31, 1976 only 23 percent of Jamaica's foreign debt was to commercial banks, whereas 29

---

*Reprinted with permission from Foreign Policy, vol. 3. no, 31, (Summer 1978), p. 3.

percent was to the IMF Oil Facility and IMF Compensatory Financing combined.

At the same time the society is deeply committed to democratic values and institutions, while the current government is politically committed to economic equality and achieving an acceptable standard of living for the mass of the population. In fact the current regime is groping its way from traditional pluralistic democracy to some form of mobilization democracy. Neither the Jamaican right and its conservative allies abroad, nor the Jamaican left and its allies in Cuba and elsewhere, are optimistic about the prospects of the present leadership's finding a political formula that will square with the island's stark economic realities. Traditional pluralistic democracy entails a private sector which functions with enough economic and political autonomy to allocate resources by its own lights. Inevitably that means the creation of entrepreneurial and professional classes with vested interests in a mass consumption society. It also entails free participation in the world market which, compounded with the physical proximity of Jamaica to the United States, means that the desired standard of living is set by the free-market Western economies whose top priority is finding export markets there, as elsewhere in the LDCs.

The problem of foreign debt is therefore an aspect of a larger problem: finding an economic equilibrium and a political formula which incorporate some meaningful expression of popular will and political participation. What distinguishes Jamaica from many other LDCs is that is still takes the latter enterprises seriously, but that cannot be taken for granted indefinitely. Given the openness of the Jamaican economy, its international economic position, and consequently its access to capital markets, will determine the island's ability to maintain a democratic political system, respect for civil liberties, and progress toward meeting the basic human needs of the mass of Jamaicans.

The core development issue in the Caribbean for the United States and the rest of the developed world is how best to respond to small states with limited economic viability. It is compounded by a number of factors. The islands' economies do not complement each other, since most of them export the same agricultural commodities and compete for the same tourists, a major source of foreign exchange. The region is deeply divided along cultural lines, with the English-speaking Caribbean countries having closer ties with each other than the Spanish- and French-speaking ones. Even within the English-speaking group, no single island is a natural leader by virtue of its size or the stature of its political leadership, and rivalry rather than regional solidarity characterizes interisland diplomacy. The Caribbean is a very small diplomatic stage for a number of leaders like Castro, Michael Manley of Jamaica, and Eric Williams of Trinidad and Tobago, who are far more interested in playing influential roles in the Third World as a whole than in the Caribbean. In addition, Trinidad's oil revenues have given it a different set of interests than its neighbors, namely to ensure that there are enough external sources of lending to prevent Trinidad from being overburdened with loan requests from other islands seeking relief from their current-account deficits.

Schemes for regional cooperation and integration, therefore, offer Jamaica no genuine solutions to its economic dilemma. The heart of that dilemma is that as poor as most of Jamaica's population is, the country as a whole has been living beyond its means at least since 1974. As a result in 1977 and 1978 it came under an austere International Monetary Fund regimen "to reduce consumption as a proportion of gross domestic product, thus making available resources to stimulate production and investment in the private sector."(1) Put another way, in the words of the head of the Jamaican operations of one of the United States-based aluminum companies, "This is a bicycle economy in which everyone wants to drive a Mercedes."(2) For the Fabian socialist government of Prime Minister Michael Manley it is especially galling to have fallen into the hands of the Western bankers on the heels of repeated attacks on "imperialism" as the cause of his country's miseries and as he began to emerge as a major Third World spokesman for a new international economic order.

In fact, the current Jamaican economic realities are such that any prime minister would be forced to look for an international solution to them. Jamaica is one of the world's most open economies. Foreign trade has traditionally accounted for about 40 percent of the island's gross domestic product. What happened in the mid-1970s is that the country's international trading position deteriorated to a point where new and harsh deprivations of an already severely deprived population were inevitable.

The most important political fact about Jamaica is its maldistribution of income. Although the island's per capita income is over $1,000, 85 percent of the population survives on less than $200 a year. The fact that the middle and upper-middle classes tend to be fairer-skinned reinforces a class distinction visible in the style and the standard of living in Kingston. Pleasant suburban homes on the hills and foothills overlook a crowded and desperately poor city of unemployed, underemployed and squatters. Fear caused by Kingston's high crime rate and the fact the victims are often middle class, is reflected in heavy security measures in the suburbs. Manley, fair-skinned himself, has cast his political lot with Jamaica's black, underprivileged majority, who have responded to his assault on those who "have run Jamaica like it was their own back yard."

Manley talks a great deal about redistribution of wealth, and he has substantially raised the taxes of the well-to-do. But redistribution could not make a dent in Jamaica's poverty - especially with the miserable performance of the Jamaican economy in recent years. In the early 1970s, the annual economic growth rate was 2.5 percent. By 1974, it was down to 1.3 percent, with negative growth rates of 2.3 percent in 1975 and 5 percent in 1976.(3) Estimated economic growth for 1977 is zero. Unemployment shot up to an official rate of 21 percent in 1975 and reached 27 percent in April 1977, the last month for which figures are available; but the true 1977 rate was acknowledged by government officials to be closer to 30 percent, and perhaps as high as 50 percent among young people in Kingston.(4) Inflation, which reached 27.2 percent in 1974, was at 18 percent in 1977.

One of the social and political implications of these statistics is a rising violent crime rate, especially in Kingston. It discourages tourists from visiting the island, causing further economic distress. In 1977, 25 policemen were shot and killed in Kingston after the state of emergency declared during the 1976 summer riots was lifted.(5)

Behind the downward economic spiral lie a number of factors. Jamaica's relative prosperity in the 1960s and early 1970s grew out of considerable foreign investment in the tourist and bauxite industries. By and large, these were one-time investments that came to a natural end just when the international oil price increases and the world recession took hold. The Jamaican balance of payments deteriorated calamitously, especially for a country that imports almost all of its food and a majority of its capital goods.

Bauxite earns 35 percent of the island's foreign exchange. Jamaica's production of bauxite, which had risen 40 percent from 1968 to 1970, fell 32 percent between 1974 and 1976, a period when world production of the mineral remained stable.(6) Both the recession and the development of alternative sources of bauxite contributed to this, but the major cause was the levy imposed by the Jamaican Government in 1974 as a means of solving the balance-of-payments deficit created by the oil price increases. In addition, the world price of sugar, a major Jamaican agricultural export, declined and the bottom dropped out of the other major foreign exchange earner, the tourist industry, which grossed $118 million in 1975, but is estimated to have grossed only $65 million in 1977. In the peak month of February, the hotel-occupancy rate fell from 71 percent in 1973 to 37 percent in 1977.(7)

The grim economic situation, combined with the socialist rhetoric of the government, has caused the flight of both domestic and foreign capital. Gross fixed capital formation declined in real terms by 1.9 percent in 1974 and by 6 percent in 1975.(8) Substantial numbers of middle-class and professional Jamaicans have fled to the United States and Canada, taking with them as much capital as they could despite government restrictions. Faced with a spate of American press reports about crime and violence in Jamaica, a decline in tourism and foreign investment, and the flight of capital and skilled Jamaicans, Manley claimed that the United States wanted him defeated in the December 1976 general elections. There is still a predisposition in government circles to believe that private conservative groups in the United States are actively trying to undermine the government. Andrew Young supports that view. Although he denied, in a Kingston press conference, that the CIA was destabilizing Jamaica, he added, "but that doesn't mean that there are not also forces that work in the area that are nongovernmental forces."

The real cause of Jamaica's economic woes, said Manley in a 1977 speech in New York, is not external meddling, but "the present system of economic arrangements [that] work unceasingly, unfailingly, and inevitably against the interests of the great majority of mankind."(9) As a result, Manley and his diplomats, at the United Nations and in North-South negotiations, have become outspoken proponents of a new international economic order involving "elements of political control in international financial arrangements, international transfers of technology, and above all international trade."(10)

Manley's casting of his economic woes in socialist rhetoric and in terms of a new international economic order serves the function of laying the blame elsewhere for the very real trials and tribulations of the population, especially inasmuch as they judge their own standard of living by American criteria. On the other hand, it masks a pragmatism and flexibility which provides a counterexample to Daniel Patrick Moynihan's claim that the Third World strain of Fabian socialism is externally confrontational and internally antidemocratic.(11) Indeed by externalizing the villains of the piece, socialist rhetoric relieves some of the domestic tensions which might otherwise, and may still, result in increased authoritarianism to make the country live within its means.

The fact is that liberal economic solutions to the island's problems were being abandoned long before Manley's People's National Party won power in 1972. Economic planning, government control of exports and imports, increased control of and revenues from the bauxite industry - just to cite a few examples - are all trends which either major Jamaican party would have been powerless to resist. Any Jamaican prime minister would have been forced by the logic of the nation's economy to seek international solutions in some form or other - increased aid and investment, improvement in the terms of trade, decreased imports, and a search for foreign markets for

Jamaican goods. The pre-Manley leadership - and the prime minister's current opposition in the Jamaican Labor Party (JLP) - would have responded by courting foreign investors and tourists. It would have requested additional development assistance partly on the grounds that Jamaica was squarely in the Western bloc and was in some danger of internal upheavals that could take unpredictable political directions. This was the course set by the first prime minister, Sir Alexander Bustamante, who announced at the time of Jamaican independence in 1962 "the irrevocable decision that Jamaica stands with the West and the United States."(12)

Since Manley's socialism has at times been a cause of considerable concern for the United States government and has tended to complicate his dealings with the international financial institutions, it is worth considering the origins and functions, as well as the implementation, of the doctrine of the present Jamaican Government.

Like its counterparts elsewhere in the Third World, Jamaican socialism is in part a vehicle for self-assertion against a colonial past and a mechanism for the creation of a sence of national pride and purpose. This is of particular importance for an island with Jamaica's history. Virtually none of the ancestors of Jamaica's population came there voluntarily. More than 90 percent of all Jamaicans are black or mulatto descendants of slaves, and many of the other 10 percent are descended from East Indian and Chinese indentured labor. As a result, the country as a whole suffers the debilitating social consequences of a slave heritage. This is true to an extent of all the Commonwealth Caribbean islands, a fact that deprives any Jamaican leader of the argument that his country has a unique heritage of misery and exploitation to be overcome by extraordinary collective effort. In 1974, when Manley wrote about the psychology of dependency, which he called the "pervasive effect of the colonial experience," he found nothing in Jamaican history to serve as an antidote:

> Neither did the heroic call to racial pride of a Marcus Garvey; nor even the momentous march to independence under Norman Manley; not even the collective experience of self-discipline of the modern trade union movement...together with the political party system, make more than a dent upon the problem.(13)

The socialism with which Manley hopes to fill the void is profoundly Fabian. As did the British Labour Party, both major Jamaican political parties grew out of trade unions, and neither was traditionally socialist. The British left behind an educated, Anglophile middle class, as well as a full complement of British political institutions and traditions. Both the political and union leadership came from that class. Michael Manley, son of Norman Manley, union leader and founder of the People's National Party (PNP), learned his political economy at the London School of Economics in the 1940s and returned to Jamaica to become a union organizer. When Manley announced in November 1974, two and one half years after taking power, that he was setting Jamaica on the path to democratic socialism, he had, in a sense, decided to mobilize his people for development through a personal campaign for the ideas of British socialist theoretician Harold Laski. Far from being a mass movement of the underprivileged or the proletariat, Jamaican socialism is the product of the British-educated leadership of the PNP - especially of the prime minister. It is a set of relatively simple ideas tirelessly preached to the population by Manley and his colleagues.

Much of the rhetoric is strongly reminiscent of the 1945 British Labour Party manifesto, with frequent references to state control of the "commanding heights of the economy," "full participatory democracy," "dynamic industrial democracy at the workplace," and an insistent invocation of equality and justice. Stressing that his socialism is a "libertarian democratic system," Manley recently defined the economic policy of his government as "a socially directed economy planned to achieve social objectives in the interest of the majority of the people."(14) Even in practice, Jamaican socialism evokes Britain in 1946 and 1947, with the gradual nationalization of key economic enterprises, such as utilities and urban transportation, and tighter government control of imports.

Yet, the trappings of a typical socialist transformation are missing. Not until late summer 1978, nearly four years after the proclamation of democratic socialism, is the country to have a five-year plan. There is no official government or party newspaper. There are no effective nationwide organizations for mobilizing youth or other sectors of the population behind the government. There is no systematic and pervasive propaganda machine. Instead, Manley restlessly roams the country, talking about justice and imperialism, and exhorting the population to greater effort.

The looseness of the Jamaican variety of Fabian socialism was illustrated by the way the government dealt with the North American-owned aluminum companies which mine the country's bauxite. Bauxite is the key to the Jamaican economy, providing 35 percent of its foreign exchange. It is also the key to United States-Jamaican relations, since at the time of Manley's first election as prime minister in 1972, the United States was importing nearly 60 percent of its bauxite from Jamaica. (The figure is still over 50 percent.)

Most of the $1 billion United States private investment in Jamaica in 1972 was concentrated in United States-owned bauxite-processing facilities, which gave American investors a considerable stake in the Jamaican status quo. The interests of the United States were spelled out in July 1973 Senate testimony by Acting Secretary of State for Inter-American Affairs Robert Hurwitch:

> From the standpoint of our own interests, this investment has helped to assure that the United States will have a reliable nearby source of alumina [an intermediate product between bauxite and aluminum]...The United States imports nearly 90 percent of its bauxite requirements and Jamaica has been the primary source of supply...The proximity of Jamaican reserves to the United States is an important economic and strategic consideration.(15)

But American and Canadian aluminum companies were operating under agreements signed with the Jamaican Government in the 1950s, when large-scale exploitation of Jamaica's considerable bauxite reserves began. The agreements, which granted over 200,000 acres to the companies as concessions, had come under increasing attack from the PNP and others in the Jamaican left.

Fear of what Manley might do with the bauxite industry was widespread during the campaign for the 1972 Jamaican elections, both in the American embassy and in the bauxite companies. The then United States ambassador, Vincent W. de Roulet, encouraged Alcoa to make a campaign contribution, illegal under Jamaican law, to Manley's opponents, the incumbent JLP - in de Roulet's words, "to explain the value of Americans in Jamaica to Jamaicans."(16)

In fact, de Roulet had been worried as early as 1969 and 1970 that even the JLP government was moving in the direction of nationalization. When he took up his ambassadorship in Kingston in late 1969, de Roulet found that the United States Overseas Private Investment Corporation (OPIC), which guarantees compensation to United States firms whose foreign investments are expropriated, was considering the issuance of $200 million in new guarantees for additional investment by the aluminum companies. Since this would have brought total OPIC exposure in Jamaica to $500 million - which he considered dangerously high, given the political climate - de Roulet vigorously opposed the new quarantees on the grounds that withholding them would warn the Jamaicans to leave the companies alone.

Ultimately, de Roulet was overruled, and the guarantees were approved in July 1970. The next month, he arranged a meeting in Washington between then Prime Minister Hugh Shearer, of the JLP, and then President Richard Nixon, after which the administration agreed to $24 million in loans to

Jamaica from the Agency for International Development (AID). Having failed in his efforts to bully the Jamaicans, de Roulet felt that the combination of the loans and the guarantees had nevertheless sent a message that American help and cooperation were contingent on not making things harder for the aluminum companies. As de Roulet later told the Senate Subcommittee on Multinational Corporations, "I think he [Shearer] got the general impression that it might make more sense to go along with the United States, which was not madly in love with the prospect of expropriation and the loss of a half-billion dollars of taxpayer money."(17)

Having taken credit for buying off the Shearer government on nationalization with AID loans and OPIC guarantees, de Roulet boasted to a Senate subcommittee in July 1973 that he had obtained a commitment from Manley during the 1071-1972 Jamaican political campaign that he would not nationalize the bauxite industry if elected, and would not even raise the issue in the campaign. In return, de Roulet claimed, he had given his own promise to Manley that the United States would not intervene in the Jamaican elections.(18) The Manley government, which had shown considerable forbearance with an ambassador who had been heard to refer to Jamaicans as "niggers," finally had enough. The day after de Roulet's Senate testimony about his deal with Manley, Jamaica finally declared him persona non grata.

The presence of influential elements in the Manley government favoring nationalization became the cause for official United State nervousness, despite Hurwitch's testimony to the Senate that "the new government has reaffirmed national policy on foreign investment with assurances that existing contracts and concessions would be honored."(19) Five months after that assessment, in January 1974, Manley demanded renegotiation of the agreements with the companies. For four months, talks continued without result. Then in May, the Jamaicans raised taxes and royalties on the companies from $30 million to nearly $200 million a year.

The companies regarded the levy as an expropriatory and unilateral abrogation of their contracts and filed claims with the International Center for the Settlement of Investment Disputes, an affiliate of the World Bank. A ruling in favor of the companies by this agency would have effectively destroyed Jamaica's credit rating with the international financial institutions, and it might well have activated congressional action prohibiting aid to countries that expropriate United State investment.

As it was, the Nixon administration, following the lead of the Treasury Department, put an immediate hold on new official lending to Jamaica. As one Treasury official describes it, it would have been "the wrong signal to give aid to a country unilaterally ripping off United State firms." A small, rural development loan of $9 million, which had been authorized by the State Department and AID out of appropriated funds a few weeks after the imposition of the levy, was stopped. (It was reinstated only in November 1976, when Jamaica had begun to sign settlements with the bauxite companies.) The Treasury Department also insisted that there be no new capital assistance and no additional OPIC insurance to Jamaica until the dispute was settled, and Secretary of State Henry Kissinger acquiesced, albeit with some reluctance. Even though many in the State Department objected to what one mid-level official called an "effort to cut Jamaica off at the knees," the embargo on new lending remained in effect until the Carter administration revoked it in early 1977.

Although the bauxite dispute triggered considerable official United State hostility, it would not by itself have caused relations to deteriorate as much as they did. By late fall 1974, it was clear that the bauxite companies were unlikely to be nationalized or expropriated. What was likely (and what ultimately happened) was that they would live with the levy and pass it on in price increases, and that a lengthy process of negotation would produce some variety of joint ownership that would assure a steady supply of bauxite to the United States. In the absence of rhetoric about nationalization and a general assault on free enterprise, the bauxite levy could be interpreted as a nationalistic economic measure motivated by the need to generate foreign exchange.

The Jamaicans, not wanting to provoke the United States unnecessarily, and not wanting to go the way of Allende's Unidad Popular, had waited until after making their move on the bauxite companies to become socialists, so that the levy would not seem to be part of an ideologically motivated, systematic socialization of the economy. Even so, they chose an unpropitious moment for the United States' leading supplier of a strategic mineral to declare itself a socialist country. Portugal, seven months after its coup, was teetering in the balance, heightening concern about Eurocommunism, South Vietnam was rapidly deteriorating, and the United States was moving to shore up friendly anti-Marxist forces in Angola.

Thus, instead of reassuring the United States that Jamaica was entering into a civilized Fabian transformation that would respect the political institutions and traditions handed down by the British, Manley's proclamation of socialism only deepened the chill between the two countries. Combined as it was with the warming of Cuban-Jamaican relations and increased rhetoric about imperialism, the modest advent of Jamaican socialism transformed what had been an economic dispute into a political one, and it ensured that the aid embargo would last for the lifetime of the Ford administration. Behind the policy was a presumption that a serious experiment in democratic socialism would result sooner or later in left- or right-wing totalitarianism.

Above all, Manley's Cuban connection provided fodder for his critics at home and abroad who sought to discredit the Jamaican Government as a tool of Castro. In fact, the warm relationship with Cuba was part of an expanded and different diplomatic role for Jamaica than that envisioned by Bustamante in 1962. Manley decided Jamaica needed to break out of its traditional reliance upon the United States and the British Commonwealth to solve its economic problems, and that he wanted to be a leader among Third World nations. To play this role, Manley had to rupture Jamaica's irrevocable commitment to the West and the United States and adopt a posture of nonalignment. That meant establishing ties with the communist world - in particular, with Cuba. Consequently, Jamaica established full diplomatic relations with Cuba in 1974, with the People's Republic of China in 1975, and with the Soviet Union in 1976. Of greater significance was the personal relationship Manley developed with Castro, aboard whose private plane he flew to a conference of nonaligned countries in Algiers in September 1974, two months before his proclamation of democratic socialism.

These initiatives allowed Manley to invoke Cuba as an example for Jamaica - a substantially black Caribbean country, with a history of slavery, economic exploitation, and colonialism, which has seemingly solved many of the problems that now plague Jamaica. As an inspiration, if not a working model, Cuba is invaluable to Manley. As one Jamaican cabinet minister put it, "When I first went to Cuba in 1961, I thought to myself, this is all very impressive, but it is a Caribbean country and it will never last. But 16 years later, there it is."

In the service of his relationship with Castro, Manley has taken positions that caused considerable controversy in the United States and increased the fears of the Jamaican middle class. For example, he has consistently defended the Cubans' military presence in Africa and has advocated a greater role for Cuba in the Caribbean region. On the day he met with Carter in December 1977, Manley told the National Press Club in Washington, D.C. that Cuba should have been invited to a World Bank conference on Caribbean development, and that Cuba should be involved in the normal business of the hemisphere. He also urged normalization of relations between Cuba and the United States.

Castro has also helped Manley cope with the Jamaican left wing. Instead of distributing machine guns for armed struggle, as some of the Jamaican left had hoped the Cubans would do, Castro has encouraged Manley to control the expansion of consumption in order to create resources for investment, and to stop acting like a trade union leader seeking a larger share of the wealth for the organized working class.

The Cuban role was especially important during late 1976 and early 1977, when the Jamaican Government was divided over what to do about the evaporation of its foreign exchange reserves. Manley had begun talks with the IMF in December 1976 for a standby agreement to meet the balance-of-payments crisis. The government's economists, led by the Bank of Jamaica, proposed a 40 percent devaluation combined with tough measures to curtail consumption and regulate non-essential imports. A group of radical economists with influence on the PNP's left proposed an alternative package, which excluded devaluation and relied instead on massive taxation of the rich and assistance from the communist world.

Deeply divided, and alarmed by the January 1977 riots in Egypt after an IMF-sponsored cut in Egyptian Government subsidies of the price of bread, Manley's government broke off talks with the IMF. Between January and April 1977, the Jamaicans explored the alternatives to an IMF agreement, including an unpublicized approach to the Soviets for aid. According to officials familiar with both sides of the discussion, the Soviets resisted the temptation to expand their role in the Caribbean by coming to Jamaica's rescue. In fact, the Soviets were so unenthusiastic about acquiring another ward in the Caribbean that they laid down prerequisites for aid that bore a striking resemblance to the standard IMF regimen for a country in Jamaica's position. There was one exception: the Soviets told Manley he was being undermined by a free press, and they insisted that he crack down on the opposition media. The Soviet attitude was that Jamaica lacked discipline and was insufficiently organized to follow through on its socialist initiatives. They refused to give aid, offering the Jamaicans only new trade agreements of modest value.(20)

By April 1977, the radical alternative had been thoroughly discredited. The projections of the government economists had been validated by the rapid disappearance of foreign exchange reserves, an increase in unemployment, and the backfiring of higher taxes on the rich, which had actually resulted in lower tax revenues. Manley reopened negotations with the IMF and worked out a package containing strict terms: severe limits on borrowing by the Jamaican Government from any source, a dual exchange rate with devaluation for nonessential imports, and a very tight incomes policy. Although the government had grave reservations about some of the terms - especially about the incomes policy, which one high Jamaican official said "will be virtually impossible for a democratic government to maintain" - it signed in August. The left was silenced when both the Cubans and the Chinese endorsed the package; but now there is talk about forming a new opposition party to the left of Manley.

The Cuban role has generally provided the leader of the existing opposition, Edward Seaga, with his major argument against the government. Seaga, a Harvard-educated businessman of Lebanese descent, is hardly a major political threat to Manley at this point. Immaculately dressed and well-groomed in the manner of an American banker, Seaga appears to be the essence of the increasingly conservative and alarmist middle class from which he draws his major support. His position, echoed by conservative United States circles, is simple: Manley is a tool of Castro.

Seaga argues that Jamaica is being systematically Cubanized under the tutelage of the head of the Cuban secret police, Manuel Pineiro. He cites two particular examples. The Jamaican Home Guard is being beefed up, with Cuban advice, to cope with the rise in violent crime and, according to Seaga, is looking more like the Cuban People's Militia, which plays a major internal security role. He also sees a similarity between the Cuban Committees for the Defense of the Revolution, which are instruments of ideological control at the local level, and the new Jamaican Community Councils, which are supposed to help regulate inflation in local communities. Manley's ultimate objectives, Seaga believes, are the creation of a one-party socialist state that controls the media, elimination of meaningful elections, and thorough regimentation of the society, with an advance commitment to support Cuban positions in international affairs.

Some American political circles question the propriety of aiding a government that continues to support Cuba. Ties between the Jamaican opposition leader, Edward Seaga, and conservative circles in the United States were reflected in Senate debate in June 1977, when a group of 30 conservative senators, led by Senator Orrin Hatch (R-Utah), opposed aid to the Manley government on the grounds that "Jamaica has become captive of Cuba through the type of leadership it now has....I am saying it is an extension of Cuba, and I am saying that they are doing the same things as Cuba."(21)

One difficulty with Seaga's argument is that the Manley government has not even begun to replicate the discipline and control that prevail in Cuba. Furthermore, in the absence of massive aid from the Soviet Union or other communist sources, Manley is locked into the Western financial system. His dependence on credit and loans from both commercial and international banks ensured restraint on leftist impulses within the government. In fact, the government's domestic policies moved to the right during 1977. As one American banker in Kingston put it, "Manley cannot nationalize us. We are his arms and legs in dealing with the outside world."

Seaga's protests notwithstanding, any Jamaican government would probably have to resort to increased control and discipline. In the absence of a foreign exchange cushion, Jamaica will have to cut consumption drastically. But any greater cut than those already made would inevitably require rationing, leading in turn to a black market, intensified police inspections, and the probable beefing up of the Home Guard to keep order - hence the government's fear that the IMF restrictions could make it difficult to maintain democracy.

Since winter 1974, Jamaica's most pressing economic need has been to overcome its balance-of-payments deficit, and debt service has become the first priority of the Bank of Jamaica - the country's central bank - in managing its foreign exchange. Rather than projecting a level of imports that is normal and letting the reserves vary, the bank has had to set a target for improvement in reserves with the import bill as the residual. While imports had been $1.2 billion in 1976, the government could not allow the figure to exceed $500 to $600 million in 1977, and has set $625 million as the 1978 ceiling. This, it is hoped, will yield reserves of $30 million by mid-1978.

The Bank of Jamaica's foreign exchange management program has been a subject of disagreement with the IMF which wanted to abolish import licensing and rely on the exchange rate to stabilize payments. Because the island imports the vast majority of its foodstuffs, the government resisted the IMF approach and proposed a food subsidy to cushion the impact of devaluation, especially on the unemployed and working poor. In additon to the food issue, the government did not want devaluation to confer a windfall benefit on the bauxite companies which would have amounted to $40 million a year. The IMF finally acquiesced in the summer of 1977 and took the unusual step of allowing as a part of the adjustment program a dual exchange rate which excluded food and bauxite from devaluation.

Part of the rationale for the 1977 standby agreement and the 1978 extended facility agreement (negotiated after Jamaica failed to meet the domestic assets test for the standby) was to improve the island's credit rating with aid donors and commercial banks. The fact is that development assistance from currently available sources in unlikely to provide an early solution to the Jamaican economic dilemma. United States aid legislation passed in 1973 and 1975 forbids AID loans for balance-of-payments support. The administration got around this in 1977 by providing Jamaica with a $9.5 million balance-of-payments loan disguised as security supporting assistance, which normally goes only to military allies as a subsidy of their defense spending. With that small exception, all United States bilateral aid will have to be for specific development projects, which may help the balance of payments in the long run, but will not relieve the immediate pressure. The same is true of the World Bank, which normally lends money only for development projects, but which is making an exceptional $30 million loan to Jamaica for balance-of-payments support.

Much of the justification for the IMF agreements has been

that they establish the creditworthiness of Jamaica and will result in increased lending from commercial banks and aid donors. While the increased United States aid program and the World Bank program loan would probably not have been forthcoming in the absence of the IMF agreement, it is by no means clear that commercial bank lending is triggered by the IMF. The major foreign commercial banks in Jamaica not only have the ability to take short-term risks in a country like Jamaica, they also have a vested interest in the solvency of the government. As the Kingston manager of one of the major United States-based banks put it, "We have to lend the government more to protect current investment. In essence we have to sink or walk on water." The principal political concern of the foreign banking community in Jamaica is the strength of the private sector. Certainly they are not bothered by socialist or radical rhetoric. As another Kingston manager of a United States bank put it, "Half the world is socialist after all. Castro's visits have no bearing on our attitude. We're indifferent to the government's ideology as long as we show a profit in the long run." The IMF presence is reassuring to be sure, since it helps protect what the bankers see as the crucial role of the private sector: "The IMF is insurance for us that the government is guided and can't do as it pleases. The IMF will assure that government economic thinking will be more or less where free enterprise would like it to be."

The World Bank has sponsored a collaborative effort of aid donors and recipients in the Caribbean to forge a regional approach to outside aid. The model which some of the sponsors of this effort - including the United States State Department - had in mind was the Marshall Plan, in the hope that the Caribbean countries would work together, in rationalizing outside aid, toward more integration. The problem is that any such effort would require a strong lead on the part of the United States. The United States could set an example by increasing aid and providing incentives for Caribbean cooperation in the form of additional resources. In the absence of major new sources of credit and capital, the burden of adjustment of Jamaica's economy to its payments position will fall most heavily on the poorest sector of the population. There is, therefore, a substantial risk of social and political instability that could threaten the democratic character of the regime.

NOTES

1. International Monetary Fund, Press Release no. 78/40, Washington, D.C., June 12, 1978.
2. Interview, Kingston, Jamaica, December 14, 1978.

3. Interamerican Development Bank, Economic and Social Progress in Latin America: 1976 (Washington, D.C., 1977) pp. 290-98.
4. Gladstone Bonnick, Acting President of the Bank of Jamaica, Interview, Kingston, Jamaica, December 20, 1977.
5. Daily Gleaner, Kingston, Jamaica, December 13, 1977.
6. International Bauxite Association, unpublished document.
7. Jamaica Tourist Board, Travel Statistics - Jamaica, unpublished.
8. Interamerican Development Bank, Economic and Social Progress, p. 290.
9. Michael Manley, speech to the Jamaica Educational and Cultural Institute, New York, New York, October 27, 1977.
10. Ibid.
11. Daniel Patrick Moynihan, "The United States in Opposition," Commentary 59, (March 1975): 31-44.
12. Alexander Bustamante, quoted in Louis Lindsay, "Colonialism and the Myth of Resource Insufficiency," in Size Self-Determination and International Relations: The Caribbean, Vaughan A. Lewis, ed. (Kingston: The Institute of Social and Economic Research, University of the West Indies, 1976), p. 61.
13. Michael Manley, The Politics of Change (London: Andre Deutsch, 1974), p. 21.
14. Manley, speech to Jamaica Educational and Cultural Institute.
15. United States Senate, Subcommittee on Multinational Corporations, Multinational Corporations and United States Foreign Policy, Part 3, 93rd Congress, 1st Session (Washington, D.C.: United States Government Printing Office, 1973), p. 149.
16. New York Times, July 17, 1976.
17. United States Senate, Multinational Corporations, p. 116.
18. Ibid.
19. Ibid., p. 149.
20. Based on interviews with high level officials in the Jamaican Government, United States multinational corporations in Jamaica, and United States Government officials.
21. Orrin Hatch, Senator, Congressional Record, June 15, 1977, pp. S9897-8.

BIBLIOGRAPHY

Bank of Jamaica. Balance of Payments of Jamaica, 1976. Kingston, Jamaica, 1977.

__________. Statistical Digest. Monthly Publication, Kingston, Jamaica.

Bell, Wendell, and Hibson, J. William. "Independent Jamaica Faces the Outside World: Attitudes of Elites After Twelve

Years of Nationhood." International Studies Quarterly 22 (March 1978): 5-48.

Bergsten, C. Fred. "A New OPEC in Bauxite." Challenge, July-August 1976, pp. 12-20.

Crile, George. "Our Man in Jamaica." Harper's, October 1974, pp. 87-96.

Davis, Stephen, "Fear in Paradise." New York Times Magazine, July 25, 1976, p. 8.

Fitzgerald, Frances. "Jamaican Limbo," Harper's, July 1977, pp. 10-14.

Foner, Nancy. "Party Politics in a Jamaican Community." Caribbean Studies 13 (July 1973): 51-64.

Interamerican Development Bank. Economic and Social Progress in Latin America: 1976. Washington, D.C., 1977.

Institute for Policy Studies. "Treasury Blocks Jamaican Funds." The Elements, August-September 1976.

Jamaica Bauxite Institute. Annual Report. Kinsgton, Jamaica, 1977.

Lewis, Vaughan A. "The Commonwealth Caribbean." In Foreign Policy-Making in Developing States, Christopher Clapham, ed. Westmead Hants, Great Britian: Saxon House, 1977, pp. 110-30.

________. ed. Size, Self-Determination and International Relations: The Caribbean. Kingston, Jamaica: Institute of Social and Economic Research, University of the West Indies, 1976.

Lowenthal, David. West Indian Societies. New York: Oxford University Press, 1972.

Manley, Michael. The Politics of Change. London: Andre Deutsch, 1974.

________. Search for Solutions. Oshawa, Ontario, Canada: Maple House, 1976.

Moynihan, Daniel Patrick. "The United States in Opposition." Commentary 59 (March 1975): 31-44.

Rosenfeld, Stephan S. "Should the U.S. Build Socialism Abroad?" Washington Post, August 19, 1977.

United States Senate, Subcommittee on Multinational Corporations. Multinational Corporations and United States Foreign Policy, Part 3. 93rd Congress, 1st Session. Washington, D.C.: U.S. Government Printing Office, 1973.

Volkman, Ernest, and Cummings, John. "Murder as Usual." Penthouse, December 1977, pp. 112-17.

8 A Compendium of IMF Troubles: Turkey, Portugal, Peru, Egypt

Robert N. McCauley

This chapter profiles the debt troubles of four countries: Turkey, Portugal, Peru, and Egypt. Stories of crisis and bargaining are vulnerable to the charge that they gloss the fundamental sources of crisis. The hope is to show how foreign capital and private creditors and domestic groups influence the choices of government officials in the midst of a foreign exchange crisis.

TURKEY

The recession in Europe and restrictions on immigration sent home 80,000 Turkish workers between 1974 and 1976. Worker remittances, which almost matched the foreign exchange earnings of exports of goods in 1973, dropped from $1.4 billion that year to less than $1.0 billion in each of 1976 and 1977. Western Europe's export of unemployment not only directly impinged on Turkey's external accounts but also forced choices that further worsened its trading position. As Kindleberger puts it, "restrictions help industrialized countries to achieve a given [low] target of inflation for a lower [reported] level of unemployment at the expense of lesser-developed nations where the trade-off is consequently worsened."(1) Turkey's economic managers predictably expanded the economy and reaped a 37 percent inflation rate in 1977. Devaluations of the Turkish lira lagged and in 1975 and 1976 the deficit on current payments reached one-twentieth of domestic production (see Table 8.1).

Turkey did not go to the Eurocurrency market to borrow money to finance its deficits with seven- or ten-years loans. Instead it fell into debt by encouraging short-term bank loans, by drawing on short-term bank credit lines, and by stretching

Table 8.1. Turkey's Balance of Payments
(in millions of dollars)

	1971	1972	1973	1974	1975	1976	1977
Goods, Services, Transfers	24	124	615	-634	-1,848	-1,964	-3,325
Merchandise exports	677	885	1,320	1,532	1,401	1,960	1,752
Merchandise imports	-1,055	-1,407	-1,880	-3,363	-4,235	-4,565	-5,158
Merchandise balance	-378	-522	-560	-1,831	-2,834	-2,605	-3,406
Service exports	219	381	546	622	616	895	819
Service imports	-390	-532	-629	-924	-1,054	-1,360	-1,841
Service balance	-171	-151	-83	-302	-438	-465	-1,022
Unrequited transfers	573	797	1,259	1,498	1,424	1,106	1,104
Long-Term Capital	217	697	360	404	1,315	2,334	1,988
Direct investment	45	43	79	88	153	28	184
Other government	188	180	215	70	84	180	233
Other	-16	473	67	247	1,078	2,127	1,571
Short-Term Capital	57	35	-590	-189	-294	-585	842
Deposit money banks	-	-	274	57	-393	-282	-
Other	57	35	-764	-245	100	-304	842

Source: IMF, International Financial Statistics 31 (October 1978): 374.

payment on trade credits. Bankers in theory at least could call in loans and credits; foreign producers are bound to halt shipments in the face of a stack of overdue and unguaranteed bills. Turkey compounded the problem of unstable foreign exchange earnings by building an unstable structure of foreign debt.

The convertible lira deposits were born of political convenience and financial imprudence. They are short-term foreign exchange loans to Turkish banks extended by foreign banks. Turkish banks sold the foreign exchange to the Central Bank and loaned the lira proceeds domestically. The Central Bank guaranteed the deposits, denominated in lira, against any loss in the value of the lira, and sold the foreign exchange to importers. In comparison to the government's borrowing directly from foreign banks, the deposit scheme had one advantage: set up in 1967 to encourage worker remittances and not used since, it required no legislative action when the need arose amid a political crisis in 1975.(2) It had severe disadvantages: the effective interest rate on the deposits stood well above what Turkey could have otherwise bargained for and the term of the loans allowed bankers to demand, if not get, repayment precisely when Turkey's external accounts could least accommodate it. By 1977, $2 billion had entered Turkey through these deposits; from the middle of that year onward, the banks of necessity have rolled them over (to the extent of $400 million in 1977).(3)

Indeed, mid-1977 represented a watershed in Turkey's international borrowing. In February, the Central Bank ceased paying out foreign exchange for all but oil and other critical goods. In March, Wells Fargo floated the last syndicated bank loan. The loan's six-month term hardly expressed confidence, however.(4) From then on, Turkey relied on debt rollovers, credit-line drawings, and unpaid supplier credits. The financial crunch lowered the real rate of growth of the economy from 7.7 percent in the period 1974 to 1976 to 5 percent in 1977. In the latter half of 1977, manufacturing plants ran from 30 to 55 percent below capacity as foreign suppliers cut deliveries.(5)

Table 8.2 profiles Turkey's short-term debt as of April 1978. The noncommercial arrears include overdue convertible lira deposits. Again, the total debt is not so insupportable as its term structure. The difference between the figures from Turkey and the statistics provided to the central banks reporting to the Bank for International Settlements (BIS) is striking (see Table 8.3).

By mid-1977, Turkey had exhausted the possibility of further bank loans and faced the cutoff of bank credit lines and supplier credits. The British export credit agency tightened in July and terminated in October the financing and guaranteeing of exports.(6) A national election in June re-

Table 8.2. Turkey's Short-Term Debt: April 1978
(in millions of dollars)

Banks	4,033
Convertible lira deposits	1,629
Banker credits	424
Noncommercial arrears	373
Overdrafts	264
Bank for International Settlements	85
Dresdner Bank	208
Commercial arrears	270
Acceptance credits	780
Trade Arrears	2,086
OECD countries	1,600
OPEC countries (Oil)	350
Other countries	136
Other Debts	538
Total	6,657

Source: Middle Eastern Economic Digest, July 14, 1978, p. 3.

turned right-of-center Prime Minister Demirel to power dependent on Mr. Erbaken of the National Salvation Party for his parliamentary majority. In arguing for any austerity measures, the prime minister collided head-on with his Islamic fundamentalist ally who was as zealous in his plans for accelerated public investment as he was ardent in his opposition to a devaluation, "a plot of the Greek lobby."(7) After an IMF team, which reportedly wanted a 20 to 25 percent devaluation, left in September,(8) a 10 percent devaluation was announced. "Too little and too late" responded bankers.(9) The devaluation in conjunction with a credit tightening and increases in prices of goods produced by public enterprises failed to win a nod from the IMF.

The current account deteriorated further in 1977 when the deficit reached 7 percent of domestic production. At the turn of the year, Mr. Ecevit convinced enough defectors from the governing coalition to assume power with a four-vote margin in parliament. Despite opposition from left-wing members of his own party, the new prime minister moved quickly to clinch the deal with the IMF. By the end of March, a 23 percent devaluation of the lira, interest rate hikes, and

Table 8.3. Domestic and Foreign Currency Positions of International Banks:* Turkey (in millions of dollars)

	Liabilities	Assets	Net
March 1976	715	1,039	324
June 1976	571	1,189	618
September 1976	405	1,503	1,098
December 1976	545	2,063	1,518
United States foreign branches	36	944	958
March 1977	455	2,311	1,856
United States foreign branches	21	1,012	991
June 1977	531	2,407	1,876
United States foreign branches	36	1,046	1,010
September 1977	546	2,377	1,831
United States foreign branches	34	1,039	1,005
December 1977	590	2,573	1,983
United States foreign branches	59	1,139	1,080
March 1978	611	2,794	2,183
United States foreign branches	41	1,133	1,092

*Banks in Group of Ten countries (Belgium/Luxembourg, Canada, France, Italy, Japan, Netherlands, Sweden, United Kingdom, United States, West Germany), and Switzerland, and foreign branches of United States banks in Group of Ten countries and Switzerland and Bahamas, Caymen Islands, Panama, Hong Kong, and Singapore.

Source: Bank for International Settlements, data in Bank of England, Quarterly Review 16 (September, December 1976), Table 23; 17 (March, June, September, December 1977), Table 22; 18 (March, June 1978), Table 22; 18 (December 1978), Table 23; Federal Reserve System, Statistical Release, June 13, 1978.

tax increases on middle- and high-income groups provided collateral for a two-year $370 million standby arrangement.

No cash under the agreement would be available until August. In April, the Turks did draw, however, a $90 million loan in compensation for slumping export receipts. For seven weeks, the Central Bank resumed payments for imports.(10)

In May, the Turkish consortium in the Organization for Economic Cooperation and Development (OECD) came together for the fourth rescheduling exercise since 1969 to defer payment on $1.5 billion in export credits and aid loans.(11) The public creditors rescheduled four-fifths of principal and interest due on long-term (over one year) loans for 30 months starting January 1977. At the insistence of representatives of the United States, they also rescheduled principal and interest falling due on short-term credits for 16 months starting at the same date. The United States had extended little in the way of such loans but the United States representatives argued that, absent their inclusion, those countries heavily exposed in long-term loans, such as the United States, would not get their fair share of Turkey's limited repayment capacity.

Turkey's private creditors will in all likelihood refinance $2.5 billion in debt for seven years with a two- or three-year grace period. During this grace period, the outstanding debt will remain fixed and only interest payments will be due. Public creditors rescheduled interest payments, but private creditors will collect them regularly. There is no reason to doubt that Turkey's public creditors, who take pains to enforce the principle of nondiscrimination among themselves, will call this comparable treatment of public and private creditors.

In the face of its foreign exchange crisis, the Turkish Government has resorted to state trading and barter. The Soviets will provide $341 million worth of goods, largely oil, in 1978 and 1979.(12) Turkey has made Iraq an unwilling recipient of Turkish goods in a barter agreement for a quarter of a billion dollars worth of oil that flowed through a Merrill Lynch-financed pipeline before deliveries ceased in January, 1978. Turkey must pay for further oil on a 20-day basis.(13) Libya will take olive oil for its oil.(14) Romania will provide equipment and oil and Iran crude oil in exchange for agricultural products and basic manufactures.(15)

Turkey's differences with its creditors surfaced noisily in August 1978. On August 7, Prime Minister Ecevit juxtaposed "stagnation in the name of stability" and "dynamic stability." Turkey's creditors' imposition of the former would lead to "grave social and political crisis and eventually to upheavals, due to a slowing down of development or to increasing unemployment."(16) A week later he blamed the United States, "some European allies," and the international banks for Turkey's financial crisis. He pilloried royally the policy prescriptions of his creditors:

> We have no intention of having our head chopped off by certain so-called solutions which fall foul of both contemporary realities and the economic and social realities of democratic Turkish society.

Finally, he linked the financial support from the West to "the nature of our future relation with them";(17) such relations presumably include the NATO alliance. These remarks may have been directed at a domestic audience, since, in late August, the government devalued the lira an average of five percent.(18)

Turkey's prospects for receiving fresh injections of capital dimmed with the sacking of Professor Sadiklar, governor of Turkey's Central Bank. Government auditors and the press, respectively, accused him of two partisan acts under the former government: juggling the books to make Turkey's reserve position look better and failing to press for austerity measures with his current fervor.(19) The Central Bank's directors rejected the auditors' report and Sadiklar charged in a press conference that the ministry of finance had refused to enforce the austerity measures announced in March 1978. A minister in the last government's cabinet has testified that Sadiklar's voice had not changed but that Mr. Erkaban of the Islamic National Salvation Party regularly drowned that voice out with proposals for massive public investment.(20)

The silencing of the voice of the Central Bank, a technocratic voice that spoke at some distance from the electorate, scares Turkey's creditors. Sadiklar had threatened not to create money to accommodate the fiscal deficit.(21) He "is more disposed than the ministry of finance to accept the International Monetary Fund's austerity prescriptions for Turkey,"(22) but the ministry of finance seems now to be calling the shots. In fact, an IMF team in Turkey delayed the first drawing envisioned for August in the April standby. Apparently, Turkey's performance disappointed the men in the field but officials of the Fund in Washington found the Turks within the letter of the agreement. The negotiations for the next tranche, slated to be drawn in November, promised to be so tough as to make a drawing before late December or January unlikely. Behind the IMF stands the Turkish cosortium of the OECD which rescheduled $1.5 billion in public loans but which has refused any new money for Turkey. Also behind the IMF stand the international banks which, with the exception of limited financing operations, have not extended new credit to Turkey.

The banks have followed the IMF in its wait-and-see attitude which, in the event, has been more wait than see. Citibank has shepherded two credit arrangements which, if anything, have reduced its exposure in Turkey. The first, a $150 million, seven-year loan at an interest spread of 1½ percent over the cost of funds, the London Inter-Bank Offer Rate (LIBOR), will directly pay off overdue trade credits. The risk of Turkey's not repaying the loan will be held by the foreign suppliers who are its immediate beneficiaries.(23) The United States Export-Import (EXIM) Bank explored such an arrangement with Citibank and Turkey at the beginning of 1978; Turkey rejected the offer of a three-year loan as too short-term and EXIM's exposure was swept into the official rescheduling. The second is a $100 million untied credit with a bump of 3/4 percent over LIBOR for the first two years and then 7/8 percent for the final three years. The risk of this loan will reside in Libya's National Libyan Arab Foreign Bank.(24) Citicorp weaves the hazard of its credit lines into a safety net of risk-bearing.

In the discussions in Zurich, representatives of the consortium of banks holding $2.5 billion of Turkey's debts do not speak as one. Many of the regional and correspondent banks that followed the large international banks into Turkey want out.(25) The unwritten rule of rescheduling calls for bearing new risk in proportion to old risk. The small banks can lever their way out, however. They can demand that their credits be well secured, say with the IMF imprimatur. As for the international banks, their larger stake in one country and their fear of default contagion do make cowards of them all. Their fortunes are inextricably bound to Turkey's coming to terms; they cannot press too hard. So, in a crunch, one observes either a concentration of risk-bearing or a tougher consortium stance than serves the immediate interest of the consortium leaders.

Agreement on refinancing $2.5 billion of bank-held debt will likely follow Turkey's next drawing on the IMF. Large banks will have to accept some of the exposure of smaller banks to conclude this arrangement. The consortium of banks that has been talking about a new loan in the $500 million range has lately taken to discussing $225 million.

PORTUGAL

Both the wake of the 1974 revolution and the tide of world recession have swamped Portugal's external accounts. The institution of cooperatives and struggle over seized land cut deliveries to the cities until imported food contributed half of the country's diet. The loss of the colonies sparked a reflex of some 800,000 souls, ten percent of the population. Workers demanded and got hefty wage increases while struggle over worker control of industry sent productivity skidding. Political turmoil joined the world recession to slow tourist traffic in 1975. Workers' remittances fell by half in 1975 and

Table 8.4. Portugal's Balance of Payments (in millions of dollars)

	1972	1973	1974	1975	1976	1977
Goods, Services, Transfers	354	341	-830	-832	-1,252	-1,477
Merchandise exports FOB	1,307	1,843	2,289	1,935	1,825	2,028
Merchandise imports FOB	-2,041	-2,753	-4,284	-3,606	-3,927	-4,534
Merchandise balance	734	-910	-1,995	-1,671	-2,102	-2,506
Service exports	961	1,248	1,369	1,053	801	908
Service imports	-753	-1,094	-1,313	-1,247	-913	-1,012
Service balance	208	-154	56	-194	-112	-104
Unrequited transfers	881	1,097	1,110	1,033	963	1,135
Long-Term Capital	-96	-141	272	-90	8	45
Direct investment	66	51	69	109	-	21
Other government	-170	-104	-83	-83	-15	28
Other	9	-88	286	-117	23	-4
Short-Term Capital	-10	-135	-26	-205	194	760
Deposit money banks	28	-7	69	-8	219	528
Other	-38	-128	95	-197	-25	232

Source: IMF, _International Financial Statistics_ 31 (October 1978): 310.

only really recovered in 1977 when the government instituted bank accounts for expatriate workers denominated in foreign currencies. Despite the price rise, Portugal imported a half more oil in late 1977 than in June 1974.

Table 8.4 shows that while the value of merchandise imports shot up over 50 percent in 1974 and started growing again after a year's pause, merchandise exports rose only by a quarter in 1974 and declined in the following years. The international banks covered a sixth and a third of Portugal's current-account deficits in 1976, and 1977, respectively (see Table 8.5). Despite an import deposit requirement and eventually a 60 percent import levy on most items as well as the highest gasoline prices in the world, Portugal's current account plunged deeper into the red in 1976 and 1977.

Henry Kissinger first proposed a $1.5 billion OECD loan for Portugal in 1976. The credit was to be extended without the usual IMF strings that might only strengthen the communist bid for power in Portugal. Congress anteed up the third that the United States promised even as it refused to hold its end of the "Safety Net," Kissinger's $25 billion credit facility for OECD countries with international payments problems.(26) Mario Soares argued that without the loan democracy in Portugal would fizzle. The Europeans and the Japanese, smarting from congressional refusal to support the American initiative and having already exposed themselves to the extent of $1.2 billion in Central Bank loans, project loans, and suppliers credits to Portugal, resisted even the $1 billion that the United States and Portugal let out they would settle for.(27) In May 1977, the foreign ministers of the Common Market and Japan rejected the United States plan for Portugal.(28) When the 11 countries Kissinger approached agreed to a $750 million loan in late June, only the United States and West Germany did not insist on austerity measures beyond those announced by Soares in February. These countries signed up for two-thirds of the package: The United States $300 million and Germany $200 million. Paul Boeker, Deputy Assistant Secretary of State and chairman of the meeting of OECD ministers, stated wishfully, "Our decision means the progress of Portuguese democracy will not be impeded by lack of balance-of-payments financing...[it is] a strong encouragement for the government of Portugal; while it represents a considerable vote of confidence in the economic policies which it is following."(29) In fact, the Europeans and Japanese followed Dr. Arthur Burns' call for "governments to resist the temptation to circumvent the IMF," and made their vote of confidence contingent on the IMF's monitoring of Portugal's economy.(30)

The United States built a financial bridge to the IMF-OECD credit while the West German Government seemingly arranged through German banks a medium-term commercial

Table 8.5. Domestic and Foreign Currency Positions of International Banks:* Portugal (in millions of dollars)

	Liabilities	Assets	Net
March 1976	786	619	-167
June 1976	741	633	-108
September 1976	755	762	7
December 1976	820	865	45
United States foreign branches	52	299	247
March 1977	774	1,042	268
United States foreign branches	78	382	304
June 1977	773	1,180	407
United States foreign branches	61	418	357
September 1977	887	1,282	395
United States foreign branches	71	377	306
December 1977	1,103	1,516	413
United States foreign branches	74	470	396
March 1978	1,441	2,210	769
United States foreign branches	101	582	481

*Banks in Group of Ten countries (Belgium/Luxembourg, Canada, France, Italy, Japan, Netherlands, Sweden, United Kingdom, United States, West Germany) and Switzerland, and foreign branches of United States banks in Group of Ten countries and Switzerland and Bahamas, Caymen Islands, Panama, Hong Kong, and Singapore.

Source: Bank for International Settlements, data in Bank of England, Quarterly Review 16 (September, December 1976), Table 23; 17 (March, June, September, December 1977), Table 22; 18 (March, June 1978), Table 22; 18 (December 1978), Table 23; Federal Reserve System, Statistical Release, June 13, 1978.

credit (see Table 8.6). The United States could not anticipate the IMF agreement by activating a Central Bank swap line as it did with Great Britain, Italy, and Mexico, nor did it want to set an official gold price by lending money against Portugal's gold as Germany had done.(31) Instead the Exchange Stabilization Fund of the Treasury coughed up a $300 million credit. A $50 million swap, renewed for $35 million in May,

Table 8.6. Foreign Credits to Portugal, 1977
(in millions of dollars)

Date	Source	Terms	Amount
February	Exchange Stabilization Fund, United States Treasury(a)	see text	300
April	IMF(b)	First credit tranche standby	49
July 27	IMF(c)	Compensatory Finance	34.5
Fourth Quarter	Commerzbank(d)	6-year 1 ½ percent above LIBOR	60
Fourth Quarter	Kredietbank(e)	6-year 1 ½ percent above LIBOR	50
Fourth Quarter	Bank of Montreal(e)	7-year 1 ¼ percent above LIBOR	100

(a) International Currency Review, vol. 9, no. 2, p. 143; Wall Street Journal, May 5, 1977, p. 10.
(b) IMF Annual Report, 1978, p., 98.
(c) Wall Street Journal, July 28, 1977, p. 29.
(d) Euromoney, March 1978, p. 20.
(e) Euromoney, October 1977, p. 69.

accounted for $85 million of these $300 million while a reciprocal gold deposit scheme took up the rest. The Portuguese Government spared itself the embarrassment of announcing the sale of the national hoard by persuading the Americans to swap ounces so that Portuguese could sell gold without affecting gross gold reserves. Only at the reversal of the swap in autumn did Portugal's accounts reflect the gold loss. Window dressing, yes, but window dressing sometimes keeps a government in power(32). Euromoney reports, "The Portuguese government is believed to have approached Commerzbank via political liaison channels with the German government."(33) The form of Germany's contribution to the OECD package in

1978, a government-insured DM420 million loan managed by Commerzbank and Westdeutsche Landesbank and provided exclusively by German banks, confirms the fellow-traveling of mark and flag in Portugal.(34)

As its creditors argued over the price of their aid, Portugal offered a succession of policy changes. On February 28, 1977, Soares announced an austerity plan addressed to the 1976 payments deficits and Portugal's friends: a 15 percent devaluation of the escudo, import restrictions including the extension of the list of commodities subject to 60 percent tax and an import deposit requirement(35) and price controls on a shopping basket of wage goods such as food and fuels. Earlier provisions for foreign currenct-denominated accounts for Portuguese workers abroad rounded out Portugal's alternative to the IMF's recommendation of a 25 percent to 30 percent devaluation.(36) A 15 percent limit on wage hikes in the face of a 1976 inflation rate of 20 percent or more and, eventually, a 1977 rate of 35 percent to 40 percent sought to lower real wages to achieve external balance and to lower the rate of inflation. Meanwhile the government took steps to return to their owners medium-sized companies seized by workers in order to lower state operating subsidies.(37)

These measures failed to satisfy the OECD ministers who met in May.(38) On June 22, two hundred thousand unionists seconded this rejection, albeit for different reasons, in demonstrations in the streets of Portugal.(39) Talks between the socialists and communists for a social pact had broken down. Portugal's Communist Party was not angling for Eurocommunist status.

In an attempt to spring the IMF approval, Vice Governor Constancio of the Bank of Portugal announced on August 26 that the escudo (E.) would be devalued one percent a month in a managed float and that interest rates would rise.(40) The Communist Party responded that "Mr. Soares was paying the price of a capitalist recovery imposed by the IMF,"(41) but the IMF was not convinced.

Before the IMF team arrived in Lisbon, Portuguese Planning Minister Gomes opened what was to be some of the most public negotiations ever for an institution with an instinct for secrecy. On return from its annual meeting in Washington, "he accused the IMF of 'an excessively conservative approach in monetary and fiscal policy.'" favoring "stagnation or recession" over "minimum growth ... to guarantee development of internal production."(47) With unemployment at a "realistic" (IMF) 15 percent, the government introduced a budget at the end of October that despite a tax rise of 15 percent foresaw a continuation of the 1977 E.60 billion deficit (then $1.5 billion).(43) An October leak revealed the IMF wanted the government deficit reduced, interest rates raised from 13 percent to 20 percent, the current-account deficit lowered to $800 million and the escudo devalued 30 percent.(44) Soares negotiated with the Communists to the left and the Social Democrats and Center Democrats to the right to win support in the National Assembly for policies acceptable to the IMF. The Communists appeared ready to join a popular front of unanimous support for the government, but the Social Democrats refused to support any program without being included in a governing coalition. In the event, Soares lost a vote of confidence on December 8 after openly soliciting Communist Party votes.(45)

Soares was back in January with the Center Democrats as partners of convenience. He rushed a program to the National Assembly that called for tax rises and a 20 percent limit on nominal wage rises. Railroad workers and teachers went on strike in protest of the plan but the assembly voted Soares its confidence in February.(46) Preliminary negotiations resumed with the IMF on February 9 but this time in less leaky Washington.

The budget that passed the National Assembly in mid-April showed the IMF to have accepted the budget deficit proposed by the Portuguese during the preceding autumn. Of course, in dollar terms the budget had shrunk about four percent, but in real terms close to 20 percent. After the IMF team arrived in Lisbon in late March, disagreements over the extent of a devaluation leaked out. On May 5 the Portuguese pre-empted the discussion by devaluing 6.5 percent and announcing that the dirty float down would be accelerated to 1.25 percent per month.(47) The IMF further settled for an 18 percent interest rate and a commitment to a $1 billion current account deficit.

Table 8.7 displays the flow of credit to Portugal since the May accord with the IMF. A performance clause in the letter of intent limiting the expansion of foreign indebtedness of the banking system to less than $1 billion during 1978 has no doubt reassured the international banks. The $300 million credit was negotiated by Finance Minister Constancio in New York in June. The 1978 credits to Portugal have price tags 1 percent over the cost of funds for seven years as opposed to 1.5 percent for six years in 1977. That change may reflect the buyers' market in the international capital market more than changes in Portugal. Furthermore, the private market may have provided Portugal with less credit in 1977 had it been left to its own devices by the Germans. The Soares government intended to borrow $700 million from international banks.

The goverment that signed the letter of intent did not last to fulfill its intentions. By July 24, Soares and the Center Democrats had fallen out over the pace of compensation and restitution for owners of expropriated property. With wage rises limited by a January low to 20 percent and inflation

Table 8.7. Foreign Credits to Portugal, First 8 Months of 1978 (in millions of dollars, unless otherwise noted)

Date	Source	Terms	Amount
May 16	United States(a)		200
June 6	IMF(b)		70
July	Commerzbank Westdeutsche Landesbank Consortium(c)	Long-term Fixed-rate	DM420
July 19	Commerzbank Westdeutsche Landesbank Consortium(d)	Multicurrency, 7-year, 1 ½ percent above LIBOR	150
August 17	AME, Banque(e) National de Paris, Chase Manhattan, Dresdner, Industrial Bank of Japan, Manufacturers Hanover Consortium	7-year, 1 percent above LIBOR	300

Note: (a) and (c) are parts of a $750 million OECD package, "in large part contingent on the successful negotiations of an upper credit tranche standby arrangement with the Fund." (IMF, Press Release #78/35, June 6, 1978).

Source: (a) The credit line was opened after assurances had been received in Washington that negotiations between Fund officials and the government had been conducted in good faith. (International Currency Review, vol. 10, no. 4, p. 127.)
(b) IMF, Press Release #78/35, June 6, 1978.
(c) "Guaranteed by the Federal Republic of Germany...," Tombstone, Euromoney, October 1978, p. 198.
(d) International Currency Review; see also Tombstone, Institutional Investor, September 1978, p. 52.
(e) Wall Street Journal, July 10, 1978, p. 20; Tombstone, Euromoney, October 1978, p. 64.

around 35 percent, the socialists did not want to "chase Communists and their allies out of the farms they illegally seized in 1975."(48)

Soares' replacement, the nonpartisan da Costa, quickened indemnification and "replaced the able Socialist finance minister Mr. Victor Constancio by a figure calculated to reassure foreign investors - the strong-willed governor of the Bank of Portugal, Mr. Silva Lopes."(49) The government did not last 16 days but until the parties agree among themselves:

> Mr. Nobre da Costa's government will be a caretaker during the long period it takes to find a way out of the political fog. The govermment will not be able to introduce legislation, but it will be able to enforce the austerity measures already enacted by its predecessor; and its competent finance minister, Mr. Silva Lopes, should be able to keep Portugal's end up in the negotiations with the International Monetary Fund.(50)

Thus, no party need take responsibility for the austerity.

PERU

In 1975 a World Bank consultative group gave a green light to loans for Peru.(51) As Table 8.8 shows, however, in the spring of 1977 the light turned red. The Peruvian mania fed on expectations of jungle oil, heavy anchovy catches, and high copper prices. Exports for 1977 fell short of projected exports by one-third, or $1 billion.(52) Amazonian oil left an expensive trans-Andean pipeline half used, the anchovies disappeared, copper held to a 150-year-old pattern of boom and bust, and sugar prices soured. Anticipated proceeds from exports were nevertheless spent, as purchases of military hardware and investment goods by the government combined to keep imports high and push Peru's merchandise account into serious deficit in 1975. Peru's borrowing (see Table 8.9) from banks abroad accounted for most "other" capital flows, while the interest charges swelled the service deficit.

Table 8.9 shows that Peru's trading position did not shift quickly after 1975 when its imbalance in goods and services exceeded one-tenth of its domestic output. Still, in 1976 the banks were prepared to finance half of Peru's current payments gap. By contrast, in 1977, the near-constant level of assets in Peru suggests a considerable demand for foreign exchange by banks (interest payments exceeded new inflows by approximately $150 million during that year).

In June 1975, the Velasco government responded to Peru's

Table 8.8. Domestic and Foreign Currency Positions of International Banks:* Peru
(in millions of dollars)

	Liabilities	Assets	Net
March 1976	429	2,477	2,048
June 1976	379	2,497	2,118
September 1976	377	2,656	2,279
December 1976	369	2,829	2,460
United States foreign branches	42	983	941
March 1977	454	3,006	2,552
United States foreign branches	73	1,056	983
June 1977	350	3,083	2,733
United States foreign branches	64	1,159	1,095
September 1977	437	2,580	2,543
United States foreign branches	77	1,086	1,009
December 1977	452	2,965	2,513
United States foreign branches	78	1,073	995
March 1978	455	3,019	2,564
United States foreign branches	115	919	804

Source: Bank for International Settlements, data in Bank of England, Quarterly Review 16 (September, December 1976), Table 23; 17 (March, June, September, December 1977), Table 22; 18 (March, June 1978), Table 22; 18 (December 1978), Table 23; Federal Reserve System, Statistical Release, June 13, 1978.

*Banks in Group of Ten countries (Belgium/Luxembourg, Canada, France, Italy, Japan, Netherlands, Sweden, United Kingdom, United States, West Germany) and Switzerland, and foreign branches of United States banks in Group of Ten countries and Switzerland and Bahamas, Caymen Islands, Panama, Hong Kong, and Singapore.

Table 8.9. Peru's Balance of Payments
(in millions of dollars)

	1971	1972	1973	1974	1975	1976	1977
Goods, Services, Transfers	-34	-31	-261	-725	-1,541	-1,198	-929
Merchandise exports FOB	870	945	1,113	1,506	1,291	1,360	1,726
Merchandise imports FOB	-730	-812	-1,097	-1,909	-2,389	-2,099	-2,164
Merchandise balance	160	133	16	-403	-1,098	-739	-438
Service exports	197	221	256	374	432	395	426
Service imports	-429	-425	-576	-744	-924	-912	-974
Service balance	-232	-204	-320	-370	-492	-514	-548
Unrequited transfers	39	40	42	48	50	58	58
Long-Term Capital	9	106	408	720	1,293	807	946
Direct investment	-58	24	70	58	316	170	55
Other government	10	81	215	435	602	447	606
Other	57	1	123	227	375	189	286
Short-Term Capital	-39	21	-10	476	-70	335	61
Deposit money banks	4	-7	-	-2	57	51	37
Other	-43	27	-10	479	-127	284	24

Source: IMF, International Financial Statistics 31 (October 1978): 302.

deteriorating external position. Finance Minister General Morales Bermudez sugar-coated subsidy cuts that boosted food and fuel prices 20 to 30 percent with wage rises that favored lower-paid workers.(53) The sol was devalued 16 percent in August after General Morales installed himself in Velasco's stead. In January 1976, Finance Minister Barua, Morales' replacement, coupled another set of price rises for food and fuel with new taxes on high-income individuals and wage increases for workers.(54)

Although its 1975 performance had made it a candidate for IMF treatment, the government, fearing the political consequences of the conditions attached to IMF help, went shopping for a substitute. The international bankers argued, reportedly at length, that Peru should go to the IMF. Finally, the banks made "the judgment that Peru's situation is somewhere between the first and second IMF tranche [sic] in seriousness."(55) American banks offered $210 million; European banks, $87 million; and Japanese and Canadian banks $45 million each.(56)

Bankers are always able to predicate their sovereign loans on certain policies and may predicate rollover or new loans on adherence to approved policies. The contract negotiated by a consortium of banks cast this "responsibility to the shareholders" in the image and likeness of an IMF agreement. The American bankers sliced the loan in two and agreed with the Peruvians on a set of performance criteria. A 44 percent devaluation, price increases, and minor budget cuts announced in June 1976 were to put them "within calling distance of their objectives,"(57) win the support of 75 percent of the banks (weighted by exposure), and release the second slice. The Peruvians would forward to the banks the report on the state of their finances by an IMF mission in December.(58) Transfer of control of the national budget from the planning office to the Finance Ministry no doubt gladdened potential creditors.(59)

The preconditions for the loan bore the distinctive mark of the banks. Peru must, said the bankers, settle with the Southern Peru Copper Company (SPCC) on back taxes owed and compensate the Marcona Mining Company for the expropriation of its newly producing iron mine. The bankers emphasized not the indebtedness of SPCC to Chase and other consortium members, but the contribution its completion would make to Peru's exports. Similarly, they spotlighted not the interlocked directorates of Marcona and the banks, but the loss of official United States capital flow were the expropriation to trigger application of the Hickenlooper amendment.(60)

Thus, the banks bid below the IMF in terms of the policies offered as collateral, particularly since precise numerical targets did not appear in the contract and local statistical inspection seemed unlikely. Too much significance should not be attached to the absence of quantified targets since the Fund, with some frequency, recognizes progress in the right direction at the expense of precise numbers. However, the preconditions concerning SPCC and Marcona bear little resemblance to the Fund's conditions. These may well create a better investment climate and release foreign exchange for debt service and profit remittance and may even require the sale of an industry to the private sector, but could not, say, require the compensation of expropriated landlords in Portugal.

If the banks aggressively bid lower and made 2¼ percent over LIBOR for their efforts,(61) they acted defensively as well. The bankers recognized the tenuous balance in Peru's cabinet between those committed to maintaining open credit lines and those entertaining a debt moratorium. If the IMF were too tough, Peru's losses from default might appear the lesser of two evils.

> One New York banker involved in those negotiations said the "main reason" the loan was approved was "to perpetuate Morales Bermudez in power." He said the banks considered Morales Bermudez ... to be their best bet to get back the money they had already put into the country.(62)

The bankers defended more than the $2.5 billion at risk in Peru if only because the epidemiology of default were unknown.

The reaction to this arrangement prompted a declaration of a firm purpose of amendment if no mea culpa from a leading participant in the arrangement: "I want no part of deals with that kind of discipline in the future."(64) The protest of the left in Peru, the disapproval of some diplomats, the uneasiness of bankers with the prospect of catching flak for unpopular government policies, and the purchase of $250 million worth of Soviet swing-wing fighter-bombers after agreement on terms of the loan all played their part in the volte-face. A sufficient explanation, however, lies in the difficulty internationl banks have in cooperating or, if you prefer, not competing. Banks have squeezed the spread between the cost of funds and the interest rate charged to 7/8, 3/4, 5/8, even ½ percent. Citibank, Manufacturers Hanover Trust, and Bank of America tried to play price leaders by standing at 1 percent in early 1977; all three have since broken ranks and joined the battle.(64) Federal Reserve Governor Wallich has instructed the banks that the spread necessary to cover bank capital costs (not the cost of funds) and risk is 1 percent.(65) Far worse than price-cutting, which pinches gains, is another form of competition that threatens real losses: competition on the paucity of information or on the laxity of policies demanded as security for a loan.(66)

When, in February 1977, a government team sounded the banks in New York, the answer uniformly pointed the Peruvians to the IMF. An IMF team arrived in March with goals of 33 percent devaluation, budget deficit restraint (through subsidy cuts, sales of enterprises to the private sector, and tax rises), and wage restraint to lower real wages 10 to 15 percent.(67) The head of the Central Bank, who negotiated with the IMF, positioned himself between the IMF, whose "extremely short-term plan" implied "excessive and unnecessary [sic] depressive effects with a high social cost," and the government which he criticized for burdening Peru with debt incurred by arms purchases.(68) The minister of finance inexplicably refused to meet the head of the IMF mission. A government commission headed by the minister of industry recommended reflation through easy money, pegged exchange rate, and increased subsidies. Finance Minister Barua resigned in mid-May.

His replacement for two months, businessman Walter Piazza, remained in office only until he confronted the cabinet with an austerity plan acceptable to the IMF. The Central Bank managers resigned with Piazza since the cabinet tightened rationing of foreign exchange and repuditated the policy of regular mini-devaluations favored by the Central Bank.(69) With the departure of these men, foreign creditors faced a general and a faithful bureaucrat in the Finance Ministry and Central Bank. The IMF team returned to Washington.

Piazza's plan found its opposition not only in the cabinet but also in the streets. In June, while the IMF team was still in Peru, and in July, unionists and others struck and rioted in provincial cities. Police and troops shot and killed upwards of 20 people. On July 19, the first successful general strike since the depression shut down Lima. Police killed six and arrested 300 communist union leaders(70) after their rebellious membership failed to support their progovernment stance.(71) The government reacted with wage increases a few days after the strike.

A representative of Citibank, Irving Friedman, visited Peru in August and again referred the government to the IMF. Meanwhile, government and foreign creditors elbowed one another: the former, requiring six-month financing of imports; the latter, tightening credit lines to local banks. Finally, in late September the cabinet approved an agreement reached between a new Central Bank head and the IMF. The IMF got a floating sol (which sank from 86 to 130 to the dollar during November and December) and accepted a gradual elimination of the forced financing of imports as well as a high 1977 deficit in exchange for subsidy cuts and tax rises to pare 60 percent off the deficit in 1978. Interest rates rises to levels approaching the inflation rate and wage hike limits to cut real wages at least 10 percent rounded out the program.(72)

Peru's fiscal deficit in 1977 - 63 billion soles (S/) or $750 million(73) - bespeaks the bargaining between the Finance Ministry and Central Bank in consultation with the IMF on the one hand, and the rest of the cabinet steeled by urban riots on the other. The following paragraph reverts to the beginning to make this point.

The original budget drawn up in 1976 called for a deficit of S/45 billion, but by January 1977, this figure had grown unofficially to S/80 billion.(74) The IMF, for its part, wanted a ceiling of S/20 billion. The finance minister of the hour, Sr. Piazza, announced a flat 8 percent expenditure cut and a public hiring freeze to keep within a budget ceiling of S/35 billion. Further, the government increased fuel prices by 50 to 100 percent and committed itself to removing the remaining consumption subsidies. The government permitted wage increases of 15 percent for the lowest paid and progressively less for the better paid. For all, however, the increase fell short of the effect on the cost of living of the subsidy cuts. When the IMF negotiating team returned to Peru in the latter half of June, it agreed, against the backdrop of accelerating riots and strikes in the cities of provincial Peru, to a budget limit of S/32.5 billion. At the cabinet meeting on July 5, Sr. Piazza urged his program as a providential fact.(75) It is not known whether the contemplated elimination of subsidies for milk or of purchases of foreign aircraft weighed more heavily in the judgment of the generals in the cabinet but, as related above, exit finance minister, Central Bank management, and IMF team. In the October agreement, the IMF resigned itself to a S/60 billion deficit. The deficit ultimately weighed in at S/63 billion.

The level of Peru's budget deficit in 1977 can hardly be described as an IMF accomplishment. It seems likely, though, that without the IMF's leverage, the deficit would have been larger by 25 percent.

The IMF tethered Peru tightly to its November 1977 undertakings: the country could draw the first installment of $11 million only in February 1978, after it had time to give evidence of mended ways. By then it was clear to the Fund that the government had not retained the agreed level of net reserves.(76) This failure reflected the cost of the government's pegging the sol at 130 to the dollar. The Fund withheld its credit, and a group of banks previously prepared to lend Peru a fresh $260 million followed suit.(77) Earlier appeals to the United States Treasury for financial help from the Exchange Stabilization Fund were denied. Many attributed this to the conjecture of the amount considered - $100 million by most accounts - with the $60 million owed to the Soviets for the purchase of aircraft in January.(78)

In May 1978, Peru and its creditors stood on the brink.

May was long since mortgaged: the government's foreign debt had a lien on 70 percent of export earnings that month.(79) Early in May, an overdue interest payment on a loan managed by Wells Fargo caused participating banks to inquire of Wells Fargo whether any bank had exercised its right to declare a default and force a syndicate vote on calling in the loan. Shortly thereafter, Occidental Petroleum, which banks with Wells Fargo, advanced a $25 million import deposit and the dollars flowed from Wells Fargo, through the Central Bank, back to Wells Fargo, thence to all the participating banks.(80) Occidental bought some goodwill it can well use in retaining its 50 percent cut of the oil it extracts in Peru. Wells Fargo may well have taken care of some participating banks that were less certain than the agent bank of the virtues of patience.

In mid-May, President Morales cleared the decks for action. With the assurance of the chiefs of the three armed services of their complete support, he relieved, first, the minister of finance and commandant of an armored brigade in Lima, General Saenz; and, second, the president of the Central Bank of ten months.(81) A career civil servant and a prominent Latin American monetarist filled these two posts.(82)

On May 15, Peru closed the loop on 10 months. Removal of subsidies bumped food prices by a half; break-even pricing wrenched administered prices for fuel, public transportation, and utilities upwards; a 15 percent devaluation of the sol and a 10 percent import tax for most items put foreign goods out of reach.(83)

Peruvians reacted to these measures as they had a year before by taking to the streets. The government responded more forcefully, however. In the week of the fifteenth, at least a dozen people died in demonstrations and riots in 28 cities and towns.(84) At the end of the week, General Morales imposed martial law, arrested labor leaders, quashed political broadcasts, detained and then deported far-left candidates for the National Assembly, and postponed for two weeks elections scheduled for June 4.

Blandishments and threats to Peru's creditors matched repression of Peruvians. Rescheduling of four-fifths of the arms debt from 1978 to 1980, some $98 million a year, assured Western bankers and governments that their forebearance would not redound to the benefit of the Soviets. The president appealed to the bankers to halve the portion of export proceeds claimed by debt service (over half in 1978, two-thirds in 1979).(85) General Morales warned obliquely on national television: "If there is no response from these international bodies in spite of the sacrifices endured by the Peruvian people, we will have to take other measures."(86)

One week after the price increases, a general strike paralyzed the main cities of Peru for two days. Police fought demonstrators, arsonists, looters, and saboteurs on the first day of the strike, and troops enforced order, if not work, on the second day.(87) Eleven died.(88) The price rises stuck.

On the first day of the general strike, Vice President Figgy of Chase Manhattan sent a telex to Dr. Moreyra of the Central Bank demanding the legal enshrinement of the first claim of a group of international banks and multinational copper companies on the earnings of the Southern Peru Copper Company.(89) Curiously, a rub in the negotiation of the bank monitoring deal in 1976 had been the "negative pledge" clause which commits the borrower not to grant any other lender greater security for his loan.(90) Special legislation is "absolutely a prior condition of further cooperation" by Chase and "banking institutions worldwide," the message threatened.(91) Chase led 60 banks in lending two-thirds of the $750 million invested by United States copper companies in SPCC's mine. The company's dollar earnings were deposited in two Central Bank accounts at Chase: one for forwarding operating costs to Peru, the other for paying interest and amortization as well as profits to the banks and corporations.

This scheme suggests a conflict between comparable treatment of all creditors and maintenance of an incentive to lend only for investment that generates foreign exchange to service debt. One should not push this notion too far, since loans for investment may simply free foreign exchange for arms or for popular consumption. The precedent of such a segregation of revenues threatens Peru's ability to manage its foreign exchange earnings. The demand in the subsequently withdrawn telex that legislation be "passed this week without fail" almost tipped the balance in favor of those in Peru who supported declaring a debt moratorium.(92)

Peru hobbled into June keeping current on interest payments while coaxing its bankers into rolling over principal a month at a time. Unpaid suppliers' credits stood at $3.46 billion, a third of which was overdue.(93) The central banks of Venezuela, Spain, Brazil, Argentina, Mexico, and the Dominican Republic danced the Latin swap by providing $85 million ($25 million, $15 million, $15 million, $15 million, $15 million, and $1 million, respectively), for two months.(94)

Despite press censorship and candidates in exile, elections were held as rescheduled on June 18. The populist party, favorably disposed to foreign investment, gathered 35 percent; the right, 26 percent; and the left surprised many by reaching 30 percent.(95) Significantly, a far-left self-styled Front of Workers, Peasants, and Students outpolled both the Communist Party and a general in the Velasco mold.

In July, the banks could not wait any longer for the IMF. Manufacturers Hanover persuaded 170 participating banks to defer until year-end $185 million in amortization payments coming due in the latter half of 1978.(96) The bankers refused the long-term rescheduling wanted by the Peruvians because of the absence of IMF monitoring. But the fear of a debt moratorium tempered the bankers' commitment to the principle of standing behind the IMF.

On August 7, 1978, the minister of finance and president of the Central Bank signed a letter of intent to the Fund. In exchange for $225 million over two and a half years, the Peruvians agreed to restrain the budget deficit, accelerate the mini-devaluations, and raise interest rates.(97) In particular, the Peruvians promised to keep the budget deficit in the neighborhood of the preceding year's. Since inflation will run 80 percent for the year, this limit, if adhered to, will almost halve the budget deficit of 1977. Interest rates ascended to 30 to 35 percent, and Dr. Moreyra wants to push them closer to the inflation rate.

The day the letter of intent was signed, Peruvian miners struck some crucial copper and iron mine as well as processing plants. By the end of the next week, miners closed down all but one of the main mines.(98) SPCC declared that a force majeur, a breach of contract beyond its control, prevented deliveries to Great Britain, Japan, and the United States;(99) the Central Bank estimated that Peru was losing $2 million a day in foreign exchange earnings.(100)

The miners wanted not so much higher wages as repeal of the so-called labor stability law that gave back to the employer the right to dismiss a worker at will. Some miners, largely trade unionists and activists, had lost their jobs during and after the 1977 general strike.(101) This reflected the reversal of the thoroughgoing job security legally guaranteed under General Velasco.(102)

The government first offered concessions to the illegal strikers, then repressed them thoroughly. The dismissed workers were tempted with cash to call off their fellows, but they refused.(103) The government then sent in the troops and broke the strike. The precedent did not prevent civil servants from taking to the streets in September over the government's plan to fire 30,000 employees.(104)

In the agreement with the Fund, the Peruvians committed themselves to refinancing 70 percent of the repayments of principal scheduled for 1979 and 1980 with a new ten-year loan with three year's grace. In addition, the $185 million in payments due from July to December 1978 and deferred in June was to be converted into a five-year loan.(105) The Peruvians had second thoughts, however, when they realized that their public creditors would be loath to reschedule 90 percent of loans due in 1979-1980. In particular, Congress has legislated comparable treatment of public and private debt (to be enforced by leverage on the debtor country). So the Peruvians have offered to repay the $185 million in 1979 in exchange for refinancing 90 percent of amortization payments for two years with a seven-year loan with a three-year grace period at 1 7/8 percent over LIBOR. The banks argue that, since the Peruvians paid the public creditors regularly in 1978, the quick repayment of the $185 million constitutes comparable treatment.

EGYPT

Arab oil dollars not only cushioned Egypt from the commodity price shocks of 1973 but also powered its growing economy through the world's worst recession in 40 years. Egypt's merchandise imports jumped over 100 percent in 1974 and more than maintained that level even as the country achieved self-sufficiency in oil by the end of 1975 (see Table 8.10). The terms on which Egypt coaxed oil dollars out of its Arab friends stiffened from outright gifts ("unrequited transfers") to long-term loans ("other" long-term capital) in 1975 and after, but the crude figures remain high.

The growth in service exports understates Egypt's gains from its workers in the booming oil states since it captures only the foreign currency converted in Egypt's parallel (unofficial) foreign exchange market and the foreign currency directly used by its owners for imports. Table 8.11 shows that workers foreign earnings on deposit with Western banks grew to some $2.8 billion by March 1978. The international banks have placed these foreign exchange deposits on the Euromarkets, thereby making Egypt a contributor to this market like the Group of Ten and OPEC countries. Egypt's immediate relation as supplier of funds to the international banking system strikingly distinguishes it from Turkey, Portugal, and Peru. Were the foreign exchange earned by Egypt's workers not merely making a whistle-stop in Cairo, Egypt might lean less on the loans from Persian Gulf states and the gulf states might well deposit more in the Eurocurrency market than they do. So the line from Egypt to the Eurocurrency market may simply reroute funds from the gulf states.

After keeping Egypt solvent with $2.6 billion in 1975 and $1 billion in 1976, the country's Persian Gulf sponsors were "suffering from aid fatigue,"(106) and established in August 1976 the Gulf Organization for the Development of Egypt (GODE) with $2 billion to finance long-term projects over five years. Earlier that year, in May, Minister of Economy Shafer emerged from negotiations with the IMF prepared to float the Egyptian pound and cut the budget $1 billion by removing food and fuel subsidies. The government twice lost its nerve after announcing its intention to follow its creditors' advice.

So Egypt required a GODE to get it to cut back. This organization extended a mere $250 million in the latter half of 1976 (despite pleas for five times that), and stalled on a $250

Table 8.10. Egypt's Balance of Payments and Growth
(in millions of dollars)

	1971	1972	1973	1974	1975	1976	1977
Goods, Services, Transfers	-207	-170	77	-327	-1,397	-807	-814
Merchandise exports FOB	851	813	1,000	1,672	1,567	1,609	1,993
Merchandise imports FOB	-1,131	-1,170	-1,429	-2,914	-3,941	-3,842	-4,121
Merchandise balance	-280	-357	-429	-1,242	-2,374	-2,233	-2,128
Service exports	182	308	421	708	1,078	1,975	2,551
Service imports	-386	-417	-556	-829	-1,178	-1,260	-1,681
Service balance	-204	-109	-135	-121	-100	715	870
Unrequited transfers (a)	278	295	641	1,035	1,076	710	445
Long-Term Capital	10	117	-62	-268	1,785	748	1,923
Direct investment	-	-	-	-	8	61	98
Other government	29	128	-54	-120	186	378	419
Other	-19	-11	-8	-148	1,591	309	1,406
Short-Term Capital	89	75	111	375	-271	-272	-1,040
Deposit money banks	-35	-15	224	375	-345	-234	-1,004
Other	124	90	-113	-	74	-38	-36
Percentage Growth Rate of							
Merchandise exports	4.2	-4.5	23.0	67.2	-6.3	2.7	23.9
Merchandise imports	4.3	69.2	36.7	68.2	52.3	83.2	29.2
Service exports	4.6	3.5	22.1	103.9	35.2	-2.5	7.3
Service imports	4.6	8.0	33.7	49.1	42.1	7.0	33.4
Real gross domestic product	4.9	3.9	3.5	3.2	4.0(b)	11.0(b)	8.0(b)

(a) > 85 percent government-to-government.
(b) Estimates.

Source: IMF, International Financial Statistics 31 (October 1978): 132.

Table 8.11. Domestic and Foreign Currency Positions of International Banks:* Egypt
(in millions of dollars)

	Liabilities	Assets	Net
March 1976	1,930	909	-1,021
June 1976	2,002	984	-1,018
September 1976	1,939	1,041	-898
December 1976	2,016	1,242	-774
United States foreign branches	319	294	-25
March 1977	2,027	1,298	-729
United States foreign branches	296	271	-25
June 1977	2,381	1,295	-1,086
United States foreign branches	385	251	-134
September 1977	2,725	1,300	-1,425
United States foreign branches	436	259	-177
December 1977	2,751	1,104	-1,647
United States foreign branches	415	187	-228
March 1978	2,886	1,248	-1,638
United States foreign branches	400	234	-166

*Banks in Group of Ten countries (Belgium/Luxembourg, Canada, France, Italy, Japan, Netherlands, Sweden, United Kingdom, United States, West Germany) and Switzerland, and foreign branches of United States banks in Group of Ten countries and Switzerland and Bahamas, Caymen Islands, Panama, Hong Kong, and Singapore.

Source: Bank for International Settlements, data in Bank of England, Quarterly Review 16 (September, December 1976), Table 23; 17 (March, June, September, December 1977), Table 22; 18 (March, June 1978), Table 22; 18 (December 1978), Table 23; Federal Reserve System, Statistical Release, June 13, 1978.

million Chase-provided, GODE-guaranteed loan. Why do the Gulf States pay banks to recycle there oil dollar? According to one banker, "The rich Arabs wanted to use the commercial banks as a buffer and get them to impose some commercial discipline on the Egyptians rather than the (perhaps more easily waived) political discipline of GODE."(107) The loan was signed on April 26, 1977, after Egypt had come to terms with the IMF.(108) So the banks collected 1 percent over the cost of funds and their front-end fees as agents who could say no for principal who could say yes.

On November 9, 1976, Sadat installed Kaissouny, the internationally respected chairman of the offshore Arab International Bank, as premier for financial and economic affairs. Kaissouny, it was felt, could make credible the open door to foreign investment by coming to terms with the IMF. He demurred at the IMF's suggestion to float the Egyptian pound, but he drew a bead on the projected 1977 budget deficit of 1,300 million Egyptian pounds (ЕE) - $3,200 million at the official rate of $2.56 per Egyptian pound or $2,300 million at the unofficial rate of $1,701 - which reflected, among other things, spending on food subsidies of ЕE 500 million.(109)

In December, Premier Salam outlined a new budget that would slice 30 percent off the deficit and 5 percent off the subsidy bill.(110) Kassiouny, however, negotiated for the IMF's qualified support for deeper cuts in the deficit and subsidy payments of 90 percent and 50 percent, respectively, without floating the pound.(111) The banker convinced the cabinet that his plan would free Egypt of dependence on its chary friends.

On Monday, January 17, 1977, government subsidies for flour, sugar, fuel, and tobacco were revoked. On Tuesday, street demonstrations ignited in just about every large Egyptian city. On Wednesday, a crowd of 30,000 looted shops, torched buses and, ultimately, fought police in Cairo while across the river other rioters trashed the watering holes of the new rich of Egypt, Libya and Saudi Arabia. The government restored the subsidies and imposed a curfew on Wednesday night, the first such drastic action since the 1952 revolution. In all, 79 people died.

The Egyptian Government blamed communists and rounded up 1,300 of the usual suspects.(112) A Kuwaiti newspaper smelled a plot to "scare the oil states."(113) Even observers who felt that the "Egyptian government is neither that cold-blooded nor that efficient" couldn't resist remarking on the absence of police at critical moments during Cairo's flare-up.(114)

Egypt's creditors heard the threat even if they couldn't identify the lips that spoke it. John Gunther, head of the Middle East Department at the IMF arrived in Cairo on Wednesday.(115) Kaissouny tendered his resignation the same day but Prime Minister Salam refused it and instead packed him off for a tour of oil capitals.(116) By Monday, January 24, the IMF had agreed to $145 million for Egypt.(117) A month later officials of Saudi Arabia, Kuwait, the United Arab Emirates and Qatar were prepared to empty $1 billion or more out of the GODE bucket.(118) Similarly, the United States decanted a suddenly liquid $200 million of its aid.(119)

The IMF affixed its seal of approval to a budget different from the one drawn up at the turn of the year. The overall deficit expanded to ЬE400 million, almost a third of the original figure but almost three times the January figure. The government upped food subsidies to ЬE350 million, midway between the original budget and the January budget.(120) Egypt changed as well. On February 10, Sadat called a referendum on legislation that provided a penalty of hard labor for life for destroying property, inciting to lawbreaking, impeding state operations, participating in demonstrations, or striking any firm.(121)

By the time the consultative group of aid donors met in May, Egypt was playing a strong hand which included $5 billion in new commitments and rollovers of indebtedness. The Egyptian representatives appear to have spoken of halving the subsidies despite the budget and of allowing free movement of capital through the market-related exchange rate. World Bank Vice President Benjenk, chairman of the meeting, foresaw a "long-term program of reform."(122)

Overall, 1977 marked a great improvement in the structure of Egypt's debt: $1.45 billion of short-term debt and $450 million in arrears emerged at year-end largely as long-term debt, with only $560 million remaining as medium- and short-term debt.(123) By August, Kaissouny and company achieved a normal lag in import payments. The GODE funds both bought food and bailed out the international banks holding overdue short-term debt.

After performing his magic on Egypt's debt, Kaissouny turned his attention to reshaping the Egyptian economy. A growing list of publicly produced industrial goods commenced to find their own price in the market. The subsidies for food and oil remained, however.(124)

In April 1978, foreign confidence in the management of Egypt's economy took a beating with the departure of Kaissouny. The austerity measures he had been pushing had not only been sharply criticized in the People's Assembly but also resisted in the cabinet, but the last straw was the cabinet's and Sadat's supporting increases in public sector salaries, wages, and imports without bothering to consult with the economic minister.(145)

Still, negotations for a three-year program with the IMF continued. The Paris Club met in June after agreement in principle on a $720 million three-year program. The Egyptians asked their creditors for $500 million in cash and $450 million in commodity aid beyond the $2.5 billion already committed. The aid givers expressed more enthusiasm for renovating and completing industrial plants already in place and for birth-control efforts than for the $17 billion five-year investment plan.(126) Rising oil exports, tourism receipts, and workers remittance justified some hope.

The three-year program than won the Fund's approval aims at a considerable shift from consumption to investment. Fixed investment will claim not 15 percent of gross domestic product as in 1974, but 26 percent in 1981.(127) The conditions reportedly include the elimination of subsidies and a rise in taxes to reduce the government deficit, and a rise in interest rates toward the rate of inflation.(128)

The Fund did not insist on floating the Egyptian pound, but it did receive assurances on further progress towards a single exchange rate.(129) Monetary targets seek to ensure that nominal wage boosts do not wipe out the effects of these policies on real incomes.

The policy changes that have followed the IMF agreement indicate the substantial concessions by the Fund. Despite a current rate of inflation in excess of 25 percent and the announced intention of reducing it to just 10 percent over three years, interest rates will rise 2 percent in 1978 from the July levels of about 5 percent.(130) So despite the ambitious investment plan, the real (inflation-adjusted) interest rates will continue to be negative.

Negotiations between Egypt and GODE again hinged on an agreement with the IMF. GODE rolled over for 25 years all payments of principal and interest on the nearly $2 billion lent to Egypt originally for ten years at 5 percent. This saved Egypt almost $100 million per year over the three-year grace period and much more thereafter. Further, the gulf states committed themselves to guarantee another private bank loan in the amount of $150 million.(131)

Egypt's creditors like its peaceful and pro-Western government and have placed Egypt in the position of a European country approaching the second year of the Marshall Plan. The worse it does, the more it gets. The United States recognized this perverse incentive and divided the second year's aid in the same proportions as the first year's. Egypt's Persian Gulf friends recognized that Egypt could do well doing badly and anticipated Dr. Burns' call for governments to stand behind the IMF. Egypt's crowds demonstrated the incompatibility of squeezing consumption and maintaining order. The creditors backed off and now hope to get Egypt to invest heavily out of its growth. This the crowds may allow.

CONCLUSION

It now remains to make explicit the three themes of the case studies. Creditors stand behind the IMF and its conditions. The OECD Turkish consortium met only after the agreement on a standby while private banks waited not for simple agreement on the standby, not for Turkey to qualify for its first drawing in September, but for Turkey to satisfy a second set of performance hurdles. The banking statistics give evidence that banks continued to lend to Portugal in 1977 and early 1978 without the collateral of Fund monitoring. It was the public creditors who heeded Dr. Burns' call not to circumvent the IMF, although the German Government may have lent its offices to Portugal in its approach to German banks. The Peruvians taught the banks the wisdom of allowing the IMF to play price leader in international lending and only peripheral players, for example, the Venezuelans, and the Soviets, eased the pressure before the IMF deal. The banks, it should be noted, perforce rolled over, explicitly or implicitly, loans to Turkey and Peru for the short term even before agreement with the IMF. Peru's creditor club met only after agreement with the IMF. Finally, Egypt's public creditors, especially its Arab friends, placed the IMF with mixed results between their treasuries and Egyptian mouths.

The reaction in Peru and Egypt forcefully draws our second conclusion. Currency devaluation, subsidy cuts, price rises for goods produced in the public sector-"getting the prices right"-all cut real wages. Real wages were falling in Peru and Portugal before the IMF arrived but its conditions meant still further cuts. Workers do not suffer from any illusion that their real wages have no relation to the prices they pay; in Peru and Egypt, they expressed such clear-headedness in riots and strikes.

If workers succeed in maintaining their real wages, then nominal wage increases lead in turn to price increases. As Richard Cooper says:

> At this point, the monetary authorities are confronted with a cruel dilemma: they can maintain tight monetary control, thereby inhibiting price increases but also inducing unemployment; or they can ease up on monetary controls, thereby validating the increases in wages and domestic prices and undercutting the relative price effects of the devaluation.(132)

The IMF conditions concerning credit expansion allow the central banks to make a pre-emptive move. Credit may expand only so much; the choice is between falling real wages or unemployment. Many central bankers would like to so tie their own hands but lack the power to do it themselves.

A general belt-tightening does not assure the long-run success of a devaluation-cum-austerity plan. Investment in export and import-competing activities will not happen without profits and the expectation of continued profits in these sectors. As Diaz Alejandro says:

> If a cut in absorption were all that was required for the long-run success of a devaluation, it would be possible, even in a democratic capitalistic economy, for all social classes to share equally in the burden of austerity. However, a reallocation of resources is also indispensable if the devaluation is to have a long-run success in making possible both full employment and balance-of-payments equilibrium. Therefore, even in the context of a general cut in absorption in a capitalist economy, better incentives, and higher real incomes must be offered to some sectors of production after a devaluation.(133)

Selective belt-tightening renders a popular reaction not unlikely. Real wages fell 28 percent in Lima <u>before</u> the May 1978 measures.(134) Even as wages in Portugal fall to 1970 levels and unemployment rises from 15 percent, civil and labor peace reigns unaccountably.(135) This quiet frustrated Finance Minister Constancio's attempt in early 1978 to use the possibility of turmoil to soften the IMF's terms.(136) In the summer of 1978, Prime Minister Ecevit concluded a pact with a confederation of labor unions to limit nominal wage boosts to rises in the cost of living.(137) Perhaps the promise will be honored in the breach. Bankers fear that the Turkish Government remains convinced that military bases and a long parliamentary record will substitute for austerity measures.

Neither Portugal nor Egypt were as burdened by debt servicing as they were anxious to secure new credits. Turkey and Peru, by contrast, wanted to get out from under the weight of their indebtedness. The third conclusion of this study concerns the process of debt relief. The conflicts of interest and the most intensive bargaining occur, curiously enough, not between creditors and debtor but among creditors. Creditors recognize the impossibility of upholding a claim to more than half a country's foreign exchange earnings, and, if a country commits itself to repayment and commits itself to the care of the IMF, they will reschedule or refinance. Since there is not a single creditor but a multiplicity of creditors, the question is who settles for what. The fear is that unmatched leniency amounts to a transfer from one creditor to another. One's liberality provides the reward for another's toughness.

Public creditors meet in creditor clubs to enforce "equal burden-sharing." When the Nkrumah-era debts of Ghana were rescheduled, the Soviets, though nonparticipants, were given a take-it-or-leave-it offer that brought them into the one bargain. In the Turkish consortium in 1978, the United States insisted that a fair distribution of the burden required the inclusion of short-term debts. The creditor club leaves undefined the relationship between public and private creditors on one hand, and the relationship among private creditors on the other.

The public creditors cannot directly enforce their terms on private creditors. They can reach through the debtor country, however, by making a comparable settlement with private creditors a condition of their debt relief.(138) What is comparable? In one sense, an equal deferral of debt is not comparable. In the United States, a deferral of aid debt is viewed dimly by the Congress while a delayed payment to the Export-Import Bank constrains its ability to finance more exports. A bank, by contrast, exists to lend money and a debt deferral means that it need not search for another borrower, perhaps no more solvent than the last. This is especially true when the Eurocurrency market is liquid.

But a government rescheduling and a bank refinancing with similar terms diverge in a more concrete sense. When a bank refinances a loan, it goes through the motions of a fresh loan with all its front-end fees. These management and participation fees come right off the top of a loan and contribute immediately to bank earnings. Banks do not generally make public these fees but the amounts can be significant, particularly for the manager banks.(139)

The OECD consortium for Turkey rescheduled interest payments as well as principal due public creditors. It remains to be seen whether the private banks follow suit. A divergence of terms for public and private creditors in this respect appears to challenge the principle of comparable burden-sharing.

The relationship among private creditors threatens more than anything else to push a foreign exchange crisis into a default. Banks holding Turkey's and Peru's debt have jostled one another in trying to reduce their exposure or in trying to enforce a first claim on foreign exchange earnings.

The scramble for a preferential claim on foreign exchange earnings has in recent memory tripped off a law suit and a "technical" default. Citibank and Bankers Trust took Manufacturers Hanover and the Export-Import Bank to court to close "an external account into which foreign exchange sufficient to meet EXIM Bank's direct and guaranteed debt service on the [electric transmission line] project would be paid by the Government's cooper marketing agency . . . on a monthly basis and directly after receipt of funds . . . from the purchasers of Zaire's copper."(140) The out-of-court settlement put EXIM at the front of a queue for the repayment of only that crecit extended after Zaire had fallen in to arrears.

In 1977, Indonesia fell into technical default on a loan syndicated by Morgan Guaranty when it was learned that the Export-Import Bank of Japan and 16 Japanese banks had cut into the creditors' line with a prior lien on oil revenues.(141) The first claim on the receipts from exports of gas to Japan secured a $1.3 billion loan for the construction of plants to liquify the natural gas. Morgan Guaranty successfully persuaded the syndicate banks not to call in the 1975 loan. Bankers' rivalries have come closest to precipitating a default.

NOTES

Turkey

1. Charles Kindleberger, "Migration, Growth and Development," OECD Observer, June 1978, p. 25.
2. Euromoney, March 1978, p. 37.
3. Financial Times, May 23, 1978 p. 2; Euromoney, September 1977, p. 19.
4. Middle Eastern Economic Digest, March 3, 1978, p. 37.
5. Middle Eastern Economic Digest, July 14, 1978, p. 3.
6. Financial Times, November 23, 1977, p. 22.
7. Journal of Commerce, September 7, 1977, p. 11.
8. Euromoney, September 1977, p. 23; New York Times, January 1, 1978, section IV, p. 2.
9. Financial Times, October 12, 1977, p. 23.
10. Middle Eastern Economic Digest, July 7, 1978, p. 51.
11. Financial Times, May 23, 1978, p. 2; Wall Street Journal, May 23, 1978, p. 6.
12. Middle Eastern Economic Digest, June 30, 1978, p. 37.
13. Middle Eastern Economic Digest, September 1, 1978, p. 38.
14. Middle Eastern Economic Digest, July 28, 1978, p. 40.
15. Middle Eastern Economic Digest, July 21, 1978, p. 37; and July 7, 1978, p. 51.
16. Middle Eastern Economic Digest, August 11, 1970, p. 43.
17. Middle Eastern Economic Digest, August 25, 1978, p. 39.
18. Ibid., pp. 38-39.
19. Foreign Report, Economist, August 30, 1978, pp. 3-4.
20. Financial Times, November 23, 1977, p. 18.
21. Middle Eastern Economic Digest, August 18, 1978, p. 35.
22. Economist, September 16, 1978, p. 73.
23. Economist, July 22, 1978, pp. 100-01.
24. Ibid.; see Tombstone, Euromoney, October 1978, p. 216.
25. Journal of Commerce, May 3, 1978, p. 3.

Portugal

26. *Washington Post*, April 20, 1977, p. A-16.
27. *New York Times*, June 23, 1977, section IV, p. 1.
28. *Wall Street Journal*, May 5, 1977, p. 10.
29. *New York Times*, June 23, 1977, section IV, p. 1.
30. Arthur F. Burns, "The Need for Order in International Finance," address to Columbia Graduate School of Business, New York, N.Y., April 12, 1977, p. 21.
31. Exchange of Stabilization Fund, Hearings, Subcommittee on International Finance, Senate Committee on Banking, Housing and Urban Affairs 95:1, October 7, 1977, p. 91.
32. Ibid., p. 93.
33. *Euromoney*, October 1977, p. 69.
34. See Tombstone, *Euromoney*, October 1978, p. 198.
35. *International Currency Review* 9: 144.
36. Ibid.
37. Ibid., p. 145.
38. *Wall Street Journal*, May 5, 1977, p. 10.
39. *New York Times*, June 23, 1977, section 4, p. 7.
40. *International Currency Review* 9: 66.
41. *New York Times*, August 27, 1977, p. 4.
42. *Financial Times*, October 6, 1977, p. 4.
43. *Financial Times*, October 31, 1977, p. 4.
44. *International Currency Review* 10: 126; and *Financial Times*, October 19, 1977, p. 4.
45. *New York Times*, November 28, 1977, p. 8; and November 9, 1977, p. 11.
46. *Euromoney*, March 1978, pp. 17-18.
47. *International Currency Review* 10: 167.
48. *Economist*, September 2, 1978, p. 46.
49. Ibid.
50. *Economist*, September 23, 1978, p. 58.

Peru

51. *Business Week*, September 15, 1977, p. 34.
52. Ibid.
53. *Andean Report*, July 1975. pp. 1-2.
54. *Latin American Economic Report*, January 23, 1976, p. 14.
55. Nancy Belliveau, "What the Peru Experiment Means," *Institutional Investor*, October 1976, p. 34.
56. *Euromoney*, March 1978, pp. 25-26.
57. Ibid.
58. *New York Times*, February 4, 1977, section IV, p. 5.
59. *Latin American Economic Report*, July 2, 1976, p. 101.
60. Belliveau, "Peru Experiment," p. 35.
61. "At the upper end of the range international banks have charged during the part year on loans to oil-importing developing countries." *American Banker*, December 8, 1978.

62. *Washington Post*, February 14, 1978, p. A-10.
63. Belliveau, "Peru Experiment," pp. 33-34.
64. *Institutional Investor*, International Edition, June 1978, p. 35.
65. Henry Wallich, "International Lending and the Euromarkets" (Address to the 1978 Euromarket Conference, London, May 9, 1978) quoted in *International Currency Review* 10: 47-50.
66. A bank, like Milton Friedman's individual who gambles on a lottery even as he insures his home against fire, takes risks at the margin but fears inframarginal losses.
67. *Latin American Economic Report*, April 22, 1977, p. 57.
68. Ibid.; and Nicholas Asheshov, "Peru's Flirtation with Disaster," *Institutional Investor*, September 1977, pp. 183-84.
69. Asheshov, "Peru's Flirtation," p. 157.
70. Ibid., p. 185.
71. *Latin American Economic Report*, October 4, 1977, p. 176.
72. *Andean Report, December 1977*, p. 226.
73. *Andean Report*, July 21, 1978, p. 217.
74. *Andean Report*, June 10, 1978, p. 81.
75. Asheshov, "Peru's Flirtation," pp. 185-86.
76. *Euromoney*, May 1978, p. 62.
77. *Wall Street Journal*, February 16, 1978, p. 35; *Latin American Economic Review*, March 17, 1978, p. 87.
78. *Andean Report*, December 1977, p. 221.
79. *International Currency Review* 10: 155.
80. *New York Times*, May 21, 1978, p. 11.
81. *International Currency Review* 10: 56.
82. *Economist*, May 20, 1978, p. 94.
83. *Bank of London and South America Review* 12 (June 1978): 323-24.
84. *New York Times*, May 24, 1978, p. 6.
85. *Financial Times*, May 23, 1978, p. 4; and June 29, 1978, p. 2.
86. *New York Times*, May 22, 1978, p. 12.
87. *New York Times*, May 24, 1978, p. 6.
88. *New York Times*, May 25, 1978, p. 7.
89. *Economist*, May 27, 1978, pp. 108-09; *International Currency Review* 10: 157.
90. *Latin American Economic Report*, January 28, 1977, p. 14.
91. *Financial Times*, May 24, 1978, p. 38.
92. *International Currency Review*, p. 157.
93. *Ibid.*
94. *New York Times*, June 9, 1978, p. 25.
95. *Economist*, June 24, 1978, p. 75.
96. *Financial Times*, July 19, 1978, p. 5.
97. *Financial Times*, August 11, 1978, p. 4.
98. *London Times*, August 19, 1978, p. 5.
99. *Wall Street Journal*, September 19, 1978, p. 16.
100. *Latin American Economic Report*, September 15, 1978, p. 288.

101. London Times, August 19, 1978, p. 5.
102. Bank of London and South America Review, p. 325.
103. Latin American Economic Report
104. Wall Street Journal, November 6, 1978, p. 16.
105. Journal of Commerce, August 11, 1978, p. 31.

Egypt

106. Business Week, October 25, 1976, p. 49.
107. Euromoney, October 1977, p. 111.
108. Middle East Economic Digest, May 5, 1977, p. 22.
109. Middle East Economic Digest, January 14, 1977, p. 3; and January 21, 1977, p. 18.
110. Ibid.
111. Middle East Economic Digest, January 28, 1977, p. 6; Economist, January 22, 1977, p. 59.
112. Washington Post, January 28, 1977, p. A-20.
113. Ibid.
114. Economist, January 29, 1977, pp. 59-60.
115. New York Times, January 24, 1977, p. 3.
116. New York Times, January 20, 1977, p. 1; and January 24, 1977, p. 3.
117. New York Times, January 25, 1977, p. 3.
118. Middle East Economic Digest, February 25, 1977, p. 18; New York Times, February 25, 1977, p. 1.
119. New York Times, February 25, 1977, p. 8.
120. Middle East Economic Digest, February 25, 1977, p. 18.
121. Middle East Economic Digest, February 18, 1977, p. 18.
122. Middle East Economic Digest, May 20, 1977, p. 3.
123. Middle East Economic Digest, June 23, 1978, p. 6.
124. Journal of Commerce, May 1, 1978, p. 31.
125. Journal of Commerce, April 24, 1978, p. 3; New York Times, January 4, 1978, p. D-3.
126. Middle East Economic Digest, June 23, 1978, pp. 6-7.
127. International Monetary Fund, Press Release No. 78/56, July 31, 1978.
128. New York Times, June 14, 1978, p. D-3.
129. Middle East Economic Digest, July 7, 1978, p. 4.
130. Ibid.
131. Middle East Economic Digest, August 11, 1978, p. 7.

Conclusion

132. Richard N. Cooper, "An Assessment of Currency Devaluation in Developing Countries," in Government & Economic Development, Gustau Ranis, ed. (New Haven: Yale University Press, 1971), p. 495.
133. Carlos F. Diaz-Alejandro, Exchange-Rate Devaluation in

a Semi-Industrialized Country (Cambridge, Mass.: Massachusetts Institute of Technology Press, 1965), p. 154.

134. Economist, September 2, 1978, p. 70.

135. New York Times, May 28, 1978, p. 14.

136. Euromoney, March 1978, p. 20.

137. Middle Eastern Economic Digest, July 28, 1978, p. 39.

138. See U.S. Treasury, Report on Developing Countries External Debt and Debt Relief Provided by the United States, January 1978, p. 51. For a dim view of the private bank proposals in Zaire, see testimony of John Moore, EXIM president in The Witteveen Facility and the OPEC Financial Surpluses, Hearings before the Senate Subcommittee on Foreign Economic Policy of the Committee on Foreign Relations, 95:1 (September 21, 23, October 6, 7, and 10, 1977), pp. 113-27.

139. Euromoney, March 1977, pp. 113-14. A loan to Liberia had a 3/8 percent participation fee; Euromoney, February 1977, p. 57. Management fees reportedly range up to 1.5 percent.

140. The Witteveen Facility and the OPEC Financial Surpluses, Hearings, p. 116.

141. Business Week, January 10, 1977, p. 27.

III

LDC Debt: Solutions and Constraints

9 Alternative Proposals for Debt Relief*

Marilyn J. Seiber

Since 1973 nonoil developing countries have been on a steep roller coaster debt climb, and concerns for their economic health and whether the lending banks and international financial institutions might follow them on a downhill ride have precipitated a flurry of debt relief prescriptions. With total nonoil developing country debt estimated by the United Nations Conference on Trade and Development at $225 billion by year-end 1977 and debt servicing absorbing 25 percent of the poorest developing countries' export earnings in 1978, a search for appropriate solutions has become a pressing international issue. This relatively sudden and vocal interest comes not only from the absolute debt figures, but also from the combination of sudden changes that have occurred in the international system. These changes include the Third World's increased unity and active efforts to restructure the international economic system, the sudden changes in current-account balances resulting from oil-related price increases, and the expanded role and importance of private commercial banks in financing developing countries' payments deficits. These factors combined with the economic and debt situation of the nonoil Third World countries have converged to focus on the need for debt relief strategies. However, debt relief - broadly defined as a reduction ex post in the present value of debt outstanding - takes on various forms depending on the policies, positions, and views on perceived need by the actors involved. India's position, for example, has been that a new,

---

*This chapter was originally prepared for presentation at the Annual Meetings of the International Studies Association, February 1978.

bold, imaginative generalized approach is needed to the solution of the chronic debt service problem of developing countries. The United States, on the other hand, believes that the magnitude of the debt problem has been greatly exaggerated, and, in fact, that debt is a short- to medium-term balance-of-payments problem.

In order to better understand the range of debt relief approaches, this chapter will first examine the background to debt relief strategies, and, second, will survey the collection of alternative proposals for debt relief. These proposals will be reviewed according to the following debt relief categories: the status quo approach; preventive measures; stop-gap arrangements; international debt duidelines; new mechanisms and old debt; adjustment, forgiveness, and transfers; and new roles for the IMF.

I. BACKGROUND TO DEBT RELIEF

The Need for Debt Relief

By the end of 1977, non-OPEC developing country debt reached new heights of $200-225 billion,(1) and according to Morgan Guaranty Trust, these countries' aggregate current-account deficit may widen by several billion dollars in 1978, implying a possible acceleration of external borrowing.(2) Eurocurrency borrowing alone - the bulk of private commercial lending - amounted to over $13.4 billion in 1977, up from the $11 billion level in 1976. Total developing country borrowings from private banks were estimated to be about $76 billion by September 1977.(3) This fast rise in external debt, particularly private debt with shorter maturities and higher interest rates, raises the question of the ability of developing countries to meet their service payments. Morgan Guaranty Trust Company reports that debt service burdens in a number of countries will rise rapidly through the early 1980s, due to the ending of grace periods and short maturities. Already one dollar of every four borrowed is used to pay past loans, and by 1980 the figure may be one out of every two dollars borrowed. Unless average loan maturities are extended, by 1985 over 65 percent of all gross borrowings will be needed for amortization payments. The United Nations Conference on Trade and Development (UNCTAD) projected that in 1978 debt servicing will absorb 25 percent of the export earnings of the world's 45 least developed countries, and for individual countries such as Mexico and Brazil, the debt-service ratio is considerably higher.

This situation has prompted calls for specific actions to ease the developing countries' intensifying debt pains and to avoid a possible crisis in the international finacial system.(4)

Scenarios on the consequence of not dealing with the Third World debt problem vary from a "doomsday" prognosis for the banking system to relegation of developing countries to "basket-case" conditions. The doomsday prediction raises the specter of multiple developing country defaults or refusals to meet payments, causing banks to panic and simultaneously call in their loans which would lead to a collapse of the international credit market. While this rendition may be extreme, the possibility of potential long-term dangers in the form of a conjunction of debt service peaks, stagnating developing country exports, and drying up of private credits can not be ruled out.(5) As for the impact on developing countries, countries such as India, argue that failure to find an effective solution to this problem will greatly add to the uncertainty and difficulties already faced by the poorer countries in implementing their development plans in an orderly manner. In the view of some developing countries, the international community has but two choices - either to abandon the goal of improved living standards for developing countries in face of massive and growing balance-of-payments deficits, or to seek international agreement for alleviating the burden by arranging to finance an increased proportion of these countries' debt.

Although the need for relief from debt burdens is widely recognized, the solution is not readily forthcoming. Although selective debt relief measures have been taken (e.g., see section on "Debt Forgiveness"), there is no agreed-upon measure that all donors have agreed to take except on a voluntary, case-by-case basis. The debt situation requires a mechanism to deal with serious contingencies without significantly undermining the integrity of the debtor-creditor relationship.(6) The search for solutions also should seek to avoid recurring debt problems. But whichever strategies are devised, according to Arthur Burns, former Federal Reserve chairman, "there is a clear need for a strong effort involving all major parties of interest."(7)

Determinants of Strategy

The "clear need for a strong effort involving all... parties" is impeded by a number of factors which affect the acceptability of proposed debt relief strategies. These include the stakes of the parties involved, the debt philosophies of the actors, and the categories of debt problems.

Debt at the Stake

The adage of "where you stand depends on where you sit" aptly applies to the participants in the debt problem-solving task, and their proposals reflect their interests. Hence, the stakes of the private commercial banks, the creditor governments, the developing countries, and the Organization of Petroleum Exporting Countries (OPEC) must be considered.

The banks. More than half of the $160 billion owed by developing countries, excluding the poorest, is due for repayment within the next two years - and most of it is owed to private banks.(8) Moreover, banks are faced with financing as much as two-thirds of the international payments imbalance expected over the next few years.(9) The banks' dilemma is that without long-term prospects for improvement of the world economy, prudence dictates increasing reluctance to loan. But without additional loans to finance the already heavily borrowed countries, banks face defaulting customers and no more hard cash flowing in. As The Economist has stated, "Banks, it seems, are at the mercy of their borrowers' willingness to repay as much as borrowers are at the mercy of banks to lend more."(10)

Thus, the banks' overriding concerns are the stability of the international financial system, assurance that the borrowing less developed countries (LDCs) will earn enough foreign exchange each year to meet loan repayments, and assurance that there will be continued safe opportunities to lend. Moreover, they are concerned that governments and official international financing institutions take on the more risky financing operations that banks otherwise would be competitively driven to support.

Creditor governments. Creditor governments have economic and political stakes in the debt issue, and the United States is particularly involved since two-thirds of private LDC loans are from United States institutions. These stakes include trade and investment flows supported by the international financial system; military and security interests which may be jeopardized by economic crisis in a developing country (e.g., Turkey); and the political support of friendly developing countries which could be undermined if economies and hence governments were to collapse from the weight of financial difficulties. Further, if debt problems escalate, industrial creditor countries may face more insistent developing country demands for increased official development assistance, commodity agreements, and trade concessions.

Developing countries. Developing countries are concerned that financing for their economic development programs will continue to be available. The poorer developing countries desire increased resource transfers on a grant or highly concessional basis. Middle- and higher-income countries, on the other hand, look to private sources of financing, easier access to capital markets, and maintenance of creditworthiness standings.

Opec. The oil-exporting surplus countries have a stake in the soundness of the international financial system in order to protect their investments. These countries have used the banks and economically strong industrial countries as buffers against the risks of recycling their surplus oil funds. Hence, stable currency values and a secure banking system are necessary to protect their assets in real terms.

The Philosophies of Debt

Proposals for debt relief also hinge on the philosophies of debt held by the actors involved. Developing countries believe that recent debt-servicing difficulties have been caused by external factors beyond their control, specifically, declining export earnings, increased import costs, inadequate balance-of-payments support facilities, stagnating flows of official development assistance, insufficient access to capital markets, and therefore an unusually heavy burden on foreign exchange resources.(11) Thus, developing countries' official position is that debt relief is a common problem requiring a common, generalized soultion. And because these problems are signs of failure and maladjustment of the international economic system, they should be resolved by reform of the system itself - hence, the "new international economic order." Moreover, debt relief is considered a legitimate form of balance-of-payments assistance and a means to increase untied, quickly disbursable resource transfers. Finally, debt relief should be considered within the framework of development objectives and plans and should be provided automatically at an early stage of emerging difficulties.

Industrial creditor countries, on the other hand, hold very different debt relief philosophies. They see the debt issue as not being amenable to any aggregated general approach. There is no general debt problem, but rather a diversity of situations. Hence, a case-by-case consideration of acute debt situations and relief eligibility is appropriate. Finally, and most important, developing countries have the major responsibility for avoiding debt difficulties and for maximizing efficient use of resource transfers. Increased focus on internal changes within the LDCs, such as balance of payments and exchange rate management, export promotion, project selection, and debt management is necessary.(12)

Categories of Debt

A third factor influencing the character of debt relief

proposals is the categories of countries with debt problems and the types of debt difficulties experienced. Some observers divide the problem in two: Mahbub ul Haq, director of the Policy Planning and Program Review Department of the World Bank, has said, "The problems of the poorest and middle-income countries should be separated. Definitely. There has been confusion up till now because they've not been separated, and it's obvious that they have very different problems."(13)

Others(14) break down the developing country debt problem into three categories: 1) the poorest countries with chronic debt problems such as India, Pakistan, Bangladesh, most of which have already been involved in official debt rescheduling agreements and which will countinue to depend on multilateral debt relief in the future; 2) countries dependent on one or two raw materials exports (usually minerals), such as Chile or Zambia, which are subject to highly fluctuating international prices and the economic activity in the industrial countries; and 3) countries which have borrowed aggressively to support rapid growth, e.g., Brazil, South Korea, but have demonstrated economic management capacities and enjoyed good credit ratings despite apparently precarious levels of debt. The latter are the higher-income, semi-industrial countries facing inflation, balance-of-payments deficits, and heavy debt service burdens.

In summary, these three major factors - the stakes of the major actors, their philosophies on debt relief, and the categories of debt problems - largely determine the positions taken on debt relief and provide the foundation for debt relief proposals.

II. ALTERNATIVE PROPOSALS FOR DEBT RELIEF

The Status Quo Approach

The status quo approach to debt relief is characterized by three views: a) the perception of LDC debt as a non-problem, b) the tenet of "more is better," and c) the study-it-more philosophy.

Debt as a Nonproblem

The view has been advanced that the debt of developing countries is not a problem. Rather, debt difficulties, should they arise, are really short- to medium-term balance-of-payments problems that require infusions of additional external resources. The real issues, then, are maintenance of aggregate demand, assurance of adequate financing for adjustment, and development assistance flows to the poorest countries. Hence, individual debt problems should be manageable, particularly with reasonable industrial country growth and available private and public financing. The international financial system should be able to cope with individual problems as they occur.

According to the United States Treasury Department, statistics on the rapid accumulation of developing country debt can be misleading, and major borrowing developing countries are doing better than the figures might indicate for three reasons:

First, inflation has greatly reduced the real value of debt previously incurred. According to one study, the total present value of debt outstanding at the end of 1972 was reduced by nearly 40 percent by inflation during the 1973-76 period.(15) Inflationary debt relief in 1973 outweighed the new debt outstanding in that year.

With regard to commercial debt, the World Bank has calculated that the growth rate of debt owed to private banks in the period 1973-76 was lower in constant prices than in preceding years.(16) Ultimately, it has been argued, inflation will have reduced the present value of debt service payments between 1973-82 far more than the total forgiveness of interest payments would have done over the same period.(17)

Second, the expansion of developing country export growth has increased these countries' capacities to service debt. The United States Treasury Department reports that outstanding medium- and long-term debt doubled between 1973 and 1977 - but so did exports. As a consequence, the ratios of debt service payments to exports in 1977 were roughly the same as in 1973.(18) Department of State Under Secretary for Economic Affairs Richard N. Cooper testified before a Senate subcommittee that merchandise exports of nonoil developing countries in 1973-76 increased about 70 percent in nominal terms compared to a 75 percent increase in their debt service.(19)

Third, many developing countries have borrowed to build up their international reserve assets. In 1976 nearly $11 billion of LDC external borrowing was used to increase reserves to $41 billion, a 25 percent increase over 1975 levels. In 1977 another $8-10 billion of borrowing was used to increase reserves.(20)

Finally, the concentration of debt reduces the magnitude of what is termed an LDC debt problem. High debt growth rates have been limited to a few upper-income countries which, in general, have the greatest capacities to service debts.

The conclusion drawn by some analysts from these facts is that alarmist cries about future debt difficulties are unwarranted - and, indeed, that developing country debt is a nonproblem.

The More-Is-Better Strategy

The more-is-better approach or "continuation of the same" policy is a strategy that follows from the debt-is-not-a-problem tenet. Therefore, no special debt actions need to be taken other than to tighten current policies for continuation along the same road. Hence, heavily borrowed developing countries will have to diligently pursue economic stabilization policies, and those with weak external positions and "loose financial policies" will have to practice fiscal and monetary restraint. Private institutions must do their part by adhering to high standards of creditworthiness and following dictates of prudence. Thus will the process of deficits, recycling, borrowing, and debt rescheduling continue into the future. As United States Treasury Secretary W. Michael Blumenthal explains, "The viability of the international system is premised on the assumption that all the players stay in the game: that banks continue lending and borrowers keep repaying interest, so that although principal may be rolled over for individual borrowers, the money continues to circulate." The biggest threat to the system is that one of the players may opt out of the game.(21) Hence, the more-is-better approach is not only the best strategy for debt relief, it is the _only_ strategy that will maintain the viability of the international financial system.

The Debt Study Concept

In order to "continue with the same," advocates suggest that it is necessary to thoroughly study the debt issue with the intent of finding means to avoid serious debt-servicing difficulties. Largely at the behest and support of the United States, the IMF/World Bank Development Committee - formally the Joint Ministerial Committee of the IMF/IBRD on the Transfer of Real Resources to the Developing Countries - decided to study the role of external borrowing in financing development. The committee's study will include:(22)

- A review of recent developing country experiences;
- An analysis of LDC policies that resulted in difficulties in debt service or reschedulings;
- An effort to identify and redress debt management problems before they reach crisis proportions;
- An examination of sources of external finance; and
- A review of the role of the multilateral development lending institutions in helping to promote more effective debt management and in lending technical assistance.

In sum, the status quo approach to debt relief rests on the premise that debt per se is not a problem, but rather difficulties arise from short- and medium-term balance-of-payments disequilibria. Hence, the system does not require alteration nor are special and general debt relief proposals necessary, for current methods of handling balance-of-payments difficulties are sufficient. However, to enhance efficiency and avoid unnecessary problems, complete understanding and, therefore, study of developing country external borrowing are required.

Preventive Measures

Three measures for preventing debt difficulties or their recurrence have beeen proposed that would involve the developing countries, creditor governments, and private banks. These are: 1) integration of external borrowing with LDC development plans, 2) increased data and information flows, and 3) tighter bank regulation and surveillance.

Development Planning

In 1964 at the first meeting of the United Nations Conference on Trade and Development, the first Secretary General, Raul Prebisch, sounded an alarm on the growing burdens of developing countries' external debt. Ideally there should be no debt problems, and to this end he advocated planning for avoidance. He proposed that external financing - borrowing, development assistance, and foreign investment - be an integral part of a country's development planning. External resources must be geared to a country's economic plan requirements, and likewise, debt composition, type, repayment, etc., must respond to the needs and conditions of each country. Outside resources should be committed in principle for the duration of the economic plan, and disbursement should be subject to fulfillment of basic conditions of the plan. If debt rescheduling is required, it similarly should not be divorced from a country's economic development policy. It must be "part and parcel" of a development program which makes provision for using the resources released by the lightening of the service burden as a result of debt adjustments.(23)

Since Prebisch's warning on debt-servicing burdens, the UNCTAD Ad Hoc Group of Governmental Experts and the Group of 19 developing countries in the Conference on International Economic Cooperation (CIEC) recommended in 1975 and 1976, respectively, that debt and servicing difficulties be treated in ways consistent with countries' development process and objectives.(24)

Information Flows

According to the United States Treasury Department,

"there is no single comprehensive source of data concerning debt, and the various sources that do exist are not easily reconcilable."(25) A Senate subcommittee staff report states that the tentative nature of the data concerning international debt and private bank lending overseas can not be emphasized too strongly - even data from official institutions. Much of the data is fairly speculative, although global trends, the relative distribution of debts and credits among participants in the financial markets, and officially extended credits can be assessed with some degree of accuracy. Yet despite considerable efforts to upgrade data collection in the last two years, "the true magnitude of debt and international lending by private banks remains a mystery....The art still is in a very primitive state."(26)

The problem stems from the inadequancy of available sources, the lack of government access to bank data, and the absence of international bank reporting requirements to the International Monetary Fund.

There are three primary sources of debt and lending data. First are the official institutional systems of a) the World Bank/IMF Debtor Reporting System (DRS); b) the Organization for Economic Cooperation and Developments (OECD), information system which augments the DRS and reviews net aid flows from the Development Assistance Committee country members; and c) the Bank for International Settlements (BIS) which monitors the international activities of banks of the Group of Ten countries plus Switzerland. All three official institutional sources - the World Bank/IMF, OECD, and BIS- differ in country coverage, types of debt, definition and concepts, and statistical aggregation.(27)

The second source of debt data is bank reporting to regulatory agencies which until recent efforts (see below) has been very inadequate. The third information source is "tombstones," or newspaper placements by the borrower or lender to announce that credits have been extended.

Among others, Arthur Burns, former chairman of the Federal Reserve System, has urged concerted and coordinated improvements in the information flow systems of debt and lending. He argues that "imperfect or incomplete information makes for inefficient markets and heightens the risk of disruptive discontinuities."(28) Hence, improved information flows are necessary for banks' analyses of creditworthiness and for official regulation of international banking activity.

Three approaches currently are being taken to improve the information gap. First, the United States bank regulatory agencies (the Federal Reserve System, the Comptroller of the Currency, and the Federal Deposit Insurance Corporation) are requiring more detailed information from banks in reports and are conducting specific surveys on the quality of United States bank lending. Second, the Bank for International Settlements is compiling and coordinating banking data supplied by central banks. The information will be made available to private lenders in order to improve risk analysis. Third, developing countries and banks are being encouraged by regulatory officials to exchange essential information. In the long run, say officials, banks will have better loans and countries will have better access to credit.

Regulation and Surveillance

Arthur Burns has asserted that the present bank regulatory system fosters "competition in laxity." To tighten regulation of United States bank lending to foreign governments, the United States Comptroller of the Currency announced in 1977 a formal interpretation of an existing law which restricts a national bank's lending to 10 percent of its total capital to a foreign government borrower. Until now banks have applied the 10 percent rule separately to central governments and government-controlled agencies and entities, even though the ultimate responsibility for the separate debts falls on the foreign central government. The proposed interpretation states that the 10 percent limitation would apply to the collective government entities unless a "means and purpose test" determines that a) the borrower has independent resources and income to pay back the loan, and b) loan proceeds would be used for the purpose for which it was borrowed.

In addition to tightened bank regulation, proposals also have been made for national and international bank surveillance mechanisms. The Federal Reserve System's Committee on Foreign Lending is considering treatment of country risk in bank examinations and has conducted informal surveys of methods used by major United States banks to define, monitor, and analyze country exposure. The New York Federal Reserve announced in May 1978 that federal bank regulators have agreed on an outline of a new supervisory approach to foreign lending. The plan is intended to identify large concentrations of foreign lending and to improve banks' internal procedures for monitoring and controlling their international loan exposure.(29) Finally, the United States Comptroller has formed a committee to study the feasibility of establishing a single supervisory unit located in Washington, D.C., to oversee federally chartered multinational banks.(30)

Another supervisory approach advocates International Monetary Fund surveillance of commercial bank loans to developing countries in order to prevent overexposure. Although not directed to banks, the Fund's supervisory powers increased in April 1978 when its Second Amendment to the Articles of Agreement entered into force. The Fund now is empowered to take the initiative in determining whether countries are complying with formally prescribed obligations to foster orderly economic growth and price stability.

Stop-Gap Arrangements

One prescription for curing the debt illness of developing countries is to increase the flows of official assistance for balance-of-payments financing and development programs. Senetor Frank Church has referred to this method of relief as "various stop-gap, finger-in-the-dike measures."(31) While these actions have helped to mitigate the financing problems of deficit countries, they have provided - relative to the magnitude of the problem - only a modest increment to previously available official sources of financing.(32) Following is a brief review of such financing actions and proposals to date.

Bilateral Flows

Official Development Assistance (ODA) flows to the developing countries from members of the Development Assistance Committee (DAC) of the OECD have been on an upward trend in nominal terms, although collectively the donor countries have not yet met the United Nations target of 0.7 percent of their GNPs. (United States ODA as a share of GNP fell from 0.25 percent in 1976 - ($4.84 billion - to 0.22 percent in 1977.) Official Development Assistance rose from $13.7 billion in 1976 to $14.7 billion in 1977, an 8 percent increase in dollar terms, but in real terms the increase was marginal. At the conclusion of the Conference on International Economic Cooperation (CIEC) Ministerial in June 1977, industrial countries agreed to establish a $1 billion Special Action Program for the poorest countries for which the United States share would be $375 million.

The World Bank Group

The World Bank Group - consisting of the International Bank for Reconstruction and Development (IBRD), the International Development Association (IDA), and the International Finance Corporation (IFC) - committed $8.75 billion for economic development assistance in fiscal year 1978, a $1.47 billion increase over the fiscal year 1977 level. Capital resources were expanded for all three institutions in 1977:

IBRD - World Bank governors approved a selective capital increase of $8.4 billion and World Bank President McNamara is urging agreement on a general capital increase in 1979.

IDA - The fifth replenishment of IDA, the World Bank's soft loan window, was negotiated for $7.6 billion to cover the three fiscal years 1978-80.

<u>IFC</u> - Approval was given for a $540 million increase in the corporation's capital structure with the expectation that "it ill play an increasingly catalytic role in stimulating investment" in developing countries.

International Monetary Fund

International Monetary Fund regular tranche and special facility resources also have been expanded, and new temporary facilities have been added.

<u>SDRs</u>. The interim committee of the IMF decided in September 1978 to issue a total of 12 billion special drawing rights (SDRs) - about $15 billion - over a three-year period, beginning spring of 1979.

<u>Quotas</u>. IMF quotas, which determine the amount of a members entitlement to borrow, were increased by 33.6 percent to SDR 39 billion under the sixth review of quotas which became effective in April 1978. A seventh quota increase of SDR 20 billion, or 50 percent, will raise quotas to SDR 59 billion, or about $73 billion.

<u>Compensatory financing facility (CFF)</u>. Access to the CFF, which provides balance-of-payments assistance for export shortfalls over a medium-term trend, was liberalized in December 1975. In the following year, 1976, facility drawings reached unprecedented levels - SDR 2.55 billion, or twice the amount drawn in the first 13 years of the facility.

<u>Oil facility</u>. A temporary oil facility was established in June 1974 to meet member countries' emergency balance-of-payments needs caused by oil price increases. Net drawings through the last purchase in June 1976 totaled SDR 6.4 billion.

<u>Subsidy account</u>. To help the poorer 18 IMF member countries meet interest payments on oil facility drawings, a subsidy fund totaling $195 million was established by voluntary contributions from industrial nations and major oil producers. The subsidy account effectively reduces the interest rate from 7.7 percent to 2.7 percent. A total of $78 million in disbursements from the account has been distributed as of June 1978.

<u>Trust fund</u>. The IMF established a trust fund in May 1976 to provide balance-of-payments assistance on concessionary terms to 61 low-income developing country members. The trust fund is financed primarily from the profits of IMF gold sales, and as of August 1978 profits distributed through the fund to developing member countries amounted to $362.6 mil-

lion. Four trust fund loan disbursements have been made as of June 1978 totaling SDR 841 million.

Supplementary financing facility. In August 1977, thirteen IMF member countries and the Swiss National Bank pledged SDR 8.6 billion, or about US$10 billion, for a supplementary financing facility, commonly referred to as the "Witteveen Facility." The new temporary lending pool will allow the IMF to expand its financial assistance to members facing serious balance-of-payments difficulties. Activation of the facility was pending United States Congressional approval of United States participation in the new fund, and in October 1978, Congress approved a $1.8 billion United States contribution, or 17 percent of the total, to the Witteveen facility.

In summary, balance-of-payments difficulties and the consequent increased borrowing by developing countries to finance their deficits have led to a massive build-up of debt. The major prescription thus far for alleviating the possible debt pains arising from servicing difficulties has been to enlarge the available official source funding. To date, this approach has worked, but as Raul Prebisch warned in 1964, "Meeting pressing obligations by assuming others which soon will become equally pressing, postpones the hour of reckoning, but is not a solution."(33)

International Debt Guidelines

Developing countries have proposed that the entire system of debt renegotiations be overhauled to allow for "adequate, equitable, consistent, and broadly comparable" treatment of countries seeking debt relief. They believe that departures from the "traditional orthodoxies" of handling developing country debt problems are essential to cope with the new trends and magnitudes of debt and to ensure continued momentum of these countries' economic growth. To this end, international rules and procedures should be established for all stages of debt reorganization including early initiation of action by the debtor country, principles governing the analysis of the country's economic situation taking into account its needs, and rules to protect the country against measures which would be inconsistent with its socioeconomic structures and development strategy.(34)

Progress on establishment of guiding principles for debt renegotiation as outlined by the developing countries has not advanced significantly. However, central principles which would serve as a basis for agreement on guidelines have been recommended, namely the five "common elements"; these elements are: a) consideration of debtors' development prospects, b) expeditious reorganization in a multilateral framework, c) nondiscrimination among creditors, d) debt relief terms in conformity with LDC debt service capacities and legitimate creditor interest, and e) flexible reorganizational arrangements, - identified by the UNCTAD Ad Hoc Group of Governmental Experts on Debt Problems of Developing Countries in 1975 and the "common norms" - initiation procedures, the debt reorganization framework, and institutional aspects, -discussed by the Intergovernmental Group of Experts in 1977. This issue of guidelines has been addressed at UNCTAD IV in 1976, at the Conference on International Economic Cooperation in 1977, and at the UNCTAD Trade and Development Board Ministerial in 1978. These efforts failed to establish machinery to convene, organize, and supervise debt reorganization according to internationally agreed principles. The UNCTAD V meeting in Manila will take up the problem again in May 1979.

New Mechanisms and Old Debt

Several new mechanisms dealing with both official and commercial debt reorganization have been proposed that would maintain the responsibilities of the borrowing developing countries to meet contractual obligations, yet would ease the weight of debt burdens caused by "bunching" of repayments. The following debt relief proposals, although in some cases vague and in formative stages, meet this qualification.

Anticipatory Rescheduling

One proposal would institute an anticipatory rescheduling mechanism for official bilateral debt.(35) The instrument would be geared to countries expecting a bunching of debt servicing payments in the 1978-82 period, e.g., those having a projected debt-service ratio exceeding, say, 22 percent. The mechanism would be financed by developed countries, and its use would be at the option of the debtor developing country after basic eligibility guidelines are met. However, in order that rescheduling does not become an aid exercise, the present value of the remaining loan balances would be preserved at the levels existing at the time of rescheduling. Hence, while servicing payments would be stretched out, interest rates would be hardened and higher payments would be made in the mid- and late-1980s. Reschedulings could be administered by OECD donor governments and/or the Paris Club. Participation would be determined by the creditor's share of the borrowing country's public debt portfolio.

Advanced rescheduling transactions prior to reaching an acute debt crisis stage are said to be justifiable because as a rule, public debt rescheduling is favored by private and multilateral institutions as it relieves foreign exchange pressures that might preclude servicing the debt owed to them. Also, rescheduling usually is accompanied by debtor country policy changes designed to improve the economy's liquidity position without sacrificing medium-term growth or harming access to capital markets.

Refinancing Facilities

Several mechanisms have been proposed that would refinance developing countries' commercial debt. The Manila Declaration of February 1976 advocated refinancing short-term commercial debt through an International Bank for Debt Redemption (IBDR) which possibly could operate under the auspices of the World Bank. The governments of the creditors would fund the facility, or guarantee or buy its bonds, in proportion to the total LDC debt to their creditors. The debtor country would use the IBDR to make payments to the private creditor, would pay interest to the IBDR, and would repay the principal to the IBDR over a period of perhaps 15 years.

An IMF discount window or "pseudo-secondary market" for LDC debts also has been proposed. Under this plan, the IMF would stand ready to purchase the commercial debt paper of developing countries that face imminent default but which also meet certain eligibility criteria (e.g., projected debt service ability, terms-of-trade developments, foreign exchange reserve holdings, etc.). Commercial debt paper would be purchased at a negotiated discount within a specified time limit from maturity, e.g., one year. Debt repayment then would be negotiated with the developing country for a longer maturity, for example, 10-15 years, and at a lower rate of interest.(36)

A variation of the preceding proposal would anticipate bunching of debt repayments, and would allow countries to retire private bank loans in favor of longer-term maturities, say 15-20 years. To discourage borrowing from the facility rather than private markets, loan interest rates would be fairly hard, possibly tied to Eurocurrency market rates. The facility's capital would be financed largely by OPEC and could be administered by the World Bank.(37)

Such refinancing schemes, according to their authors, would forestall liquidity crises by their anticipatory character of spreading bunched payments. In addition, their existence as a "lender of last resort" would infuse confidence and stability into the international financial system and psychologically may prevent a crisis situation.

Long-Term Private Fund

A banker from the Grindlays Bank Group in London has counseled concern about the maturity structure of commercial debt at the end of this decade.(38) Because commercial banks may be reluctant to continue their larger-than-usual role in financing developing countries balance-of-payments deficits and because official institutions are unlikely and unable to supply an appreciable increase in long-term funds, he queries, "Why not [tap] the non-bank private investor?" There is historic precedent for this strategy, for example, he believes when the British in the nineteenth century provided certain countries with almost all their external funds, and by 1914 held 4 billion pounds in foreign government bonds. Today with the enormous increase in knowledge about developing countries, debt relief through restructuring could be obtained by encouraging some method of tapping long-term resources from, say pension funds and insurance companies. A concerted effort should be undertaken to reactivate the private capital market and to convince today's private or nonbank institutional investor that risks are not significantly greater but that rewards can be.

Advantages would be universal. For developing countries, bunching would be ironed out, cash flow management would be easier, future borrowing requirements for meeting debt amortization would decrease, and in times of economic stress, a country's defenses will be strengthened by having longer maturities. For commercial banks, long-term private sources would represent a complementary source of funding, not a substitute, and strains on the commercial banking system would be lightened.

Public-Private Safety Net

For middle-income countries whose short- to medium-term borrowing structures are heavily commercial, Mahbub ul Haq has proposed a public-private safety net for which the leading bank lenders would arrange with the banks and governments of the middle-income countries the establishment of a $5-10 billion safety net. The middle-income countries have become semi-industrialized, and their concern is having continued access to capital markets. Yet short-term liquidity crises can occur from time to time, and in case of need "there would be a safety net to catch them. They won't fall on the ground."(30)

Loan Guarantees

In a recent version on loan guarantees (variations of which have been considered by the World Bank and other institutions for a number of years), the governor of the Bank of Greece, Xenophon Zolatas, proposed at the Annual Meetings of the International Monetary Fund/World Bank in September 1977 that oil-producing countries and industrial nations join together to establish an international institution to guarantee private, international development loans. The organization would assure that loans were being made for productive purposes and would cooperate with the IMF.(40) Such an insurance agency could secure and enlarge the flow of development funds from the private capital markets into developing countries, and in the process would open the commercial credit window to many low-income countries which currently do not have access.(41) Zolatas proposes two alternative approaches and suggests central principles applicable to both schemes. The first approach would have an existing international agency, such as the World Bank, operate the insurance fund with industrialized countries acting as guarantors. The second approach would call for private international financial institutions to act as guarantors by voluntarily assuming a share of the total risk associate with the international insurance fund. Either form of the insurance scheme would require improved information to lenders, operations by sound banking principles, partial guarantees and callable funds, and an income-generating plan to build reserves.(42) Loans to developing countries would be covered up to 90 percent, and the borrowing country would pay the charge that would have been levied in the absence of a guarantee. Defaults would be declared only after mandatory consultation among the insurance fund, the private lending institutions, and the borrower.

Adjustment, Forgiveness, and Transfers

A number of proposals have been offered that would alter and rewrite the current terms of developing country debt, would forgive debt owed, or would infuse new net resources to alleviate debt burdens. The following reviews these strategies.

Retroactive Adjustment

In January 1978, the Secretary General of UNCTAD, Gamani Corea, asked for consideration of a retroactive adjustment scheme for the poorer countries that would rewrite the terms of 15-year-old loans to match the terms of concessional loans given today. Debt service payments of these loans reflect the terms of assistance prevailing when the world economic outlook was more encouraging, reasons Corea, and the grant element of today's loans have increased.

At the UNCTAD Trade and Development Board Ministerial in March 1978, developed country donors agreed to "seek to adopt measures for adjustment of terms or other equivalent measures as a means of improving net flows of development assistance."(43) This adjustment of terms of past bilateral assistance - referred to as "ex post terms correction," or EPTC - will be at the discretion and direction of the creditors;

that is, means, conditions, and choice of debtor countries will remain the prerogative of the donors.

Debt Forgiveness

As part of the above plan, Gamani Corea also proposed that the richer nations convert the loans of the poorest 29 countries - which have outstanding official debts of less than $7 billion - to grants. This action combined with the above grant element increases would save the poorer countries $600 million per year over the next five years. Thus far (October 1978), seven countries - Canada, Japan, the Netherlands, Sweden, Switzerland, the United Kingdom, and West Germany - have acted to cancel debts of the poorest countries.

In May 1976 an elaborate scheme which combines elements of grant conversion and refinancing was proposed.(44) The strategy would forgive official long-term government claims on the basis of countries' per capita income levels, specifically by 75 percent, 50 percent, and 25 percent for low-, medium-, and high-income countries respectively. This debt forgiveness would be accompanied by refinancing suppliers' credits and private commercial loans on softer terms.

Finally, the International Development and Food Assistance Act of 1978 authorizes the United States president, on a case-by-case basis, to permit the least developed countries to pay both interest and principal due on past foreign assistance loans into local currency accounts to be used for development activities in the particular country. In addition, the president may waive interest payments due on past loans if he determines that the country would be unable to use all of the local currency authority.

Resource Transfers

Although a great deal of emphasis for debt relief has been directed to the poorest developing countries, it should not be concluded that the middle-income countries will not be having debt servicing problems in the future. The middle-income countries have concluded that they do not want debt relief. Rather, their concerns are for a) easier, assured, and continued access to the international capital markets, and b) assured rollovers of their short-term debts as they fall due. Therefore, new institutional means are being called for that would assure increased access to capital markets by the middle-income countries. This task has been addressed by the Working Group on Access to Capital Markets of the IMF/IBRD Development Committee in the last year and a half.

For both the poorer and middle-income developing countries, it has been proposed that large-scale resource transfers - a Marshall Plan-type of assistance effort - be made available to rectify the underlying cause of debt servicing difficulties - the problem of underdevelopment. This Marshall Plan program, believe its proponents, should be viewed as a new frontier of growth much as Europe and Japan after World War II were seen as frontiers of growth and objects of massive assistance.(45)

In summary, one category of debt relief involves a large transfer of resources and may take varying forms depending on the debt situations of various groups of countries. Whether this transfer is in the form of debt adjustment and forgiveness for the poorest, access to capital markets for the middle-income, or massive infusions of capital to alter underlying economic structures, the message is clear: developing country debt problems require more doses of resources than the incremental ad hoc transfers that have caused the debt to build but have not allowed for repayment capabilities. Repayment capabilities require larger and easier capital infusions.

New Roles for the IMF

Many equated the collapse of Bretton Woods in the early 1970s with the demise and death of the International Monetary Fund. In retrospect, the obituary was premature. Recently bankers and governments alike have come to rally around the Fund, thrusting on it a mandate to rescue the world monetary system - and developing country debt problems at the same time. The IMF already takes part in debt reschedulings and refinancing through technical expertise, its granting "certificates of good standing" to LDC economies, and its supplying funds for balance-of-payments financing. Although the IMF has provided only about 6 percent of the aggregate payments deficit financing in the three years since oil prices increased, the psychological, political, and economic consequences of its actions are far greater than a 6 percent figure might indicate. Hence, new IMF roles and greater IMF-private bank cooperation have been proposed.

New IMF Roles

One banker has commented that, rather than establish a new system of safety nets or a financing agency, it would be preferable to enlarge the role of the IMF.(46) Arthur Burns, United States Treasury Secretary W. Michael Blumenthal and Chase Manhattan Chairman David Rockefeller all agree that a) IMF lending should be increased, b) stringent conditions on IMF loans to ensure future creditworthiness should continue, and c) IMF lending should be more closely coordinated with the lending activities of private banks.(47)

Charles Ganoe of the Fidelity Bank in Philadelphia also

has proposed that consideration be given to such ideas as a reserve subtraction account to strengthen the role of SDRs, new rules to promote coordination of domestic economic policies, and the interposition of the IMF as an additional intermediary between private capital markets and sovereign borrowers.(48) In addition, the IMF could issue its own bonds and notes and relend the proceeds to developing countries. Of even greater benefit, believes Ganoe, would be the expansion and broadening of the IMF to make it a central bank of the world. Mahbub ul Haq of the World Bank supports this idea. "In order to provide short-term credit to meet the genuine needs of all parts of the world, it is absolutely necessary to agree on the concept of an International Central Bank."(49)

IMF-Bank Cooperation

Increasingly banks and bank regulators have called for forms of greater cooperation with the IMF on either a formal or informal basis. The areas of cooperation have focused mainly on information flows and joint IMF-bank financing. The intent is that banks would be better able to analyze the creditworthiness of a borrowing country, would be more assured of the country taking economic stabilization actions, and would share the lending risk in the case of cofinancing. Views of such a cooperative IMF-bank relationship are mixed and mainly favor increased informal links as opposed to new formal arrangements.

In May 1977 Treasury Secretary Blumenthal proposed more formal IMF-bank links in dealing with debtor countries.(50) For Blumenthal, IMF-bank cooperation would include IMF provision of staff reports and economic assessments to private lenders (the reports are now confidential), IMF participation in developing policy conditions for loans, and participation in cofinancing packages.

Most bankers - as well as the IMF - are cool to having formal bank links with the IMF, and in some opinions, the scope for IMF-bank cooperation is exaggerated. Dr. Friedman of Citibank and James R. Greene, President of American Express International Banking Corporation, both assert that commercial banks can not allow the IMF to determine their lending strategies. Nor, they believe, can the IMF appear as a debt collection agency for the banks.

However, Arthur Burns and Henry Wallich believe that IMF reports could be made available to banks in a "suitably sanitized form." Burns does not suggest that texts of the Fund's country evaluations be handed around private banking circles, but some sharing of information within the limits imposed by confidentiality could be arranged. On the other hand, Rimmer de Vries of Morgan Guaranty Trust believes that "banks would not give out confidential information on its customers and there isn't any reason why the Fund should do so either."(51)

Several problems could arise from closer IMF-bank cooperation. First, the Fund worries about being held responsible for bad loans made by banks. Second, to what extent and with which banks would cooperation occur? The Fund could be charged with favoritism of American banks. Third, the breaching of confidentiality could make countries less forthcoming with the Fund, and the IMF staff might be less candid in their reporting, thus adversely affecting IMF data and analysis. Finally, the IMF would be less apolitical and would appear to be in the creditors' corner "against" the debtor developing countries. Thus, the IMF executive directors have not been keen on the idea of increased cooperation, and the matter has been all but dropped.

Despite the array of proposals, it appears that the International Monetary Fund will continue to carry out its mandate as overseer of the world's monetary system and will not take on new functions and linkages with private banks. Its only debt relief activities would be direct through technical assistance in official debt relief negotations, and indirect through increased balance of payments financing capabilities via the Witteveen Facility, increased SDRs, and expanded quotas.

CONCLUSION

Having reviewed the range of debt relief proposals, several comments and observations come to mind.

First, no one debt solution or mechanism for providing developing countries relief from their growing debt burdens will be adequate to the task. The Third World is not monolithic; nor therefore should there be a monolithic cure for debt problems. One "giant negotiation" will not work. As one Third Worlder said, "There is no single prescription for the debt problem. If one were offered, it would be sold."(52)

Second, debt relief is dependent on more than a package of new proposals, specific actions, and unique mechanisms. There is more to the solution of debt relief than having Third World countries "get their houses in order" by appropriate debt management, economic development policies, and productive investment plans. The heart of debt solutions lies in the "underlying structures" of developing countries and the international economic system. In the last analysis, debt relief solutions are dependent on the general health of the international economy, the pace of industrial country economic growth, the openness of economies to trade without barriers and protectionism, and the avoidance of sudden and extreme oil price rises.

Third, in seeking solutions and proposals for debt relief, little has been said on the role and participation of the developing countries in shaping the relief strategies (other than official positions). By and large, the Third World has been treated as a passive bystander waiting for something to be done for their countries and for their debt. More should be said on cooperation among themselves to tackle the problems. Possibilities have been suggested(53) for self-help opportunities including national foreign loan guarantee schemes, local institutions for supplying assistance and market trend information, and joint efforts among small groups of LDCs having comparable needs for information and easier capital market access. Shared systems to provide information and collect and distribute data on events, market trends, lenders and borrowers would be useful. And institutions modeled on a merchant bank or consortium bank could serve several countries. Perhaps the UNCTAD Committee on Economic Cooperation Among Developing Countries can focus on the debt aspect of cooperation in finding self-help methods for easing debt difficulties.

Fourth, it appears that the banks also have been on the sidelines waiting in the wings for governments to negotiate solutions, provide information and better data systems, supply increased resource transfers, and enforce conditionality and economic austerity measures. Perhaps this coat-tail riding is not so necessary and banks should begin to seek solutions acceptable to their interests and the needs of borrowing countries without being undergirded by government relief solutions.

Fifth, little mention in the above debt relief proposals is made of the role of OPEC and the potentials for direct and participating debt relief actions. Their continued reliance on industrial country capital markets for safe investing and indirect recycling of petrodollars to the poorer nations appears to be taken for granted. Surely their responsibilities for increased involvement in finding debt relief solutions should be emphasized and encouraged.

Sixth, it appears that the diplomatic debt "jaw-boning" goes on while the old processes of struggling with patchwork, ad hoc debt relief continues. One can question therefore whether the apparent intransigence on both sides of the North-South dialogue is only buying time and treading on thin ice until it cracks from the weight of accumulated debt; or whether this stalling is an indication that there really is not a need to find new solutions to an old problem. Perhaps there is no need if the concern is only the continued abilities of poor countries to service their debts. But if the concern is also about development progress as well as debt servicing capacities, then new efforts by the two sides should be exerted to meet the requirements for both.

Finally, with the array of debt relief proposals that have been offered by academics, bankers, and government officials, there is no lack of ideas or means to resolve the problems of debt in the Third World. What is unsettling is that both sides of the official negotiations are either unaware of the needs and possibilities or, worse yet, are not truly interested in finding solutions. However, it is apparent that any debt relief actions likely to be taken in international negotiating fora will be based as much on political concerns as on economic necessities.

In conclusion, with the exception of a few cases of debt forgiveness and the principle of retroactive adjustment, Third World debt relief decisions are not being made - but not because there is a lack of available proposals. The political will to do so must support the economic capacities for action. Nor will one solution or package of solutions be sufficient. Negotiators must look beyond the narrow confines of specific debt relief acts to the broader concerns affecting debt servicing abilities. Debt relief is a matter of both short-term and long-term structural actions. In the long-run debt relief must be viewed as a kind of pump-priming for Third World countries in order for them to function in the world economy on a self-sustaining basis. And it is up to both the industrial and developing countries to cooperate and work together to enable them to do so. Only then will all countries benefit from the fruits of the international economy.

NOTES

1. Don Shannon, "U.S. Cool to Write-Off of Debts," Washington Post, December 18, 1977, p. A-45; see also "Heavy Borrowing on International Marts Expected to Continue in '78, Analysts Say," Wall Street Journal, December 12, 1977, p. 9.
2. Morgan Guaranty Trust Company, "International Credit Markets," World Financial Markets, December 1977, p. 9.
3. "Financing the LDCs: The Role of the Euromarkets, Euromoney, November 1977, p. 79.
4. Udo E. Simonis, "Some Considerations on the External Public Debt of LDCs," Intereconomics, no. 7/8 (July/August, 1977) p. 204; see also Jerome B. Cohen, "Awash on a Sea of Debt - Bankers and LDCs," Bankers Magazine 160 (Summer 1977): 20; and Karin Lissakers, International Debt, the Banks and U. S. Foreign Policy, A staff report, Subcommittee on Foreign Economic Policy of the Committee on Foreign Relations, United States Senate (Washington, D. C.: U.S. Government Printing Office, 1977), p. 33.
5. Gordon W. Smith, The External Debt Prospects of the

Non-Oil Developing Countries, NIEO Series (Washington, D.C.: Overseas Development Council, 1977), p. 51.
6. Ibid., p. 4.
7. Arthur F. Burns "The Need for Order in International Finance" (Address before the Columbia School of Business, April 1977) in Federal Reserve Bank of Richmond 63 (July/August 1977): 14.
8. "Heimann Calls the Shots for Overseas Lending," Economist, January 14, 1978, p. 99.
9. Ann Crittenden, "Coordination Urged in World Banking," New York Times, November 17, 1977, p. 63.
10. "Heimann Calls the Shots,", p. 100.
11. International Monetary Fund, United Nations General Assembly - Thirty-Second Session ("General Assembly Resolution 32/187, Provisional Text, 'Debt Problems of Developing Countries'"), SM/78/10, 27 pp.
12. Marilyn J. Seiber, "Developing Country Debt: What Price Development?" January 10, 1977, unpublished, pp. 24-32.
13. Mahbub ul Haq, Interview, Washington, D.C., January 26, 1978.
14. Smith, External Debt, pp. 3, 33-34; see also Paul M. Watson, "Debt Problems of the Developing World" (Discussion paper for dinner seminar, Overseas Development Council, May 10, 1977, Washington, D.C., p. 5.
15. Watson, "Debt Problems," p. 4.
16. U.S. Department of the Treasury, Report on the External Debt of Developing Countries and on Debt Relief Provided by the United States, Washington, D.C., January 1978, p. 36.
17. Smith, External Debt, p. 6.
18. U.S. Department of the Treasury, Debt Report, p. 37.
19. Richard N. Cooper, "International Debt: Current Issues and Implications," Statement before the Subcommittee on International Finance of the Senate Committee on Banking, Housing and Urban Affairs, August 29, 1977 (Washington, D.C.: Department of State, 1977), p. 3.
20. U.S. Department of the Treasury, Debt Report, p. 37.
21. Lissakers, International Debt, p. 61.
22. U.S. Department of the Treasury, Debt Report, p. 47.
23. Raul Prebisch, Towards a New Trade Policy for Development, Report of the Secretary General of the United Nations Conference on Trade and Development, Sales no. 64.IIB.4 (New York: United Nations, 1964), pp. 46-47.
24. See Debt Problems of Developing Countries, Report of the Ad Hoc Group of Governmental Experts on Its Third Session, Geneva, February 25 - March 7, 1975 (New York: United Nations, 1975), 10 pp.; see also Department of State, "Proposals Submitted by the G-19 on the Problems of Indebtedness of Developing Countries of the Financial Affairs Commission," unclassified, September 16, 1976, p. 6.
25. U.S. Department of the Treasury, Debt Report, p. 16.

26. Lissakers, International Debt, pp. 27, 30.
27. U.S. Department of the Treasury, Debt Report.
28. Burns, "The Need for Order," p. 15.
29. "Control of Banks' Foreign Lending Advances in U.S." Asian Wall Street Journal, May 15, 1978, p. 2.
30. "Panel to Mull Regulating of Multinational Banks," Wall Street Journal, May 24, 1978, p. 8.
31. Lissakers, International Debt, p. vi.
32. Cohen, "Awash on a Sea," p. 21.
33. Prebisch, Towards New Trade Policy, p. 46.
34. U.S. Department of State, "Proposals Submitted by the G-19," p. 2.
35. Smith, External Debt, pp. 4, 53-55.
36. S. Stanley Katz, "A Secondary Market for LDC Debt: Alternative to Rescheduling," U.S. Department of Commerce, unpublished, February 12, 1977.
37. Smith, External Debt, pp. 4-5, 55-59.
38. Proposed by Anthony Greayer in "Financing the LDCs: The Role of the Euromarkets," Euromoney, November 1977, pp. 81, 83.
39. Haq, interview.
40. Alena Wels, "International Loan Guarantee Unit Urged," Journal of Commerce, October 11, 1977, p. 1.
41. Xenophon Zolatas, "A Proposal for a New Fund to Insure Against Euromarket Defaults," Euromoney, April 1978, p. 77.
42. Ibid., p. 81.
43. "Industrialized Countries Meet at UNCTAD, Agree to Help Relieve Poor Nations' Debt," Wall Street Journal, March 13, 1978, p. 20.
44. Proposed by Peter Kenen, cited in Smith, External Debt, pp. 45, 48.
45. U.S. House of Representatives, Hearings on International Banking Operations, Subcommittee on Financial Institutions, Supervision, Regulation, and Insurance of the Committee on Banking, Finance and Foreign Affairs, March 23, 24, April 5, 6, 1977 (Washington, D.C.: U.S. Government Printing Office, 1977), p. 217.
46. Cohen, "Awash on a Sea," pp. 21-22.
47. Lissakers, International Debt, p. 62.
48. Charles S. Ganoe, "Problem Loans to Less Developed Countries" (Speech to the 1978 Financial Conference, the Conference Board, New York, N.Y., February 15, 1978), pp. 12-13.
49. Mahbub ul Haq, The Third World and the International Economic Order, ODC Development Paper 22 (Washington, D.C.: Overseas Development Council, September 1976): 25.
50. Cited in Lissakers, International Debt, p. 64.
51. Alena Wels, "IMF-Banking Cooperation Under Fire," Journal of Commerce, June 17, 1977, p. 21.
52. Abdel Meguid, "The Conference on Technical Cooperation

Among Developing Countries" (Speech before the Washington, D.C. chapter of the Society for International Development, Washington, D.C. January 17, 1978).

53. Paul A. Wellons, Borrowing by Developing Countries in the Eurocurrency Market (Paris: OEDC, 1977), pp. 390-91.

BIBLIOGRAPHY

Books and Journals

"Bankers Feel Pressure to Keep Recycling." Business Week, January 30, 1978, pp. 24-25.

Burns, Arthur F. "The Need For Order in International Finance." Address before the Columbia School of Business, April 1977. Federal Reserve Bank of Richmond 63 (July/August 1977): 13-18.

Cohen, Jerome B. "Awash on a Sea of Debt - Banks and LDCs." Bankers Magazine 160 (Summer 1977): 19-22.

"Financing the LDCs: The Role of the Euromarket." Euromoney, November 1977, pp. 76-83.

Haq, Mahbub ul. The Third World and the International Economic Order. ODC Paper 22, Washington, D.C.: Overseas Development Council, 1976. 54 pp.

"Heimann Calls the Shots for Overseas Lending." Economist, January 14, 1978, pp. 99-100.

Hughes, Helen. "The External Debt of Developing Countries." Finance and Development 14 (December 1977): 22-25.

Morgan Guaranty Trust Company. "International Credit Markets." World Financial Markets, December 1977, pp. 3-13.

Simonis, Udo E. "Some Considerations on the External Public Debt of LDCs." Intereconomics, no. 7/8 (Summer 1977), pp. 204-07.

Smith, Gordon W. The External Debt Prospects of the Non-Oil Exporting Develping Countries. NIEO Series. Washington, D.C.: Overseas Development Council, Summer 1977. 63 pp.

Wallich, Henry C. "The Critical Information Gap." Euromoney, November 1977, p. 11.

Watson, Paul M. "Debt Problems of the Development World." Discussion paper for dinner seminar, Overseas Development Council, Washington, D.C., May 17, 1977. 12 pp.

Wellons, Paul A. Borrowing by Developing Countries in the Eurocurrency Market. Paris: OECD, 1977. 449 pp.

Zolatas, Xenophon. "A Proposal for a New Fund to Insure Against Euromarket Defaults." Euromoney, April 1978, pp. 77-83.

Newspapers and Speeches

"Bank-IMF Links Over-Exaggerate?" Journal of Commerce, November 3, 1977, p. 3.

"Control of Banks' Foreign Lending Advances in U.S." Asian Wall Street Journal, May 15, 1978, p. 2.

"Debt Service is Seen Slicing Export Income of Poorest Nations." Wall Street Journal, December 12, 1977, p. 31.

"Foreign Exposure of U.S. Banks Listed in Latest Report." Wall Street Journal, January 17, 1978, p. 8.

Ganoe, Charles S. "Problem Loans to Less Developed Countries." Speech to the 1978 Financial Conference. The Conference Board, New York, N.Y., February 15, 1977. Advanced text. 14 pp.

"IMF Clears $32 Million in Subsidy Payments to Group of 18 Nations." Wall Street Journal, June 17, 1977.

"IMF Pays $30.4 Million to Subsidize Interest on Its oil-Import Loans." Wall Street Journal, June 15, 1978, p. 32.

"Industrialized Countries Meet at UNCTAD, Agree to Relieve Poor Nations' Debt." Wall Street Journal, March 13, 1978, p. 20.

Meguid, Abdel. "The United Nations 1978 Initiative: The Conference on Technical Cooperation Among Developing Countries." Speech before the Washington, D.C. chapter of the Society for International Development, January 17, 1978.

"Panel to Mull Regulating of Multinational Banks." Wall Street Journal, May 24, 1978, p. 8.

Shannon, Don. "U.S. Cool to Write-Off Debts." Washington Post, December 18, 1977, p. A-45.

Silk, Leonard. "Witteveen Successor to Face Problems of Slump and Debt." New York Times, September 11, 1977, p. 37.

"U.N. Official Asks an Easing of Debt for Poor Countries." Wall Street Journal, January 24, 1978, p. 16.

"U.S. Banks Having Overseas Branches to Give more Data." Wall Street Journal, May 9, 1978, p. 36.

Wels, Alena. "IMF-Banking Cooperation Under Fire." Journal of Commerce, June 17, 1977, pp. 1, 21.

_______. "International Loan Guarantee Unit Urged." Journal of Commerce, October 11, 1977, pp. 1, 19.

Government and International Organizations: Documents and Publications

Bank for International Settlements. "Professor Wallich Discusses International Debt Problems. Press Review. Statement before the Subcommittee on International Finance, Committee on Banking, Housing and Urban Affairs of the Senate, August 29, 1977, pp. 3-6.

Cooper, Richard N. "International Debt: Current Issues and Implications." Statement before the Subcommittee on International Finance of the Senate Committe on Banking, Housing, and Urban Affairs, Washington, D.C., Department of State, August 29, 1977, 7 pp.

International Monetary Fund. "Debt Problems of Developing Countries." General Assembly Resolution 32/187. United Nations General Assembly, Thirty-second Session. SM/78/10, January 10, 1978. 27 pp.

_______. Press Release no. 78/60, August 4, 1978, 7 pp.

Katz, S. Stanley. "A Secondary Market for the LDC: Alternative to Rescheduling." U.S. Department of Commerce, unpublished, February 12, 1977, 5 pp.

Lissakers, Karin. International Debt, the Banks, and U.S. Foreign Policy. Staff report, Subcommittee on Foreign Economic Policy of the Senate Committee on Foreign Relations. Washington, D.C.: U.S. Government Printing Office, 1977. 68 pp.

National Advisory Council on International and Monetary Policies. International Finance. Annual Report to the President and Congress, July 1, 1975 to June 20, 1976. Washington, D.C.: U.S. Government Printing Office, January 1977. 309 pp.

Prebisch, Raul. Towards a New Trade Policy for Development. Report of the Secretary General of the United Nations Conference on Trade and Development. New York: United Nations Publication. Sales no. 64.II.B.4 1964. 125 pp.

United Nations Conference on Trade and Development. Debt Problems of Developing Countries. Report of the Ad Hoc Group of Governmental Experts in Its Third Session (Geneva, February 25 - March 7, 1975) TD/B/545. Geneva: UNCTAD, 1975. 10 pp.

U.S. Department of State. "Proposals Submitted by the G-19 on the Problems of Indebtedness of Developing Countries in the Financial Affairs Commission." OECD P 26985, unclassified, September 16, 1976. 8 pp.

U.S. Department of the Treasury. Report on the External Debt of Developing Countries and on Debt Relief Provided by the United States. Report to Congress, January 1978. 81 pp.

U.S. House of Representatives. Hearings on International Banking Operations. March 23, 24, April 5, 6, 1977. Subcommittee on Financial Institutions, Supervision, Regulation and Insurance of the Committee on Banking, Finance and Foreign Affairs, Washington, D.C.: U.S. Government Printing Office, 1977.

Interviews

Ganoe, Charles, S. Senior Executive vice-president, Fidelity Bank, Philadelphia, Pa. Telephone interview, January 24, 1978.

Haq, Mabub ul. Director of the Policy Planning and Program Review Department of the World Bank. Washington, D.C., January 26, 1978.

10 United States Congressional Restraints: The Ties that Bind

Jane D'Arista

In the decades following World War II, United States public and private investment played a unique role in rebuilding industrial countries and inaugurating a new era of economic development in the Third World. Since 1946, $194.6 billion of public funds has been transferred from the United States to other countries as loans and grants for economic and military assistance.(1) Nevertheless, even recipients who acknowledge the generosity of these transfers often see United States economic leadership as less than successful. They argue that what once was appropriately termed economic leadership has been transformed into economic interdependence. The failure of United States international economic policy is reflected in its attempts to isolate its domestic economy from the interdependent world economy which it has helped to create.

It is thought that United States policy makers see international economic issues as separate and subordinate to domestic interests; that they tend to underestimate the impact of internal United States policies on other countries and ignore the frustrations of foreign political leaders in coping with these impacts. Those who hold such a view would have to acknowledge that Americans are now more aware than in the past of interdependence between their economy and the economies of other nations. But this awareness is coming at a time when conflicts between domestic and international policies are more likely to arise than in earlier periods. In no area are these potential conflicts more evident or more poignant than in the recent shift in congressional attitudes toward developing countries.

Several recent legislative proposals have prompted new attempts to define the United States posture toward lesser developed countries. Debates on the Panama Canal Treaty, the foreign assistance legislation, and the International Monetary Fund's Supplementary Financing (or Witteveen) Facility are especially useful in analyzing congressional views. The issues covered in debates involve reassessments of political and military relationships, trade, human rights, the design of development programs, and the role of private bank lending to developing countries. Some of these issues are still in the formative stage without clear evidence of a trend in policy. Nevertheless, there is evidence to suggest that a shift in congressional attitudes toward developing countries is underway and that, as is true for other policy issues, the congressional view differs from that of the administration.

The following sections attempt to summarize some of the congressional positions taken in legislative discussions during the Ninety-fifth Congress. It is by no means a complete account and, like any selective appraisal, necessarily shortchanges some points of view while exaggerating the importance of others. Other analyses with differing conclusions can be readily formulated by those familiar with the issues. But it is doubtful that any appraisal would conclude that Congress has strengthened its commitment to help developing nations in achieving their aspirations.

FOREIGN ASSISTANCE: TO WHOM AND HOW MUCH?

Development assistance measured as a percentage of Organization for Economic Cooperation and Development (OECD) donor countries' GNP dropped in 1977 to 0.31 percent, its lowest level during the present decade. A dwindling in United States bilateral aid and in United States contributions for multilateral assistance has weighed heavily in the decline.(2) Congress has cut back administration requests for appropriations and has declined to fund commitments made by the Treasury to multilateral lending institutions.

A coalition of liberals concerned with human rights and conservatives dedicated to the overall reduction of federal expenditures has succeeded in introducing a larger congressional role in shaping aid policies, even when aid is to be channeled through multilateral institutions. For example, Congress has expressly directed that bilateral aid be given only to the poorer populations in developing countries. Recently, it expanded its "New Directions" policies to require that United States officials give priority to meeting basic human needs as opposed to investing in infrastructure or export-oriented industry, and focus on development programs which promote labor-intensive light capital technology. Because the Agency for International Development (AID) has been willing to cooperate in achieving these objectives, the House Appropriations Committee has proposed increases in funding for AID's programs while cutting funding for the multilateral banks. As Congressman Clarence Long, chairman of the subcommittee with jurisdiction over the foreign assistance appropriations bill, explained:

> If the House supports our efforts to reduce funding to the multilateral banks until they recast their aid programs and become more accountable to the U.S. Congress, we could have a better chance of success of making them do in fact what they have claimed to have been doing.(3)

This approach is seen as "negative" for aid by both individuals and organizations interested in development. But it is frustratingly difficult to categorize the congressional attitudes responsible for the "New Directions" approach, since much of the impetus for its adoption comes from members who are committed to assisting development programs. However, some of these members have openly discussed their difficulties in justifying expenditures to aid foreign countries when unemployment is high at home and when leaders of some of the poorer countries of the world parade their personal extravagance on the world stage.(4)

Perhaps an absence of generosity on the part of their constituents has made members of Congress adopt positions which can be more easily justified. Thus, they can vote for foreign aid if they can assure the unemployed, the inflation-ridden farmers, workers, and pensioners back in their districts, that it is actually going to people less fortunate than they - people to whom unemployment insurance, food stamps, school lunch programs, aid to dependent children, and Medicare would seem princely gifts. And, increasingly members feel it necessary to ensure that United States funds are not used to build export industries which will enrich the few, ignore the needs of the majority, produce goods which compete with goods produced in the United States and thereby threaten United States jobs.

There has been concern that the more advanced developing countries are pulling further ahead of the less advanced and that, within the more advanced LDCs, the distribution of income has become less, rather than more, equitable.* The

---

*Congress is only one of many sources for this view. David C. Beek has expressed similar concerns,(5) as has Michael Lipton. Lipton argues that: "The most fundamental class conflict in the poor countries of the world today is not between labor and capital. Nor is it between foreign and national interests. It is between the rural classes and the urban classes."(6)

shift in official lending to the poorer countries began in the late 1960s when it was discovered that the rate of growth of the higher income countries had accelerated from 6 to 7 percent over the decade while that of the poorer countries fell from 4 to 2 percent over the same period. The sudden increase in Eurocurrency borrowing by the higher-income countries in the early 1970s widened the disparities in growth among developing countries. Ten developing countries with access to private bank loans were able to increase industrial production and real imports by 9 percent a year between 1965 and 1973, while production and imports grew by less than 4 percent in other LDCs. As a result, those ten countries now have over half of the combined gross national product of all LDCs but only a quarter of the population of the developing world.(7) The growth rates of the higher income LDCs over the past decade were higher than those of most industrial countries as well.

Between 1973 and 1976, five countries - Brazil, the Philippines, South Korea, Thailand and Taiwan - also outperformed industrial countries in terms of the rise in export volume.(8) In 1976, the United States reported a trade deficit with LDCs. For the first time, developing countries sold more goods to the United States than they bought.(9) Their combined payments deficit improved significantly as a result, dropping from $38.2 billion in 1975 to $25.8 billion in 1976.(10) Most of the improvement was enjoyed by the higher-income countries.

HELPING THE POOR HELP THEMSELVES

In several ways, Congress's aid policies reflect frustration in the face of thwarted objectives. The poor country recipients of United States aid have not developed very rapidly as of late, and the better-off LDCs are perceived - rightly or wrongly - as a competitive threat. Lack of LDC success gives ground for despair; too much LDC success seems grounds for fear. Representative Silvio Conte of Massachusetts during floor debate on the foreign assistance appropriations bill summed up congressmen's concern with the poor:

> Yes, true progress has been achieved, but we cannot stop now. Man continues to press the generous bounty of nature and often with sad results. At this time, 930 million persons in the developing world are undernourished. 1.2 billion do not have access to safe drinking water. 800 million lack basic housing. 800 million are deprived of fundamental health care sources. And 1.1 bil-

> lion lack even the most rudimentary education. Our foreign assistance programs deal specifically with the means by which we challenge this grim reality and deal with the dangers that we will face as fellow-travellers on the planet earth.(11)

The frustration with the enormity of the problem surfaced in the Appropriations Committee's report on the bill: "Even if the total U.S. foreign assistance effort could be directed to several of the neediest countries of the world, there would still not be enough funds available to cure all their ills."(12) Thus, the committee concluded that the "only hope of ever ameliorating world poverty is to adopt a totally fresh approach to development assistance."(13) It also recommended that, in view of the "critical shortage of capital resources available for needed assistance programs ... every effort should be made by the agencies to phase out aid to recipient nations as quickly as it is determined no further U.S. aid is required."(14)

The "New Directions" approach adopted by Congress is one attempt to square the circles of widespread poverty and limited funds for official aid. It emphasizes the use of light capital technology in development assistance projects. As described by the Appropriations Committee report, its purpose is to:

> ... harness the vast reserves of idle labor time which exist in all developing nations, enabling poor nations to generate their own capital. Light capital technology (or intermediate, or appropriate technology, as this approach is variously called) consists of using inexpensive tools and simple techniques which make use of the abundant resource of idle labor time and which save enough labor at busy seasons - such as harvest and planting times - to enable the work to be done but do not save so much labor as to eliminate jobs and create more idleness and unemployment. Examples of this technology are animal-drawn plows and seeders, five to ten horsepower tillers, small grain threshers and driers, hand-operated irrigation pumps, simple grain storage bins, manually operated corn and peanut shellers, and "intermediate" road construction equipment (like ox-carts for earth-moving and mini-compaction devices) instead of large bulldozers, graders, and earth movers.
>
> ... this simple, inexpensive equipment should be produced within the poor countries themselves, again through techniques emphasizing labor and the

> saving of capital. Home-grown technology not only minimizes the need for foreign aid, but, more importantly, it creates jobs in towns and smaller cities and generates the income to buy the greater output of farm and industry. Home-grown technology also creates a body of skills which are needed for maintenance and repair....
>
> Technologies on this small scale will give the poor nations the means to effect their own development, with donor countries supplying only initial ideas and enough materials for indigenous labor to get started. It would be an interesting challenge to name any nation which has ever developed in any other way than endogenously.(15)

The committee's emphasis on endogenous development implies a degree of disengagement from international markets. Some congressmen support policies aimed at import substitution to relieve developing countries of their vulnerability to changes in the business cycle in industrial countries. In debates on aid, few congressmen have urged an increase in exports from developing countries. There is, in fact, some concern about LDC export trends. The report of the Appropriations Committee states:

> The Committee is very concerned with Export-Import Bank financing of overseas production in certain overcapacity industries or commodities that cause injury to United States producers. The specific concern has been centered on the overseas production of iron and steel products. Although the Committee is certainly not advocating a protectionist stance regarding United States trade or assistance to foreign countries, it does have difficulty understanding why we have to provide help in financing producers of competitive commodities in order to qualify as supporters of free enterprise. Because of Congressional concern in this area, the Committee has included a general provision that would prohibit direct foreign assistance, the Export-Import Bank and the Overseas Private Investment Corporation from financing the production of any commodity for export, if it is in surplus on world markets and if the assistance will cause substantial injury to United States producers of the same, similar or competing commodity.(16)

In contrast to this view is that of some of the more staunch defenders of aid programs. These congressmen argue that aid transfers benefit the United States by increasing exports and jobs. They do not favor disengagement from international trade as a solution for the problems of developing countries. Rather, they see continued development and an increase in trade between the less and more developed countries as the necessary spur to continued economic growth, worldwide. The role of developing countries in this scenario was described by Representative Conte:

> There is little doubt that the world's greatest reservoir of marginal productivity is the still underdeveloped and under-utilized physical and human resources of the developing countries. Foreign assistance is a key to releasing this untapped potential. By raising the purchasing power of these nations, releasing new resources and developing new markets for both poor and rich, higher levels of economic activity can be created within and between all countries. In essence, the developing nations of the South could, over the next two decades, become one of the crucial engine of growth in this world.

The argument that LDCs are important markets for United States exports has so far failed to persuade Congress that increasing aid is in the interest of the United States. And even if all the cuts made so far could be restored, United States official development assistance would still be only a small fraction of the aggregate flows of funds to developing countries. Thus, it could be argued that the views of Congress on aid will have little impact on either the design or probability of success of development programs. But, even if this were so, the concerns expressed could have significant effects in other policy areas which are equally important to the developing countries.

The higher-income countries have more to gain or lose from United States trade than from aid. Most have been phased out of United States bilateral assistance programs over the last several years. From their point of view, the trade implications of the "New Directions" approach may seem more threatening than the aid cuts. Trade restrictions could hamper their ability to repay present debt, jeopardize their prospects for future borrowing, and lessen their hopes for further development.

CONGRESSIONAL VIEWS ON PRIVATE BANK LENDING AND THE WITTEVEEN FACILITY

If Congress is concerned about the effects of official assistance - i.e., its failure to alleviate poverty, its alleged contributions to creating disparities in income distribution among and within developing countries, to creating over-capacity in certain industries and commodities and to increasing the volume of exports which compete with United States manufactures - what must be its attitude toward private bank lending to developing countries? In recent years, the volume of bank loans to LDCs has greatly outstripped official flows of funds. (It is generally agreed that LDCs financed about 60 percent of their current-account deficits between 1973 and 1976 by borrowing from Eurocurrency banks.) Most of these loans - 87 percent in the case of United States banks -(18) were made to ten higher- or middle-income countries and were used to finance the much larger payments deficits they incurred as a consequence of the oil price increase, the rise in prices of food and manufactured goods, the drop in commodity prices, and the 1974-1975 recession in industrial countries.

The rise in private bank lending to LDCs after 1973 was seen as both necessary and inevitable by both the Ford and Carter administrations. It was the means for recycling OPEC (and German and Japanese) surpluses to deficit countries. Financing their deficits allowed LDCs to adjust more gradually to the increased cost of food, oil, and manufactures and the decline in prices and demand for commodities. Bank financing thus helped maintain the level of imports needed to sustain growth in the higher income LDCs and thereby contributed to political stability. This was especially true in countries like Jamaica where wage-goods such as food figured prominently in the import bill. (See Chapter 7, by Daniel O'Flaherty, in this book.) It also helped some industrial countries to maintain their export volumes to LDCs and thereby made the 1974-1975 recession less severe than it might otherwise have been.(19)

Congressional attitudes toward private bank lending to LDCs have been heterogeneous. Some members see graduation from dependence on aid to access to private markets as one of the goals of aid policies. These members are not necessarily committed to laissez faire economic policies as a general rule. But they recognize that there is only so much to go around and aid is best reserved for the worst cases.(20)

Other members, equally concerned with the poorest people in developing countries, see rising levels of private bank debt as a menace to future development efforts. Since bank loans are medium-term at best, they subject LDCs to higher debt-service ratios than would long-term official assistance or private equity investment. Servicing bank debts of unrealistically short maturities drains resources and leads to cutbacks in public expenditures which may fall most heavily on the poor. Members who hold this view constituted as a group the greatest obstacle to smooth passage of the Witteveen Facility.(21)

To these members, the problem which the Witteveen Facility addresses has been exacerbated as much by the escalation of LDC bank borrowing as by the much greater payments surpluses and deficits attributed to the oil price increase. They do not see the Witteveen Facility as a bail-out for banks - the amount of funds involved is much too small for that purpose - but they questioned the wisdom of using the Facility to bestow an IMF "Good Housekeeping seal of approval" on countries so that they can continue to borrow from banks. One congressman suggested this might be "like putting a Band-Aid on a cancer."(22) It would not address the fundamental issues of how to reduce payments surpluses and deficits, the appropriateness of private bank lending to governments to finance payments deficits or the appropriateness of IMF conditionality. In addition, it suggested a too-cozy relationship between the IMF and the multinational banks to members who thought the interests of public and private finance were different and should not be blurred.(23)

As the result of a sustained campaign by members of the Banking Committee, the House amended the Witteveen proposal to ensure that the United States position on the use of the Witteveen Facility would reflect a policy favoring comparability of treatment of public and private creditors in cases of debt rescheduling where official United States credits are involved. It also adopted a "human rights, human needs" amendment. This amendment instructed United States officials to initiate discussions within the IMF concerning appropriate stabilization policies designed to meet basic human needs, to take steps to ensure that fund programs do not contribute to the deprivation of basic human needs or the violation of human rights, and to report to Congress on the effects of fund policies in borrowing countries on the ability of the poor to obtain adequate supplies of food, shelter, and clothing, as well a public services and employment.(24)

The adoption of these amendments resulted in substantially wider House support for the legislation which passed on a vote of 267 to 125.(25) The Senate, however, defeated the "human needs" amendment and it has been modified by the Conference Committee. The amendment which deals with comparable treatment for both public and private lenders in debt rescheduling, was not offered in the Senate but, since it was adopted as United States policy by the Treasury in January 1978, it was accepted by the Conference Committee.

THE LINK BETWEEN DEBT AND TRADE

The House Appropriations Committee has castigated the Export-Import Bank and the World Bank for making loans to the steel, textile, and shoe industries in developing countries which have resulted in overcapacity in these industries and in undercutting the competitive position of United States manufacturers in import-competing industries.(26) So far, however, the Representatives have not explored the possibility that private bank loans to LDCs might have undesirable effects on United States trade and competition. The Witteveen debate made no reference to trade issues. But these issues were raised in the Senate Banking Committee's hearings on international debt in August 1977. Senator Jacob K. Javits, appearing as a witness, argued:

> We must realize ... that foreign borrowing cannot be a substitute for [LDC] export earnings. A strong export performance is the indispensible base for a sustained use of foreign credits. The developed countries must, therefore, increase the opportunities for trade expansion with - and among - the developing world; accelerate technology transfers; and give greater encouragement private sector investment on fair terms to investors and most countries in the developing areas of the world.(27)

Senator Javits' statement implies, as has discussion outside Congress, that the escalation of private bank lending since 1973 has added new pressures for development policies oriented toward export production. The degree of pressure and its implications for trade policy were also acknowledged by another witness before the Senate Banking Commitee, Frederick Heldring, president of the Philadelphia National Bank, who said:

> I do believe that we ought to buy all the products without restrictions that developing countries have to offer us.
>
> It really does not make sense, on the one hand, for the United States to be lending to a country and then say, yes, but you cannot service your debt by selling us this, that, or the other thing. That doesn't make sense to me at all.(28)

Whether Mr. Heldring is referring to official or private United States lending to developing countries is unclear. Private lending has now outstripped official credits and almost no bilateral assistance is being given to countries which are major exporters of manufactured goods. Thus, it could be argued that Mr. Heldring has imputed an official status to private United States lending which some members of Congress have been anxious to repudiate. In any event, his remarks tend to support Albert Fishlow's comment that bankers have become the new champions of freer trade and open access to markets.(29)

But another banker, Richard D. Hill, chairman of the board of the First National Bank of Boston, called attention to the political problems which increases in LDC exports might cause:

> Obviously, the United States, as the world's largest and most affluent economy, must provide other countries with fair and open access to its markets. As has been stated many times, it is particularly important that less-developed countries be assured of opportunities to export their products.
>
> Nevertheless, in the short run, at least, this can have a notably adverse impact on various industries and on regional employment within our borders. As a New England bank, we must be sensitive to the domestic consequences of our trade policies. Our region has experienced keen import competition in some industries, especially shoes, with serious local consequences. One solution is a larger and more effective program of adjustment assistance aimed at retraining workers and retooling industries which have lost their ability to compete. Unless this is done more effectively, we can only opt for more protection.
>
> The impact of expanded imports on employment in the United States will remain a significant issue in Congress. While it may be beyond the immediate attention of this subcommittee, the subject is one that must, nevertheless, be included in any discussion of international debt.(30)

The subject was not the immediate conern of the Senate subcommittee, but it has been discussed elsewhere, and there is general agreement on the need for a better integration of international financial and trade policies.(31) The administration's position is not inconsistent with such a view, but the relationship between private debt and trade and the potential for conflict between United States domestic and international objectives are issues which so far have been ignored by United States officials. One who has anticipated conflicts is Comptroller of the Currency John G. Heimann. In a speech to international bankers in April 1978, he warned them not to place themselves "in an untenable position of loan repayment being predicated upon future national trade policies."(32) But, with some 80 percent of their LDC lending going to Brazil, Mexico, South Korea, Taiwan, and other exporters of manufactures, the banks were probably in such a position long before that date.

REGULATORY ISSUES

Congressional interest in international banking activities dates back to the beginning of its expansion in the 1960s when Senator Javits played a leading part in urging a larger role for United States banks in international finance.(33) But the failure of a Lebanese bank in 1965 and the closing of its insolvent New York branch called attention to the fact that international banks operated outside domestic regulatory systems and that this could cause problems for regulatory authorities. Opportunities for fraud and unsound banking practices were enhanced by the absence of outside examination and supervision. Failures could occur without warning and without safeguards for depositors. In 1967, the first of a series of bills was introduced which would require foreign banks in the United States to conform to domestic banking practices and regulatory restraints. Such a bill passed the House in July 1976 but was not acted on in the Senate. In August 1978, it was finally enacted by both Houses.

Congress has also been concerned about the activities of United States banks abroad. Their involvement in currency speculation was the issue under discussion in 1973.(34) In 1974 and 1975, the failure of Franklin National Bank and the impact of the Herstatt failure were the major issues.(35) In 1976, the House Banking Committee held hearings and published a study of United States banks abroad as part of its overall review of Financial Institutions and the Nation's Economy (FINE). The main concern of the FINE study was to call attention to findings which indicated that the absence of regulation of international banking operations tended to undermine the effectiveness of domestic regulation. It also discussed the impact of international banking on domestic and international monetary policies, the problem of concentration in international lending, and the risks involved in direct loans to countries to finance payments deficits.(36)

Another problem stressed by the FINE study was the lack of data on international lending operations. A General Accounting Office report to Congress on bank regulation in January 1977 also complained about the absence of data and inadequate regulation of overseas operations.(37) During the 1977 hearings on international debt, Under Secretary of the Treasury Anthony Solomon told the Senate Banking Committee that when he first began to look at the problem, he was "shocked" by the inadequacy of the information available.(38)

United States regulatory authorities in collaboration with the Bank for International Settlements have recently begun to collect data on the Eurocurrency market which at least identifies borrowers and depositors by country. Beginning with data for June 30, 1977, the Federal Reserve Board and the Comptroller of the Currency began to issue biennial surveys of United States banks which add to the country data a breakdown of foreign loans to banks, public borrowers and private nonbank borrowers. It also provides a limited breakdown of loan maturities and data on bank commitments. As yet there is no sectoral data on foreign lending and it is impossible to analyze international financial flows by industry.

One result of the Federal Reserve's Country Exposure Lending Survey was to call attention to the subtantial commitment of United States banks to a small group of high- and middle-income developing countries. Ten countries - Argentina, Brazil, Chile, Korea, Malaysia, Mexico, Peru, the Philippines, Taiwan, and Thailand - accounted for $34.9 billion or 86.9 percent of the $40.1 billion loaned to all non-oil-exporting developing ountries. United States bank loans to LDCs were 24.4 percent of total foreign loans of $164.2 billion. Claims on Brazil and Mexico - $10.6 billion and $11.3 billion, respectively - amounted to 13.3 percent of total loans and 55 percent of loans to all LDCs.(39)

The concentration of lending by groups of United States banks was also marked. Of 199 lending banks, the nine largest* accounted for 63 percent of United States bank loans to LDCs. Loan concentrations in relation to bank capital were even more striking. (The 119 United States banks surveyed reported aggregate equity capital and loan loss reserves of $36,175 million. The nine largest banks reported $16,130 million of capital funds.) The ratio of LDC loans to capital for all 119 lending banks was 111 percent but rose to 157 percent for the nine largest. Loans to LDC public sector borrowers aggregated 49.2 percent of capital for all lending banks, 70.6 percent for the nine largest. Total United States bank loans to Brazil and Mexico were 29.3 percent and 31.3 percent of capital, respectively, but were 42.3 percent and 38.4 percent of the capital of the nine largest banks. Public sector loans to these two countries were 10.3 and 16.3 percent of capital

---

*The nine banks in this group are: Bank of America, Citibank, Chase Manhattan Bank, Manufacturers Hanover Trust Co., Morgan Guaranty Trust Co., Chemical Bank, Bankers Trust Co., Continential Illinois National Bank and Trust Co., and First Chicago Bank.

for the entire group of banks, and 15.8 percent and 20.3 percent of capital for the top banks.(40)

It is often argued that concern for capital ratios has little meaning in the highly leveraged environment of international banking; a more significant measure of exposure - LDC loans as a percentage of total bank assets - indicates that there is little cause for alarm. Loans to Brazil and Mexico are about 3 percent of total assets for the largest United States banks. That is also the approximate ratio of domestic consumer loans to total assets for these banks. Their domestic real estate loans are about 5 percent of assets, roughly the same ratio as capital (equity and loan loss reserves). But United States banks loaned only $22 billion to real estate investment trusts (REITs) - far less than the $42 billion loaned to LDCs - and the loss of income on even that small portion of their portfolio had a dramatic effect of profits.(41)

Members of Congress have repeatedly asked regulatory authorities if United States banks are overextended in foreign lending. Federal Reserve Board Governor Henry C. Wallich's response to Senator H. John Heinz reflects the tone of most of what they have been told: While some banks have concentrations in particular countries, they are "not of a sort that one would say immediately are unsustainable.(42)

But some key members* of both Houses have seen the problem of loan concentration and the possible erosion of regulatory safeguards in foreign lending as major concerns.(43) Thus, it can be expected that Comptroller Heimann's effort to apply the statutory limit on loans to one borrower to foreign public sector lending will receive congressional support.(44) The Comptroller's guidelines on foreign lending in relation to bank capital may have been a contributing factor in the decline in United States banks' LDC lending from $20 billion in 1976 to $13 billion in 1977. Other factors were the reduction in LDC growth rates, improvement in developing countries' current accounts, smaller increases in OPEC deposits, an increase in OPEC borrowing and a pick-up in domestic business loan demand. It is likely that the focus on lending limits will influence the level of United States bank lending in the future as well. As has been true for official assistance, a larger share of private bank lending to developing countries will probably shift to banks in other industrial countries. Such a

---

*Among these key members are Chairman Henry S. Reuss and Subcommittee Chairman Fernand J. St Germain of the House Banking Commitee; Senator Frank Church, ranking Majority Member and Subcommittee Chairman, Senate Foreign Relations Committee; and Chairman William Proxmire of the Senate Banking Commitee.

shift may be viewed by Congress as both reasonable and desirable.

OTHER POLICY ISSUES

The 1977 House hearings on international banking operations betrayed an uneasiness on the part of all participating subcommittee members. Concern for the political aspects of international bank lending was a major theme of the hearings. The disinterested nature of United States banks' support for the Panama Canal Treaty was questioned in view of their loans to the Panamanian Government and the tax-free status granted by it to their operations. The implications for United States policy of large OPEC deposits in United States banks and of loans to communist countries were among the specific topics discussed.(45) Some subcommitee members saw private lending as ignoring and undercutting the more even-handed distribution of resources expected of official lending, suspecting that the banks might be "red-lining" certain countries and contributing to political instability.(46) Others thought bank lending to Brazil, Chile, and other countries had lessened the effectiveness of the United States human rights policy.(47)

The subcommittee hearings also questioned why it was considered proper for United States banks to help share-out the deficits created by the oil price increases.(48) While this question did not focus on the use of the private banking system as an instrument in executing policies considered desirable by the United States government, the testimony of the Treasury and State Department witnesses imply that such a role in United States international monetary policy has been assigned to the banks.(49) Congress is clearly not unsympathetic toward the use of the private sector to effect domestic economic policy. But subcommittee members of both parties were less willing to endorse its use in international policy. The attitude of a majority of the subcommittee members seemed to be reflected in the remarks of one who said:

> ... there is no overwhelming inclination to bail out large banking institutions of our own. The money center banks must recognize that they are bearing the risks of their loans alone.(50)

It is not likely that many Members of Congress would adopt a different view. And, inherent in such a view is a degree of hostility toward a greater expansion of United States bank lending to LDCs. So far, only a few preliminary questions concerning the United States role as lender of last resort have been asked, but there is growing concern that either the United States must accept a larger volume of imports from LDCs to facilitate loan repayments or accept whatever consequences befall bank with loans to countries which cannot earn the needed foreign exchange by exporting.

It is likely that the growth in imports from developing countries and United States trade deficits with individual LDCs will stimulate congressional interest in the links between LDC debt and trade. The alternatives open to the United States - to encourage greater acceptance of LDC imports by other industrial countries and OPEC and an increase in OPEC or industrial country lending to LDCs - may lessen LDC demand for United States exports. Such trade-offs indicate that it is increasingly difficult for the United States to isolate its domestic economy from international policy objectives.

To encourage other nations to assume larger burdens and responsibilities in implementing international economic policies would reflect a greater United States acceptance of economic interdependence. It would also be seen by some as an abnegation of United States economic leadership. There are those who argue that the United States must continue to play this role since no other single nation can, and because protectionist regional blocks are apt to spring up in the absence of a central economic power, threatening fragmentation and decline in world trade.

It could be argued, however, that the ability to separate its domestic economy from the rest of the world was critical to the success of United States economic leadership. If the United States were willing to accept painful domestic adjustments for the sake of the economic well-being of the world as a whole, it would be the first nation to do so. A more realistic position for the United States would be to attempt further rationalization of interdependence along the lines set out in the Multilateral Trade Negotiations (MTN).

It is expected that the MTN will be completed in early 1979 and congressional discussion will begin in the spring. Recognition by Congress that the multilateral framework provided by the MTN for continuing negotiation and discussion is more important than particular concessions will be critical in developing a structure for resolving conflicts between United States domestic and international objectives in an increasingly interdependent world economy.

NOTES

1. Foreign Assistance and Related Programs Appropriations Bill, 1974 House Report No. 95-1250, from the Committee on Appropriations, 95th Congress, 2nd Session, June 1, 1978, pp. 10-11.

2. IMF Survey, July 2, 1978, pp. 102, 200.
3. Congressional Record, July 31, 1978, p. H 7548.
4. Remarks of Representative Millicent Fenwick, Transcript of Proceedings, Committee on Banking, Finance, and Urban Affairs, Markup on H.R. 9214, to amend the Bretton Woods Agreements Act, January 23, 1978, p. 56; and remarks of Representative Virginia Smith, Congressional Record, July 31, 1978, p. H 7557.
5. David C. Beek, "Commercial Bank Lending to Developing Countries," Federal Reserve Bank of New York, Quarterly Review, Summer 1977, pp. 5-6.
6. Michael Lipton, Why Poor People Stay Poor (Cambridge, Mass.: Harvard University Press, 1977), p. 13.
7. Beek, "Commercial Bank Lending," pp. 5-6.
8. Robert Solomon, "A Perspective on the Debt of Developing Countries," Brookings Papers on Economic Activity 2 (1977): 493.
9. Albert Fishlow, "Debt Remains a Problem," Foreign Policy 30 (Spring 1978): 139.
10. Solomon, "Perspective on Debt," pp. 481, 483.
11. Congressional Record, July 31, 1978, p. H 7554.
12. Foreign Assistance and Related Programs Appropriations Bills, p. 4.
13. Ibid., p. 6.
14. Ibid., p. 4.
15. Ibid., p. 6.
16. Ibid., pp. 56-57.
17. Congressional Record, July 31, 1978, p. H 7554; see also testimony of Dr. Ronald E. Muller, International Banking Operations, Hearing before the Subcommittee on Financial Institutions Supervision, Regulation and Insurance, House Banking, Finance and Urban Affairs Committee, 95th Congress, 1st Session, April 6, 1977, pp. 833-35.
18. Federal Reserve Board, Country Exposure Lending Survey, January 1978.
19. Testimony of C. Fred Bergsten, Assistant Secretary for International Affairs, Treasury Department, and Paul H. Boeker, Deputy Assistant Secretary for Economic and Business Affairs, State Department, International Banking Operations, pp. 546-55; testimony of Anthony M. Solomon, Undersecretary of the Treasury for Monetary Affairs, International Debt, Hearings before the Subcommittee on International Finance, Senate Banking, Housing and Urban Affairs Committee, 95th Congress, 1st Session, August 29, 1977, pp. 26-37.
20. Foreign Assistance and Related Programs Appropriations Bills, p. 4.
21. See remarks of Representatives Parren J. Mitchell and John J. Cavanaugh, Transcript of Proceedings, Markup on H.R. 9214, January 23, 1978.
22. Remarks of Representative Stanley Lundine, U.S. Partic-

ipation in the Supplementary Financing Facility of the International Monetary Fund, Hearings before the Subcommittee on International Trade, Investment and Monetary Policy, House Committee on Banking, Finance and Urban Affairs, 95th Congress, 1st Session, September 20, 1977, p. 86.
23. Representative John J. Cavanaugh's comments on the testimony of Undersecretary of the Treasury Anthony M. Solomon and Undersecretary of State Richard N. Cooper illustrate this view:

> I think that there are substantive questions as to what is the relationship between IMF funding, public funding, government funding and private funding of this whole world economic system, and what is the U.S. role in it. I think if you get your back up as both of your statements did today, defending the stability of American banks in all of their transactions and in all the countries around the world, some of which I don't think are defensible, they were bad business judgments, and I think we ought to have some acquiescence in that if we are going to say that the American banking industry has made all perfect judgments in all their international busines decision, and this facility will not assist in relieving some of the consequences of those judgments. We are going to be in [a] non-win situation.

(U.S. Participation in the Supplementary Financing Facility of the International Monetary Fund, p. 77.) See also remarks of Representative Fernand J. St. Germain, International Banking Operations, p. 625.
24. Congressional Record, February 23, 1978, pp. H 1395 - H 1438.
25. Ibid., p. H 1438.
26. See Foreign Assistance and Related Programs Appropriations Bills, pp. 56-57. Shortly after the committee report was issued, the Export-Import Bank cleared two direct loans to steel producers in Iran and Brazil. It loaned $17.9 million at 7.75% interest to National Iranian Steel to buy furnaces and other U.S. equipment. The bank loanded $7.22 million and guaranteed $4.8 million of private credits to Companhia Siderurgica Nacional of Brazil at 8% interest to purchase U.S. equipment and to expand steel-making facilities. (Wall Street Journal, July 25, 1978).
27. International Debt, p. 16.
28. Ibid., p. 136.
29. Fishlow, "Debt Remains Problem," p. 141.
30. International Debt, pp. 129-30.
31. Interim Report of the Meeting on Alternative Solutions of

the External Public Debt Problem of the Developing Countries, El Colegio de Mexico, October 27-30, 1977, pp. 5, 8, 15, 26; and Fishlow, "Debt Remains Problem," pp. 140-41.
32. American Banker, April 5, 1978.
33. Nomination of James J. Saxon to be Comptroller of the Currency, Hearing before the Senate Committee on Banking and Currency, 87th Congress, 2nd Session, February 6, 1962, pp. 19-20.
34. Economic Report of the President, Hearings before the Joint Economic Committee, 93rd Congress, 1st Session, February 20, 1973.
35. Bank Failures-Regulatory Reform-Financial Privacy, part 2, Hearings before the subcommittee on Financial Institutions Supervision, Regulation and Insurance, House Committee on Banking, Currency and Housing, 94th Congress, 1st Session, July 16, 17, 21, 1975. Adequacy of the Office of the Comptroller of the Currency's Supervision of Franklin National Bank, House Report No. 94-1669, from the Committee on Government Operations, 94th Congress, 2nd Session, September 23, 1976, 42 pp.
36. Jane D'Arista, "U.S. Banks Abroad," Financial Institutions and the Nations Economy (Compendium of papers prepared for the FINE Study, Book II, House Committee on Banking, Currency and Housing, 94th Congress, 2nd Session, June 1976).
37. Federal Supervision of State and National Banks (A study by the Comptroller General of the United States, January 31, 1977); see also International Banking Operations, pp. 67-70, 246-59.
38. International Debt, p. 41.
39. Country Exposure Lending Survey, January 1978.
40. Federal Reserve Board, data supplied to the House Committee on Banking, Finance and Urban Affairs, May 10, 1978.
41. Country Exposure Lending Survey, Federal Reserve Board Call Report Data, January 1978.
42. Internationl Debt, p. 87.
43. Letters from Representative Henry S. Reuss, Chairman of the House Committee on Banking, Finance and Urban Affairs, to Secretary of the Treasury U. Michael Blumenthal, Federal Reserve Board Governor Arthur F. Burns, Comptroller of the Currency John G. Heimann, Federal Deposit Insurance Corporation Chairman George A. LeMaistre, December 15, 1977; International Banking Opeations, pp. 1-2; 41, 281, 633-35; Multinational Corporations and United States Foreign Policy, Part 15, Hearings before the Subcommittee on Multinational Corporations, Senate Committee on Foreign Relations, 94th Congress, 1st Session, March 1975; International Debt, the Banks, and U.S. Foreign Policy, Staff Report to the Subcommittee on Foreign Economic Policy, Senate Committee on Foreign Relations, 95th Congress, 1st Session, August 1977;

p. v; and International Debt, pp. 89, 92, 99.
44. Economist, January 14, 1978, pp. 99-100; and Financial Times, February 6, 1978.
45. International Banking Operations, pp. 30-32, 42, 293, 621, 623-25, 720-22, 740.
46. Ibid., pp. 25, 35-37.
47. Ibid., pp. 54-55, 736-38.
48. Ibid., p. 602.
49. See International Banking Operations, pp. 546-55; and International Debt, pp. 26-37.
50. Remarks of Representative Jim Leach, International Banking Operations, p. 621.

BIBLIOGRAPHY

Beek, David, C. "Commercial Bank Lending to Developing Countries." Federal Reserve Bank of New York Quarterly Review 2 (Summer 1977): 1-8.

"Controls on U.S. Banks and their Lending Activities." Financial Times, February 6, 1978.

El Colegio de Mexico. Interim Report of the Meeting on Alternative Solutions of the External Debt Problem of Developing Countries. October 27-30, 1977. 36 pp.

"Exim Bank Clears Loans for Steel Producers." Wall Street Journal, July 25, 1978.

Federal Reserve Board. Country Exposure Lending Survey. Press Release, January 16, 1978.

Fishlow, Albert. "Debt Remains a Problem." Foreign Policy, no. 30 (Spring 1978), pp. 133-43.

General Accounting Office. Federal Supervision of State and National Banks. Study by the Comptroller General of the United States, January 31, 1977.

"Heimann Calls the Shots for Overseas Lending." Economist, January 14, 1978, pp. 99-100.

"Heimann Says Risk of Lending Overseas Invite Regulation Unless Banks Control Selves." American Banker, April 5, 1978.

International Monetary Fund. IMF Survey, July 3, 1978, pp. 102, 200.

Lipton, Michael. Why Poor People Stay Poor. Cambridge, Mass.: Harvard University Press, 1977.

Solomon, Robert. "A Perspective on the Debt Problems of Developing Countries." Brooking Papers on Economic Activity 2 (1977): 479-510.

U.S. House of Representatives. Adequacy of the Comptroller of the Currency's Supervision of Franklin National Bank. House Report no. 94-1669, from the Committee on Government Operations, 94th Congress, 2nd Session, September 23, 1976. 42 pp.

_______. Bank Failures-Regulatory Reform-Financial Privacy, part 2. Hearings before the Subcommittee on Financial Institutions Supervision, Regulation and Insurance, Committee on Banking Currency and Housing 94th Congress, 1st Session, July 1975.

_______. Congressional Record. February 23, 1978, pp. H 1395-H 1438; and July 31, 1978, pp. H 7548-H 7560.

_______. Economic Report of the President. Hearings before the Joint Economic Committee. 93rd Congress, 1st Session, February 20, 1973.

_______. Financial Institutions and the Nation's Economy. Compendium of papers prepared for the FINE study, Book II, Part 4. Committee on Banking, Currency and Housing, 94th Congress, 2nd Session, June 1976.

_______. International Debt, the Banks, and U.S. Foreign Policy. Staff report to the Subcommittee on Foreign Economic Relations, 95th Congress, 1st Session, August 1977.

_______. Multinational Corporations and United States Foreign Policy, Part 15. Hearings before the Subcommittee on Multinational Corporations, Committee on Foreign Relations, 94th Congress, 1st Session, March 1975.

_______. Nomination of James J. Saxon to be Comptroller of the Currency. Hearings before the Committee on Banking and Currency, 87th Congress, 2nd Session, February 1962.

11 The International Monetary Fund and LDC Debt

Carl R. Neu

INTRODUCTION

Most discussions of developing country debt turn eventually to the need for some international body responsible for surveillance and perhaps regulation of international borrowing and lending. Some observers have suggested the establishment of an international "lender of last resort" to provide emergency financing whenever the failure of a sovereign borrower to meet its international obligations threatens the stability of international financial arrangements. Increasingly in recent years, the International Monetary Fund (IMF) has been cited as potentially the proper institution to assume these responsibilities. It is argued that the established international character of the IMF makes it well suited for this role, and many see a greater responsibility for international financial stability as a logical extension of the Fund's traditional responsibilities for monetary stability.

To an extent, the IMF already performs some of the functions of a financial regulator, but major changes in the nature and operations of the Fund would be required if it were to expand this role or to become a true lender of last resort. This chapter describes briefly the Fund's present role in providing financing for developing countries. Special attention is given to the size of the IMF lending and the conditions attached to IMF financing. The chapter concludes with a consideration of the prospects for the Fund's becoming an international lender of last resort.

THE PURPOSE OF THE IMF

Since its establishment in 1947, the IMF has been the primary institution responsible for the maintenance of a smoothly operating international monetary system. Through the years, the actions required of the Fund to fulfill this responsibility have changed as the nature of the international monetary system has changed. Until the early 1970s, the Fund's primary function was the management of a system of fixed exchange rates. Today, in a regime of floating rates, its major function it to encourage its member nations to adopt policies that will facilitate the international flow of trade and capital and to avoid actions that would restrict these flows.(1) What has remained unchanged through the years, however, is the Fund's responsibility for promoting a liberal system of international trade and capital movements.

The principal instrument by which the Fund discharges these duties is its lending to member nations. This lending is designed to aid countries facing current-account deficits and whose currencies are under downward pressure. The rationale behind this design is that a country that finds itself in such a situation may have no recourse but to impose restrictive trade policies or severely contractionary domestic economic policies, or to allow the value of its currency to fall abruptly. Such actions would reduce the exports of other nations, which in turn might respond by trade restrictions and devaluations of their own. By such a chain of events, a temporary disturbance in a few countries could lead to a general adoption of restrictive trade policies or a round of competitive devaluations that would harm all nations. Permanent changes in the world economy could bring about similar results if countries responded by adopting restrictive trade policies rather than by making necessary internal economic adjustments. By providing financing, the Fund can allow countries in temporary difficulty to avoid restrictive policies and give those facing more permanent problems time to adjust in ways that will no be harmful to other nations.

As other chapters in this book have pointed out, any widespread failure of nations - whether developed or developing - to meet their debt servicing requirements could result in a large-scale contraction of international credit. Such a contraction would have seriously detrimental effects both on international trade and on worldwide economic growth. It is clearly among the IMF's responsibilities to aid in avoiding such situations by encouraging careful and deliberate adjustment to eliminate balance-of-payments problems and by doing whatever it can to maintain an international financial environment conducive to the flow of needed international credit.

THE SIZE OF IMF LENDING

What is perhaps most striking in view of the Fund's very great responsibilities is the relatively small scale of IMF lending. During the years 1974 through 1977, net IMF lending averaged only about $3.8 billion a year. During that same period, however, the aggregate deficit of all nations running current-account deficits was in the neighborhood of $80 billion per year. Thus, the IMF was supplying less than 5 percent of all of the required current-account financing in these four years. By comparison, during these same four years, total international private lending averaged some $53 billion per year, nearly 14 times greater than the amount of IMF lending.(2)

The relative importance of IMF lending changes very little if one considers only lending to nonoil-exporting developing nations. During the years 1974 through 1978, these nations had combined current-account deficits of about $28 billion per year. The IMF provided only about $1.4 billion per year to these developing countries and thus provided only about 5 percent of their current-account financing. In 1977, the net flow of IMF leading to these countries was negative, as repayments by nonoil LDCs to the IMF in 1977 exceeded new Fund lending to these countries by about $186 million. During the four years 1974 through 1978, the nonoil LDCs obtained more than $15 billion per year from private capital markets.

The relatively small share of international lending accounted for by the IMF is a reflection of the Fund's limited resources. Although Fund holdings of currencies are quite large - more than SDR 41 billion (about $52 billion) - only a fraction of these holdings can be used for making loans to members. Many nations whose currency is held by the Fund are themselves running large current-account deficits or have reserve assets that are inadequate to maintain orderly markets for their currencies. Fund lending of these currencies might only exacerbate the difficulties of the deficit nations supplying the currency, and thus Fund holdings of these currencies are not usable for making loans.

The determination of which currencies are usable at a given time is based on the Fund's assessment of the strength of member countries' current-account and reserve positions. The Fund does not make public which currencies it considers usable at any given time, but from time to time it does publish its total holdings of usable currencies. At the end of IMF fiscal year 1977 (April 30, 1977), holdings of usable currencies stood at only SDR 4.5 billion. Since that time, another SDR 5 or 6 billion in usable currencies has been added by the coming into force in April 1978 of the increased quotas approved under the sixth General Review of Quotas. The Fund has an additional SDR 2.5 billion available to it for use in particular circumstances under the terms of the General Arrangements to Borrow (GAB).(3) Finally, as much as SDR 8.7 billion could be added to the Fund's holdings of usable currencies if the proposed Supplementary Financing Facility (more commonly known as the Witteveen Facility) is approved by the necessary individual governments. As of the fall of 1978, approval of United States participation in the facility was still pending before the United States Congress, and its chances of being approved were far from certain. A seventh General Review of Quotas is now underway, but because the process of approval and ratification of further quota increases by member nations is usually quite lengthy, the increased holdings of usable currencies resulting from quota increases approved in this review will probably not be available until 1981. For the next few years, then, the IMF will have at most about SDR 22 billion - and maybe only SDR 13 billion - at its disposal for net lending. If total international lending continues at its current levels - and there is no evidence that suggests that it will not - the IMF will remain a source for only a small fraction of all international finance.

IMF CONDITIONALITY

But the importance of IMF lending does not arise from the size of this lending. Instead, it arises from the "conditionality" of Fund lending - the ability of the Fund to require that its borrowers adopt economic policies that will lead to reductions in payments imbalances and will insure that that borrower's external financial affairs are maintained in good order.

Conditionality is usually seen as a necessary adjunct to lending that is intended to finance a current-account deficit. Financing is necessary to provide a deficit nation with the time required to make deliberate adjustments to changed circumstances. But because this adjustment can be politically and socially painful for many nations, there is also a need for some institutions that will, in addition to supplying financing, insist on the adoption of policies that will lead to adjustment. Through the conditions associated with its loans, the IMF encourages adjustment that will not be accomplished at the expense of other nations. In attaching these conditions to its loans, the IMF is unique among international lenders.

Some other international lenders impose conditions on borrowers, but none for the same purposes as the IMF does. The multilateral development banks, for example, require that the funds they lend be used for specific development projects. Bilateral loans from governments often carry conditions about how borrowed funds are to be used or about where they must be spent. Only the IMF, however, regularly requires that policies be adopted that will facilitate the smooth operation of the international financial system.

Private lenders - who provide the largest fraction of international lending - have been loath to involve themselves in the internal affairs of borrowing nations, for both political and business reasons. Most international banks have a variety of financial interests in potential borrowing countries, and these interests make it important for the banks to maintain good relations with host governments. Involvement in domestic economic policy could threaten these relations. Further, it is difficult for any one bank to impose stringent conditions on a borrower because the opportunity often exists for the borrower to take its business elsewhere. If conditions imposed by banks are to be effective, most of the major international banks must stand behind the conditions. Finally, few banks have the staff or the data necessary to determine what measures are required to correct payments imbalances in particular nations.

Similarly, governments are often unwilling to appear to be dictating internal economic policies when making loans to other governments. Borrowing nations may also find it politically difficult to accept conditions - even reasonable ones - that are imposed by foreign governments. As a result, bilateral loans rarely carry conditions that encourage economic adjustment.

The IMF is particularly well suited for providing conditional financing. Because the Fund is an international body with no direct interests other than maintaining order in the international financial system, borrowing nations are more willing to accept conditions imposed by the IMF than those imposed by commercial banks or other governments. In fact, governments often welcome IMF conditions because these conditions often provide a justification for politically difficult measures. It is also difficult for a nation to avoid IMF conditions by turning elsewhere for financing; commercial banks have in general been wary of lending to nation with large borrowing needs that have not first submitted to Fund conditions. The Fund is also better supplied with information than are the commercial banks. To receive a loan from the Fund, a nation must report data relevant to its present and prospective economic situation. Some of these data are not available to private lenders, and the Fund is generally regarded as having better information on the prospects of particular countries than other lenders have.

As a result of its ability to impose conditions on its borrowers, the IMF has in recent years come increasingly to be accepted by private lenders as a dependable certifier of international creditworthiness. Throughout the lifetime of an IMF standby arrangement, the Fund monitors a nation's compliance with the agreed-upon conditions. If the nation in question fails to carry out the actions required, the Fund will cancel the credit line represented by the standby arrangement. Thus, a decision by the Fund to provide a line of credit to a particular nation is widely seen as a sign that that nation has agreed to adopt policies that will guarantee repayment of foreign loans. Further, the Fund will undertake to make sure that all the promised policies will in fact be implemented. Wth this kind of assurance of good financial behavior, private lenders are much more willing to lend to the country in question.

Thus, it is often argued that the size of IMF lending is not really important. Instead, it is argued, what matters is the fact that the IMF agrees to lend any money at all to a particular country. The Fund is seen as controlling not only its resources, but also the resources of private lenders; unless a government comes to terms with the IMF, it will not receive private financing from abroad. Proponents of this view point to recent events in Peru. The government at first rejected IMF conditions, choosing instead to seek financing from private lenders. When private lenders proved unwilling to extend credit without a guarantee that the government would adopt what the banks considered prudent economic policies, Peru was forced to go back to the IMF and to submit to Fund conditions in order to establish its creditworthiness. Similarly, the United States Government and the government of a number of other developed nations extended a line of credit to Portugal in 1976 on the condition that Portugal first conclude a standby agreement with the IMF.

Because of the powerful influence that IMF lending can have on the flow of other international financing, a number of observers have in recent years been looking more closely at the effects of IMF conditionality, and some have questioned whether the conditions imposed by the IMF are always well suited to solving the problems facing borrowing countries - especially borrowing developing countries.(4) Fund conditions are widely seen as being quite conservative in nature and placing a heavy emphasis on monetary policy. Typically, Fund conditions are concerned with the rate of credit expansion, the size of the government deficit, exchange rate policies, trade policies, levels of foreign borrowing, and the maintenance of "adequate" reserves of foreign exchange. The focus of IMF conditions is usually on the short term; conditions are designed to stabilize the external payments of a borrowing nation within two or three years. Seldom is direct consideration given to such matters as the composition of government spending, the choice between investment and consumption (either public or private), government price and wage policies, or how the current payments difficulties relate to the longer-term economic goals of the borrowing country.

There are good reasons for the Fund's reticence to go

beyond these areas traditionally included among its conditions. A definite focus on the short-term situation reduces the chance that the Fund will be seen as a source of long-term development finance. By restricting itself to relatively technical matters of monetary and exchange rate policies, the Fund is able to avoid more politically charged issues of resource allocation within an economy.

Some have argued, however, that this narrowly focused, politically neutral orientation is becoming increasingly irrelevant to the problems confronting developing countries. The adjustments that need to be made by these countries are by their nature long term and involve major restructing of economies. The transition to an economy, for example, less dependent on imported oil, more highly industrialized, or with significantly improved agricultural productivity will in many countries require major new investment and perhaps significant redistributions of resources among individuals, among industries, and between the private and public sectors of the economy. Unless the IMF addresses these issues directly, it is argued, Fund conditionality will have only a minimal effect on the rate at which these transitions are accomplished. Indeed, in some cases it has been argued that the conservative nature and short-term focus of Fund conditions has hindered the process of economic development.

For all its attempts to restrict itself to technical issues, the Fund cannot help imposing conditions that have political content. Monetary policies and exchange rate policies do affect the distribution of resources within an economy and can in part determine the rate and character of economic development. As long as the Fund is already involved in such political issues, critics ask, why should it not extend its concern to include a wider set of relevant economic issues?

THE IMF AS A LENDER OF LAST RESORT

The high volume of international lending and the apparently precarious position of some borrowing nations that have characterized the last few years have led some observers to urge the establishment of some institution to serve as a international "lender of last resort." By standing ready to provide financing to countries in need and without access to financing from any other source, this institution would provide some insurance against the sort of contraction of international credit that is postulated as a possible result of a simultaneous failure by several borrowing nations to meet their obligations under existing loan agreements. Presumably, the interest rates and conditions associated with loans made by this lender of last resort would be such as to discourage nations from seeking such loans except in the most extreme cases. With such an institution in operation, it is argued, commercial banks would face greatly reduced risks in their international lending and would be more likely to continue making financing available even to borrowers experiencing some difficulties. Thus, the likelihood that any nation would be without access to financing and would therefore be forced to turn to this lender of last resort would be reduced.

Opponents of such a scheme argue that it would serve only as a "bail-out" for commercial banks and would in the long run actually reduce the financing available to LDCs. In this view, the commercial banks have overextended themselves in their international lending - lending more (particularly to the developing nations) than the borrowing nations can realistically be expected to repay or refinance within the maturity of the loans. In some cases, the banks may find themselves with no choices other than to accept rescheduling or postponement of repayments or to make further loans to allow the borrower to continue to make payments on the original loans. If the latter course is chosen, the rescheduling of repayments is merely postponed.(5)

Commercial banks could extricate themselves from such a situation without losses only if loans from some new source, such as the lender of last resort, became available. These new loans would allow debtor countries to repay their private creditors, who would in turn reduce their exposure in marginal countries by refusing to make further loans. Thus, it is argued that the establishment of an international lender of last resort would provide no new financing to developing countries. Instead, it would serve simply to let private lenders off the hook, by assuming the risks inherent in what are often seen as imprudent loans made by these lenders.

Because of its unique position as an international institution with established procedures for imposing conditions on borrowers and for monitoring compliance with these conditions, the IMF is most often cited by proponents of the lender-of-last-resort concept as the appropriate body for undertaking such responsibilities. Opponents of the idea have also focused on the Fund, using arguments similar to those given above to argue against recent proposals for expansion of the Fund's resources.

Perhaps the most important thing to point out in this connection is that the Fund is not now and in the near future is unlikely to be in a position to serve as a lender of last resort. This is primarily because of the small size of IMF resources compared to the magnitude of LDC debt. Estimates of the total size of disbursed LDC debt at the end of 1977 are in the range of $240 billion, with perhaps 40 percent of this amount owed to private lenders. At present, IMF resources for lending are only in the range of $16 billion or $17 billion.

More resources may be available if the Witteveen Facility is finally established, but if LDC debt continues to grow at the rate of the last few years, the potential need for emergency financing will far outstrip these new resources.

Total IMF resources, however, do not impose the only limitation of how much credit is available to a country from the IMF. In most cases, the amount a country can borrow from the Fund is limited to about two times the amount of its quota in the Fund.(6) Approval of the Witteveen Facility will make available to a borrowing country an additional line of credit roughly equal to its quota. Table 11.1 provides an example of how serious a limitation this restriction places on the Fund's ability to serve as a lender of last resort. The first column shows the amount of disbursed public or publicly guaranteed debt owed by selected countries at the end of 1976 (the last year for which complete data are available). The next two columns show each country's quota in the Fund and the ratio of debt to private lenders to quota. Many of these countries have already drawn heavily on the Fund, and less than the usual amount of IMF credit is therefore available to these countries. The last column shows much much each country had drawn from the Fund as of July 31, 1978. For nearly all of the countries listed in this table, outstanding debts have increased significantly since 1976, and it is clear that the amounts of Fund lending available are sufficiently small as to prohibit the Fund's acting as an effective lender of last resort except in a very few cases. Similarly, it seems unlikely that any expected increase in Fund quotas or resources will allow any significant reduction in private exposure in LDCs or serve to "bail out" private lenders.

Even if IMF resources were sufficient to allow commercial banks to reduce their exposure in LDCs, there is little to indicate that the banks concerned would do so. In recent years, international lending has accounted for a growing share in the earnings of commercial banks,(7) and these banks have suffered much lower loss rates on their international lending (particularly sovereign lending) than they have on their domestic lending.(8) This does not guarantee, of course, that losses will not be higher in the future. What it does indicates, though, is that international lending has been highly profitable for private lenders, and there is no reason for them to reduce their international lending unless for some reason the risks involved were to increase substantially. Increased resources for the IMF could not help but decrease these risks, and indeed the prevailing view among commercial bankers is that official lending (particularly IMF lending) and private lending are complements rather than substitutes.(9)

Table 11.1. Debt to Private Lenders, IMF Quotas, and Drawings from the IMF of Selected Countries

Country	Total Public Debt (Including Undispensed) Owed to Private Lenders December 31, 1976 (in millions of dollars)	IMF Quota (in millions of dollars)	Debt/Quota (percent)	IMF Drawings July 31, 1978 (as percent of quota)
Argentina	4,019	674	596	19
Brazil	10,750	838	1,283	2
Chile	1,618	273	593	148
Colombia	895	243	368	--
Costa Rica	292	52	562	91
Dominican Republic	234	69	339	91
Greece	2,066	233	887	114
Guyana	168	32	528	129
Jamaica	528	93	568	203
Korea, Republic of	5,125	202	2,537	192
Malaysia	1,639	319	514	3
Mexico	13,363	674	1,983	67
Nicaragua	428	43	995	11
Panama	887	57	1,556	112
Paraguay	138	29	476	--
Peru	2,585	207	1,249	129
Portugal	931	217	429	159
Spain	4,338	702	618	126
Syria	209	79	265	25
Turkey	687	252	273	252
Yugoslavia	730	349	209	89
Zaire	2,002	192	1,043	163
Zambia	562	178	316	163

Sources: Debt: World Bank, Annual Report, 1978, pp. 124-125; Quotas and Drawings: IMF, International Financial Statistics, September 1977.

THE FUTURE ROLE OF THE IMF

As we have seen in the preceding sections, unless IMF resources are greatly expanded the Fund will remain the source of only a very small fraction of total international lending. The prospects for the expansion of IMF assets of sufficient size to allow the Fund to play a substantially larger direct role appear dim. Even an increase in quotas of 40 or 50 percent (the largest increases now being talked about) coming into force in the early 1980s would allow the Fund to do little more than keep pace with the expected continued rapid growth in international lending from other sources.

Of course, other sources of funds are available to the IMF in addition to quota increases. It is generally believed that the IMF's articles of agreement would allow it to raise funds by selling bonds in international bond markets. A number of observers (and particularly some seeking to avoid the necessity of placing government funds at the disposal of the IMF) have urged the IMF to take such action, but there is no sign at present that the Fund is prepared to alter its traditional mode of operations and approach private investors directly.

One is forced to conclude, then, that there is little prospect of the IMF's assuming the responsibilities of an international lender of last resort. Indeed, it seems much more likely that the Fund will continue to act more as a lender of _first_ resort, providing credit in a timely fashion to nations in difficulties and allowing these nations time to negotiate larger lines of credit with commercial lenders. Certainly the IMF will not be able to provide any important assistance in the unlikely event that international economic or political developments should bring about widespread interruptions in debt servicing by LDCs. At best, the Fund can be relied upon to provide temporary, stop-gap financing for one or two countries which need time to make more extensive arrangements.

With only a relatively small direct role to play in providing international credit, the IMF is likely to remain an important force in international finance only if the Fund's conditionality remains an essential element in the international financial system. The prospects for the Fund's continued importance on this score are nearly certain; private lenders are becoming increasingly dependent on the IMF's certification of a country's creditworthiness in making their own lending decisions. Although the coordination between commercial banks and the IMF is far from perfect, in most marginal cases in recent years commercial lenders have refused to extend credit until the borrower has reached agreement with the IMF on what steps are to be taken to eliminate the conditions that require large amounts of international credit.

In recent years commercial lenders have been urging the IMF to share its information on economic conditions in particular countries with private lenders, allowing private lenders to make better and more independent assessments of the risks involved in particular loans. The Fund is able, however, to collect much of the information it does only because this information will be kept confidential, and it would be difficult for the IMF to make these data available only to some small group of banks without making it available to all banks. Greater sharing of information, then, is likely to mean publication of heretofore confidential information and therefore such sharing seems unlikely. Thus far the IMF has given no sign that it might consider such arrangement.

Closer coordination between the Fund and commercial banks is probably still in the interests of both, however. It would provide greater leverage for the Fund and reduced risks for the banks. It might even be in the interests of borrowing countries if such coordination facilitated negotiation with commercial lenders. It is possible that in the future this coordination might take the form of more direct involveent of the IMF in the deliberations of "creditors clubs" with responsibility for working out credit packages for countries in financial difficulty. It is probably unrealistic to expect anything in the nature of joint financing arrangements involving the Fund and commercial banks; such arrangements would seriously threaten the Fund's independence and would greatly complicate the Fund's efforts to maintain the confidentiality of proprietary information.

Finally, if the IMF's role as a guarantor of good international financial behavior and a certifier of creditworthiness continues to increase in importance, the Fund will come under increasing pressure to maintain rather narrow technical standards for how nations in balance-of-payments difficulty should act. Private lenders will demand firm assurances that they will be repaid and borrowing nations, aware that the IMF in large measure controls their access to private credit markets, will be particularly sensitive to any Fund conditions that appears to have important political content. For these reasons, it seems unlikely that there will be any dramatic change in the nature of Fund conditionality. At most, one might expect some increase in the duration of IMF standby arrangements and loan maturities. Major attempts to make IMF conditions more consonant with particular long-term development strategies, however, seem unlikely. The emphasis in IMF conditionality will probably remain narrowly focused on short-term correction of international payments imbalances.

NOTES

1. Under the amendments to the Fund's Articles of Agreement adopted in April 1978, the Fund will undertake "surveillance" of members exchange rate policies. What actions the Fund will actually be able to take to affect these policies is uncertain.

2. This figure for private international lending includes foreign and international bond issues and publicized Euro-currency credits. Excluded are supplier credits and unpublicized transactions. Data are from Borrowing in International Capital Markets, published quarterly by the World Bank.

3. In the early 1960s, it was feared that balance-of-payments support for the largest of the industrial countries would require financing in excess of the Fund's ability to provide it. To meet this potential need, special arrangements were made between the Fund and 11 major industrial nations (Belgium, Canada, France, the Federal Republic of Germany, Italy, Japan, the Netherlands, Sweden, Switzerland, the United Kingdom, and the United States). Under these arrangements, called the General Arrangements to Borrow (GAB), the Fund may borrow up to certain limits from any of these nations for the purpose of making loans to some other members of the group. Total resources available under the GAB are about SDR 6.6 billion, but usable currencies remaining to be drawn amount to only about SDR 2.5 billion.

4. For a concise discussion of these issues, see the testimony of Professor Richard S. Eckaus before the Joint Economic Committee, 95th Congress, 1st Session, April 21, 1977.

5. The recent financial arrangements between Zaire and its private creditors are an example of this kind of dilemma. In 1976, Zaire fell into arrears on its international loan repayments. Zaire's official creditors (foreign governments and international institutions) agreed to a rescheduling of debt, but private creditors refused to accept such a rescheduling, preferring instead to provide a new package of loans and to require that Zaire continue to meet its obligations under the terms of the old loans. The effect of this action was much the same as rescheduling; in either case, the commercial banks would be postponing repayment of their original loan.

6. In certain circumstances, nations may make larger drawings from the IMF. For a concise treatment of the amounts available in various circumstances, see "Supplement on the Fund," IMF Survey, Fall 1976.

7. In 1976, international lending accounted for nearly half of the earnings of 13 large U.S. international banks. See International Debt, the Banks, and U.S. Foreign Policy, Hearings before the Subcommittee on Foreign Economic Policy, Senate

Committee on Foreign Relations, 95th Congress, 1st Session, August 1977.

8. Bank for International Settlements, Forty-Seventh Annual Report: 1st April 1976 - 31st March 1977 (Basle, Switzerland: June 1977), p. 102.

9. For a banker's view on this subject, see Irving S. Friedman, The Emerging Role of Private Banks in the Developing World (New York: Citicorp, 1977), pp. 52-53.

IV

The Problem Redefined

12 Three Windows on LDC Debt: LDCs, the Banks, and the United States National Interest*

Robert W. Russell

Growth in the external debt of developing countries has been outpaced by growth in interest in the question of whether LDC debt is excessive. The perspectives of borrowers and lenders, public officials and private participants can hardly be expected to coincide on the issue. The appropriate level of debt for development purposes may be different from the appropriate level of debt for the safety and soundness of the principal lenders: the banks of developed countries. International debt can have a bearing on the foreign policies of both borrowing and lending countries even when it has little effect on economic conditions. LDC debt is considered here from three perspectives: 1) the development needs of LDCs, 2) the safety and soundness of United States banks, and 3) the United States national interest.

DEBT FOR DEVELOPMENT

With few exceptions the debt levels of developing countries appear too low to support optimum rates of economic development. Increasing debt, the accounting manifestation of capital inflow, is an essential part of the development process; that is, it is essential if development is to proceed at a lively pace. The importance of foreign capital investment in the historical development process of the United States, Canada,

*Author's note: The views expressed are my own and do not necessarily reflect those of the institutions and persons with whom I am associated.

Australia and New Zealand is well known. Korea, Taiwan, the Philippines, Brazil and Mexico are achieving a rapid rate of economic growth today through reliance on foreign capital inflows, including a large proportion of debt to foreign banks. Other countries are attempting to do likewise. Indeed, the effort to achieve development goals accounts for the buildup of developing country debt.(1)

The sudden expansion in developing country debt which began in 1973 was largely due to factors beyond the control of the LDCs themselves. The oil price increases contributed significantly to increased current-account deficits in 1974, but in subsequent years the world recession, not oil prices, accounted for the largest portion of the mounting deficits of LDCs. Slow growth in the Organization for Economic Cooperation and Development (OECD) countries, not excessive monetary expansion in LDCs, caused the current-account deterioration in developing countries, and remains the principal threat to a smooth workout of accumulated debt service obligations.(2)

Capital flows to developing countries make sense for investors as well as for the LDCs. The rate of return on investments in developing countries is higher than the rate of return on investments in the developed world.(3) New production facilities in developing countries can take advantage of the latest technology and organizational efficiencies, as well as lower-cost labor. From the standpoint of optimal allocation of the world's resources, as well as from the viewpoint of the private investor, investment in developing countries is rational.

The general inadequacy for development purposes of capital flows to the developing countries is accentuated by the skewedness of the flows which occur. Private capital flows in all forms - stock and bond purchases, direct investment, and bank loans - are directed to the least poor of the poor countries. More advanced developing countries generally provide a more hospitable climate for private capital investment and maintain steadier and higher levels of economic growth. Charles Ganoe has illustrated, with respect to United States bank claims the pronounced concentration in higher-income LDCs (See Chapter 9).(4) The same phenomenon is reflected in Eurobond issues and Eurocurrency placements generally.

The profile of official development assistance (ODA) is skewed in the opposite direction: the poorest countries receive more ODA than do the advanced developing countries.(5) (See Table 12.1.) Furthermore, ODA with the largest concessional elements is concentrated in the poorest countries. It is precisely this group of poorest countries with debt arising almost exclusively from ODA for which debt relief may be appropriate and necessary. Debt cancellation for the poorest 29 countries (see Table 12.2) would cost the ODA donor countries very

Table 12.1. Estimated External Medium-Term and Long-Term Debt of Developing Countries:* December 1976 (in billions of US$)

	Low-Income Countries(a)	Middle-Income Countries	Oil-Exporting Countries(b)	Total
From official creditors	26	41	13	80
From private creditors(c)	3	70	16	89
Total	29	111	29	169

*This represents a total of 80 countries; it excludes southern Europe except Turkey and all territorial dependencies.

(a) Countries with a per capita income below $265 in 1975.
(b) Algeria, Ecuador, Gabon, Indonesia, Iran, Iraq and Venezuela.
(c) Includes debt publicly guaranteed by developing countries and other debt from private sources.

Source: Helen Hughes, "The External Debt of Developing Countries," _Finance and Development_ 14 (December 1977): 24.

little ($500 million per year in interest and capital payments), but greatly improve growth prospects in the recipient countries. As _The Economist_ notes:

> Nearly 95% of the 29 poorest ldcs external debt is official debt to other governments (compared with only about 65% for the debt of all ldcs). In 1976 these poorest 29 received only 1.1% of the private funds going from the rich countries to all ldcs. Relief to them would neither encourage them to ignore their private debts (as bankers fear) nor enable them to pay mountains of debt back to the banks and then start borrowing more (as taxpayers fear). The mountains don't exist.(6)

Table 12.2. The Twenty-nine Poorest Countries, 1975

	Total Outstanding Debt (disbursed)	Debt Service (in millions of dollars)	Debt Service Ratio*
Afghanistan	787	23	10
Bangladesh	1,622	70	16
Benin	99	9	7
Botswana	263	20	12
Bhutan	0	0	0
Burundi	15	2	6
Central African Empire	92	11	14
Chad	70	6	5
Ethiopia	387	32	9
Gambia	14	NA	NA
Guinea	211	24	NA
Haiti	62	6	5
Laos	25	2	NA
Lesotho	13	NA	NA
Malawi	262	17	9
Maldives	1	NA	NA
Mali	327	6	5
Nepal	37	5	NA
Niger	114	13	NA
Rwanda	22	1	2
Sikkim	NA	NA	NA
Somalia	257	5	4
Sudan	1,191	158	30
Tanzania	839	38	8
Uganda	209	29	11
Upper Volta	63	8	6
Yemen Arab Republic	243	17	5
Yemen PDR	101	4	1
Western Samoa	16	1	5

*Total debt service as percentage of total exports of goods and services.

NA = not available.

Source: OECD, cited in The Economist, "Relief for the Poorest," March 4, 1978, p. 75.

Countries holding debt to private creditors are in a different situation, for which different treatment is appropriate, as was recognized at the United Nations Conference on Trade and Development (UNCTAD) board meeting in September, 1977:

> No debt relief was being sought in respect of developing countries with access to private capital markets: here the problem was thought to lie not in the amount of debt but rather in an unbalanced debt maturity structure. The solution to problems faced by some of these countries might be found in long-term re-financing through officially sponsored credit facilities.(7)

LDC debt to private creditors is concentrated too heavily in short-term maturities and bears high interest rates. American Express reports that in 1976 "nearly 90% of syndicated Eurocurrency bank credits carried a final maturity of 5 to 8 years."(8) American Express estimates that, whereas only 60 percent of all LDC debts will have matured by 1983, 95 percent of the Euroloans extended in 1976 will have come due for repayment by 1983. Edgard Kröller of the OECD staff estimates that the "average interest cost of private debt outstanding is currently around 9 percent - twice what it was ten years ago and 2 ½ times as high as on official debt."(9)

The point is not how this debt will be repaid - developing countries should remain capital importers - but how the debt will be replaced or rolled over. As Henry Wallich has observed, "So long as the debt and its service does not outgrow a reasonable proportion to the productive capacity and particularly the exports of the economy, creditworthiness and the ability to refund and roll over can be maintained."(10) This means that the capital acquired through debt must be used for investment rather than consumption, and especially for investment which boosts exports or reduces imports. But this export-based strategy for managing LDC debt relies heavily upon growth in the developed economies and an absence of trade protectionism. Albert Fishlow has observed that the debt problem is ultimately a trade problem:

> Repayment requires consistent, rapidly growing exports from developing countries as the basis for reducing their current account deficits. It is not clear that the global environment will favor such increasing competition.(11)

Recession in the OECD countries or a resurgence of protectionist barriers against imports from LDCs could presage serious debt servicing difficulties for advanced LDCs. The period from 1978 to 1981 is of particular concern because during that period debt servicing costs will increase more rapidly than export earnings. The judgments of creditors will determine whether LDCs receive the capital flow necessary to roll over existing debt and even expand indebtedness.

In cases where debt service obligations cannot be met on schedule, debt restructuring should be accomplished promptly on terms which insure that the same problem will no re-emerge in a year or two. Debt renegotiation, basically a stretching out of old seven-year credits to something nearer to fifteen-year terms, should be regarded as an acceptable solution for all parties. Restructured debt seems far preferable to drastic deflationary measures in the debtor country or outright default.

Increasing LDC debt is a natural concomitant of development, and from that perspective, the concern should be with maintaining the economic conditions which succor world trade and economic growth, and, thereby, debt and development. But development is a long-term process and LDC economies are susceptible to greater cyclical fluctuations than are developed economies. There is a need for capital which is committed for ten to twenty years, which far exceeds customary terms on commercial bank loans.

Larger capital flows on longer terms are possible if both developed and developing countries follow sound economic policies. Indeed, Robert Aliber concluded from a study of relative growth rates that:

> The developing countries - and the world - would be better off if a larger share of the world's capital were invested in them - as long as one can make the assumption that the differences in growth rates (and the implied differences in marginal interest rates in the industrial countries and the developing countries) are large relative to additional risks associated with these credits.(12)

The challenge is to enable LDCs to attract the traditional sources of longer-term private capital - bond issues and foreign direct investment - not bank credits.

THE SAFETY OF UNITED STATES BANKS

Discussion in the United States of LDC debt has been dominated by the question of whether debt owed to United States banks endangers the safety of the banks. On an aggregate global basis, the evidence seems incontrovertible that United States banks are not excessively exposed. A survey of foreign lending by large United States banks indicates that as of December 31, 1977, cross-border and cross-currency claims on residents of nonoil-producing LDCs amounted to approximately $47 billion.(13) Total consolidated assets of the United States banking system, by contrast, were $1,231 billion in June 1977. Loss rates on international lending have been very low (roughly one-third of one percent, compared to three-quarters of one percent on domestic loans). Rates of return on international lending have been well above those for domestic loans. Aggregate data indicate that United States banks as a group are not excessively exposed in individual developing countries, although lending is concentrated in a few countries: Brazil ($11.7 billion); Mexico ($10.9 billion); Korea ($3.3 billion); Taiwan ($2.7 billion); and the Philippines ($2.0 billion).(14)

Aggregate data do not begin to answer the question, however, of whether particular United States banks might be overexposed in particular foreign countries, or whether that situation, if it exists, would endanger the banking system in general. Because data on individual bank exposure is confidential, one can only speculate on the exposure of individual United States banks in individual foreign countries.

If any United States banks are exposed to the extent that a default by a foreign country could endanger the bank's capital position, only a small number of banks are likely to be in that state. United States banks can be grouped into three tiers with respect to the scale of their international business. First-tier banks, the top nine United States banks, are so large and diversified that it seems unlikely that debt repayment difficulty in a particular foreign country could endanger one of these United States banks. If one of the first-tier banks were endangered, the Federal Reserve would almost certainly find it necessary to enable the bank to continue to operate. The domestic as well as the international roles of the largest United States banks make it highly unlikely that they would be allowed to simply close their doors.

Second-tier United States banks, that is, those banks with assets of more than a billion dollars, are likely to engage in substantial foreign lending, but have modest capital resources. Within this group of banks there may be instances of excessive exposure in particular foreign countries. These banks tend to specialize in types of foreign lending or lending within certain world regions. These are also the banks to whom bank regulators have most often addressed cautionary remarks about foreign lending, foreign exchange trading and other international banking practices.

Finally, the third tier of United States banks consists of the smaller banks that do some international business but for whom international banking is a very minor part of their operations. These banks, with a few exceptions, conduct so little international business that they would not be in grave difficulty even if they took substantial losses on the international side.

The two key elements in prudent lending practice are thorough analysis of risk and risk diversification. Both could be improved with respect to international lending. Risk analysis in international lending depends upon the quality of information available to the creditor. Henry Wallich has warned that "ignorance is not bliss where credit is concerned," and cautioned that: "If there are banks that, in competing for loans, also engage in a competition in laxity with respect to debtor information, they surely are storing up trouble for both themselves and the debtor."(15)

Information on the economic prospects for individual countries is becoming more available and more reliable. Even so, it remains quite difficult to estimate export earnings.(16) Information on debt maturities is still more difficult to acquire.

One would assume that LDCs would readily provide maturity profiles and that lenders would insist upon them if they were not immediately proferred. Such is not the case. Nothing is more difficult to obtain than the maturity profile of the external debt of a developing country. Lenders should insist that developing countries provide maturity data on their external debt. The International Monetary Fund could take the lead in pressing LDCs to provide such profiles.

A device sometimes suggested to enhance investor confidence is lending on the basis of assigned export earnings. But assignment adds little to the investor's protection. The country's entire economy must be assessed in the context of the global economy. If a country faces general economic difficulty in managing its debt, cross-default provisions make it unlikely that differential treatment will be provided for particular loans, despite contracts to assign export earnings. Thus, investors should continuously review country debt maturity profiles and watch them against projected export earnings, rather than relying upon specific export earnings assigned to pay off particular obligations.

To ensure that banks diversify their lending risks in LDCs, single borrower limits could be applied more effectively to country exposure. The Comptroller of the Currency, John Heimann, recently issued a regulation which tightens the application of the ten percent of capital limit on national bank loans to a single foreign public borrower. To be considered a separate entity for purposes of the ten percent limit, a foreign public agency or government subdivision would have to be responsible for its own financial accounts and have a separate revenue stream under its control. The lending bank should have documentation of such facts. The regulation should have a modest precautionary effect on the distribution of United States national bank lending and on LDC borrowing.

The limits applied to national banks ought to apply to

state banks, too, but they do not. State-chartered banks in New York, for example may lend sums equal to 25 percent of their capital to single borrowers. The same is true for state-regulated banks in certain other states. If single borrower limits are desirable for prudential reason they should apply to all United States banks, not just national banks.

The basic difficulty with single borrower limits is that they do not control the country exposure of the bank. Some banks are said to have more than 100 percent of their capital exposed in foreign countries, principally in the larger advanced LDCs, Brazil, Mexico and Korea, for example. From the standpoint of the safety of United States banks, concern should be focused upon the exposure of individual banks in individual countries, not on aggregate levels of United States bank lending to foreign countries or loans to public borrowers. The semiannual surveys now conducted by the federal regulatory agencies provide the basis for closer supervision of individual bank exposure.(17)

In some respects concern about United States bank loans to LDCs has been exaggerated. There has been a tendency to confuse default on debt with debt repudiation or with true inability to pay. Debt repudiation and true inability to repay are unlikely. As Robert Aliber has noted, a country's failure to pay on schedule does not necessarily indicate that external indebtedness is too large, rather failure to repay on schedule may say more about the level of a country's international reserves, its views on whether it might be able to increase its net aid receipts by delaying repayment, and its willingness to adjust its exchange rate to maintain its international competitiveness.(18) Furthermore, to the extent that refinancing (as opposed to debt repudiation) provides benefits to developing countries and creates some opportunity costs to the banks, it can lead to better judgment on the part of banks and a better balance between international and domestic lending. A moderate risk of default together with occasional necessary debt reschedulings does not endanger United States banks, but can help to keep risk assessments honest. Too frequently United States banks take no losses in either actual or opportunity cost terms on reschedulings. The prospect that a number of countries will reschedule their external debt should not be taken as evidence that the system will collapse or that banks will not be repaid.

LDC DEBT AND THE UNITED STATES NATIONAL INTEREST

The principal consideration from the standpoint of the United States national interest must be the soundness of the international economy. Marina v.N. Whitman has urged the

United States to shed any illusions that the state of the international economy and the United States economy are separable:

> Exports today account for more than 10 percent of the U.S. gross national product. About a quarter of the profits of U.S. nonfinancial corporations is accounted for by foreign earnings. It is estimated that at least one out of every eight manufacturing workers in this country is producing for export. Economic interdependence is today a two-way proposition. The U.S. economy cannot remain healthy unless the international economy and the delicate and complex network of financial relationships that undergird it remain healthy as well.(19)

The United States also has major foreign policy interests in many of the countries with heavy debt burdens. Turkey, Greece, Italy and Portugal are NATO allies. Security treaties link the United States and Korea, the Republic of China, the Philippines, Spain, and all the Latin American republics. In other cases, such as Zaire and Indonesia, the security linkage is less formal but nonetheless tangible. As noted in a staff report to the Subcommittee on Foreign Economic Policy of the Senate Foreign Relations Committee, the United Sates "can hardly afford to stand by and watch the economies of these countries collapse, or to have their governments undermined politically by financial difficulties."(20)

The importance to the United States of continued economic development in LDC countries as well as the soundness of the United States banking system has led to the suggestion that a closer link be established between United States foreign policy and the lending policies of United States banks. The difficulty of maintaining a solid wall separating private bank lending and foreign policy is readily apparent in several recent cases.

In Zaire in 1977 the reluctance of private bank creditors to reschedule Zaire's debt to them on terms comparable to those provided by foreign government creditors threatened to impede the recovery of the economy of Zaire. The United States Government has a substantial foreign policy interest in the future of Zaire, as well as an interest in repayment of AID and Export-Import Bank credits. It is not surprising that United States foreign policy and the interests of the private banking community came into conflict in Zaire during the debt rescheduling negotiations.(21) Private banks ultimately provided financial arrangements approximating "comparable treatment," but only under strong governmental pressure to do so.

Indonesia went through a similar episode. Financial mismanagement of the Indonesian state oil company, Pertamina, resulted in a severe debt repayment problem in the early 1970s. The United States, from a foreign policy perspective, was eager to see the creditworthiness of Indonesia and Pertamina restored. As part of its recovery program, the Indonesian Government pledged to the IMF that external borrowing would not exceed specific ceilings. In turn, the IMF provided standby credit to enable Indonesia to manage the huge Pertamina debt. The State Department encouraged United States banks to abide by the terms of the Indonesian pledge to the IMF; that is, to refrain from extending credits which evaded the purpose or letter of that pledge. Furthermore, the State Department discouraged United States banks from declaring the Pertamina debts in default and thereby upset efforts by the Indonesian Government to get the situation in hand. The banks did not always accede to the State Department's representations, nor did United Sates bank regulatory agencies incorporate the foreign policy considerations in their supervisory actions.(22)

Potential conflicts between United States banks and United States foreign policy will grow as United States bank financing of the debt of advanced developing countries continues to increase. Some observers take the view that there should therefore be further mingling of the lines separating private sector decisions on international finance from public policy considerations. But attempting to include United States foreign policy considerations in private bank decisions on financing and refinancing could entail a larger measure of government regulation of foreign lending by United States banks than would be consistent with the efficiency of the private sector. The result could be resource misallocations and an increasing regulatory burden upon the United States Government. In addition, foreign misunderstandings of the purpose and intent of United States policy could arise.

It would seem better to keep public policy and private investment at arm's length to the extent possible. In fact, it may make sense to preserve the distance between the two sectors, by insisting that representations by the State Department to United States banks be limited to insuring that foreign lending and refinancing decisions do not diminish the likelihood of prompt servicing of public credits, and that all parties agree to comparable terms for rescheduling or refinancing private as well as public credits where necessary.

The difficulty in the renegotiation of credits to Zaire arose because private banks attempted to resist an extension of credit to Zaire on terms comparable to those provided by the renegotiation of official credits. The behavior of the banks, although perfectly understandable, was inconsistent with the interests of the public creditors, including the United States Government.(23) The United States properly insisted upon renegotiation of the private credits on terms comparable to those offered by the public sector. The Department of the Treasury recently restated United States policy on debt renegotiations. The strong affirmation therein of the principle of comparable treatment should help to avoid future misunderstandings.(24)

It has been suggested that as in the Indonesian case, when a country has arranged with the International Monetary Fund for a standby or other credit, the Department of State together with other agencies of the United States Government should see that United States banks conform their lending practices to whatever promises the country has made to the IMF. State Department personnel, however, have neither the experience nor the legal authority to supervise United States bank lending. Injecting foreign policy considerations into private bank decision making through State Department representation could mean restraint on profitable opportunities for United States bank lending in some cases and encouragement for imprudent United States bank involvement in others. United States foreign policy actions already have an indirect influence on the behavior of private bankers; a direct official role seems likely to exacerbate both the problems of foreign policy and bank soundness.

United States economic policies may also affect bank lending to LDCs, and there is reason to ask whether there is a built-in bias toward foreign lending. The rapid growth of foreign loans by United States banks, especially the largest United States banks, may reflect not only an objective evaluation that the marginal return on investment in LDCs is more profitable than on domestic loans, but that United States public policies tend to stimulate or subsidize foreign lending. Chief among these would seem to be the prohibition on interstate branching by United States banks, favorable tax treatment of foreign corporate earnings, and accounting and bank regulatory policies which tend to understate the risk involved in international lending.(25)

The net effect of such public policies would seem to be to make foreign loan safer and more profitable than domestic loans, not as a matter of deliberate policy to assist development in poorer countries, but as an accidental consequence. Because the rate of return on capital ought to be naturally higher for loans to developing countries than loans within developed countries, there is no need to stimulate or subsidize foreign lending in general at the expense of domestic lending. Rather, development policy should concentrate on trade and financial measures which help developing countries maintain and enhance their natural attraction for private capital flows. Policies on taxation, accounting, and bank regulation which are neutral with respect to foreign versus domestic lending are optimal, both for U.S. economic well-being and international development.

CONCLUSION

LDC debt is too low, not too high, for development purposes. The problem for the developing countries is how to earn foreign exchange and thereby remain creditworthy, not how to pay off the creditors. The critical variable are growth rates and trade policies in the developed countries, not the developing countries. Debt forgiveness for the poorest LDCs would be a humane and helpful step, but neither debt forgiveness nor debt repudiation are likely or useful for the advanced LDCs who hold the bulk of the debt, much of it owed to banks.

The banks do not appear to be overexposed in a general sense nor likely to be endangered by anything short of widespread and severe economic recession. Banks do need to improve their information base for country lending and continue to diversify risks; bank regulators should see that prudent practices are followed. Banks will need to be prepared to restructure and refinance LDC debt on a case-by-case basis, and banks, governments, and the public should begin to regard debt renegotiation as a normal occurrence, not the sounding of an alarm.

The United States has strong economic and foreign policy interests in the development of LDCs, and, therefore, in a well-managed and expanding LDC debt system. The highest priorities for United States policy, which happily serve both domestic and international interests, should be steady economy growth and a liberal trading policy. Banks should neither be encouraged nor discouraged with respect to lending to LDCs. Any attempt to "guide" private international lending would raise more problems than it would solve. LDCs can be expected to offer attractive investment opportunities as long as the major developed economies are expanding steadily and trade is flowing freely. No special stimulus is needed for the private sector to seek out such profitable opportunities in LDCs, and no special restraints on the resulting capital flows, other than those necessary to sound banking practices, are warranted.

NOTES

1. W. H. Bruce Brittain, "Developing Countries' External Debt and the Private Banks," Banca Nazionale del Lavoro Quarterly Review, no. 123 (December 1977), pp. 365-80.

2. Ibid., pp. 374, 380.
3. Robert Z. Aliber, "Living with Developing Country Debt," Llyods Bank Review, September 1977, pp. 40-41.
4. Charles S. Ganoe, "Loans to LDCs: Five Myths," Journal of Commercial Bank Lending, November 1977, pp. 18-27.
5. Helen Hughes, "The External Debt of Developing Countries," Finance and Development 14 (December 1977): 24.
6. "Relief for the Poorest," Economist, March 4, 1978, p. 75
7. Ursula Wassermann, "UNCTAD: The External Indebtedness of Developing Countries," Journal of World Trade Law 12 (January-February 1978): 76.
8. The Amex Bank Review 3 (March 25, 1977): 4.
9. Edgar Kröller, "The Debt Problem of Developing Countries: A Challenge to the International Community," OECD Observer, no. 90 (January 1978), p. 28.
10. Henry C. Wallich, "U.S. Lending Abroad: The View from the Fed," Institutional Investor, June 16, 1978.
11. Albert Fishlow, "Debt Remains a Problem," Foreign Policy, no. 30 (Spring 1978), p. 134.
12. Aliber, "Living with Developing Country Debt," p. 41.
13. "Country Exposure Lending Survey," Comptroller of the Currency News Release, June 8, 1978.
14. Ibid.
15. Wallich, "U.S. Lending Abroad."
16. Declan Duff and Ian Peacock, "Refinancing of Sovereign Debt," Banker, December 1977.
17. For a summary of the Comptroller's view of country risk, see Harold D. Schuler, "Evaluation of Risk in International Lending: A Bank Examiner's Perspective," Key Issues in International Banking, Proceedings of a Conference held in October 1977, Conference Series no. 18, The Federal Reserve Bank of Boston, pp. 136-53.
18. Aliber, "Living with Developing Country Debt," p. 38.

I am indebted to Dr. Lawrence G. Franko for pointing out that the structure of a country's economy (price elasticities of supply and demand for imports and exports) may preclude sudden increases in foreign exchange earnings through exchange rate changes or other measures in response to external economic shocks. It is an open question whether countries should manage reserves and debt so as to insure themselves against such risks or whether lenders should expect them to do so.

19. Marina v. N. Whitman, "Bridging the Gap," Foreign Policy, no. 30 (Spring 1978), p. 156.
20. "International Debt, the Banks, and U.S. Foreign Policy," (Staff Report prepared for use of the Subcommittee on Foreign Domestic Policy, Committee on Foreign Relations, U.S. Senate, 95th Congress, 1st Session, August 1977), p. 7.
21. International Debt, Hearings before the Subcommittee on

International Finance of the Committee on Banking, Housing and Urban Affairs, U.S. Senate 95th Congress, 1st Session, August 29, 30, 1977, pp. 181-84; and The Witteveen Facility and the OPEC Financial Surpluses, Hearings before the Subcommittee on Foreign Relations, U.S. Senate, 95th Congress, 1st Session, September 21, 23, October 6, 7, 10, 1977, pp. 113-27 and 146-50.
22. Witteveen Facility, pp. 83-112.
23. The bankers' perspective has been clearly stated by Dr. Irving S. Friedman, Senior vice-president of Citibank:

> Private banks must approach the question of a developing country's debt-service problems on the basis of (1) the fundamental distinction between the developing country's debt to official creditors (governments and official international financial institutions) and debt to private creditors; (2) the assignment of the highest priority to servicing the private debt; and (3) the fundamental assumption that debts to private banks must be serviced as scheduled.

The Emerging Role of Private Banks in the Developing World (New York: Citicorp, 1977), p. 69.
24. U.S. Department of the Treasury, Press Release, January 5, 1978; reprinted in the Congressional Record, February 23, 1978, p. H 1402.
25. The Financial Accounting Standards Board (FASB) backed down on a proposed standard with respect to "troubled credits" which could have compelled banks to disclose and perhaps write down loans in cases of roll-overs or stretch-outs. The final product, Statement of Financial Accounting Standards No. 15, "Accounting by Debtors and Creditors for Troubled Debt Restructurings," issued in June 1977, permits banks to carry weak loans to LDCs at face value. See Chicago Tribune, April 18, 1977, section 6, p. 8, for criticism of the FASB action.

BIBLIOGRAPHY

Aliber, Robert Z. "Living with Developing Country Debt." Lloyds Bank Review, September 1977, pp. 34-44.

The Amex Bank Review (London).

Brittain, W. H. Bruce. "Developing Countries' External Debt and the Private Banks." Banca Nazionale del Lavoro Quarterly Review, no. 123 (December 1977), pp. 365-80.

"Country Exposure Lending Survey." Comptroller of the Currency, News Release, semi-annual.

Duff. Declan, and Peacock, Ian. "Refinancing of Sovereign Debt." *Banker*, December 1977.

Economist. (London).

Fishlow, Albert. "Debt Remains a Problem." *Foreign Policy*, no. 30 (Spring 1978), pp. 133-43.

Friedman, Irving S. *The Emerging Role of Private Banks in the Developing World*. New York: Citicorp, 1977.

Ganoe, Charles. "Loans to LDCs: Five Myths." *Journal of Commercial Bank Lending*, November 1977, pp. 18-27.

Hughes, Helen. "The External Debt of Developing Countries." *Finance and Development* 14 (December 1977): 22-25.

International Debt. Hearings before the Subcommittee on International Finance of the Committee on Banking, Housing and Urban Affairs, U.S. Senate, 95th Congress, 1st Session, August 29, 30, 1977.

International Debt, the Banks, and U.S. Foreign Policy. Staff report prepared for use of the Subcommittee on Foreign Economic Policy, Committee on Foreign Relations, U.S. Senate, 95th Congress, 1st Session, August 1977, Committee Print.

Kröller, Edgar. "The Debt Problem of Developing Countries: A Challenge to the International Community." *OECD Observer*, no. 90 (January 1978), pp. 25-29.

Schuler, Harold D. "Evaluation of Rise in International Lending: A Bank Examiner's Perspective." *Key Issues in International Banking*, Proceedings of Conference held October 1978. Conference Series no. 18, the Federal Reserve Bank of Boston, pp. 136-53.

Wallich, Henry C. "U.S. Lending Abroad: The View from the Fed." *Institutional Investor*, June 16, 1978.

Wasserman, Ursula. "UNCTAD: The External Indebtedness of Developing Countries." *Journal of World Trade Law* 12 (January-February 1978): 74-83.

Whitman, Marina v. N. "Bridging the Gap." *Foreign Policy*, no. 30 (Spring 1978), pp. 148-56.

The Witteveen Facility and the OPEC Financial Surpluses. Hearings before the Subcommittee on Foreign Economic Policy of the Committee on Foreign Relations, U.S. Senate, 95th Congress, 1st Session, September 21, 23, October 6, 7, 10, 1977.

13 The International Debt of Developing Countries and Global Economic Adjustment

William A. Noellert

INTRODUCTION

The international debt of developing countries (1) has historically been the concern of the multilateral lending institutions established after World War II and various organizations and scholars concerned with the economic development of these countries. The problem was to define the limits of external indebtedness which these countries could assume and the appropriate terms on which aid should therefore be provided.(2) In the mid-1970s the international debt of the developing countries became part of a broader concern with the financial stability of the world monetary system.(3) The combination of intense competition among banks in the Eurocurrency market and distrust of the ability of developing countries to sensibly manage their own financial affairs created the image of a severe world financial contraction caused by the default of major developing country borrowers. However, by the summer of 1978, the specter of major defaults causing an international financial contraction had vanished. The developing countries continued to borrow, methods were found to deal with problem countries like Zaire and Peru, and the financial press focused on a new source of international monetary instability - the decline of the U.S. dollar in relation to other major currencies. It would appear that the recent alarm voiced by many about the external indebtedness of developing countries had been overstated. Developing country debt seems to be once again returning to the province of finance officers and development economists as one aspect of the problem of economic growth.

The objective of this chapter is to present an alternative framework for analyzing recent trends in the accumulation of external debt by developing countries, particularly the rapid expansion in commercial bank debt. The reason is not that the "development" framework or the "financial stability" framework are wrong. Rather, from the perspective of the global economy, both approaches are inadequate for understanding the significance of developing country borrowing in the past decade and thereby its significance for the future. The alternative framework that will be presented is the analysis of developing country debt in the context of the international adjustment problems arising from the disintegration of the Bretton Woods adjustable-peg exchange rate system. Once this framework is laid out, the global significance of international borrowing by developing countries can be presented.

INTERNATIONAL ADJUSTMENT AND DEVELOPING COUNTRY DEBT

Conceptually, the definition of balance-of-payments adjustment is straightforward. The classical concept of real adjustment refers to "a marginal reallocation of productive resources and exchanges of goods and services under the influence of changes in relative prices, incomes, and exchange rates."(4) Simply stated, the adjustment process requires a country with a current-account deficit to undergo monetary deflation or currency devaluation, or the surplus country to undergo monetary inflation or currency revaluation, or some combination of the two. The alternatives to real adjustment is the financing of payments imbalance with short-term capital movements. However, such process obviously has limits in terms of a given country's access to sufficient means of financing and, at least theoretically, is only considered appropriate for temporary and nonrepetitive equilibrium disturbances.

The problem of international adjustment becomes less straightforward when the history of the world economy is examined. An analysis of global current-account balances in the postwar era shows an ever-changing pattern of deficits and surpluses and continual struggle by various national governments to minimize the costs of adjustment to these imbalances.(5) The disintegration of the Bretton Woods exchange rate system occurred because of a failure to reach international agreement over the distribution of adjustment costs under the rules of that system. The fundamental cause of the need for structural adjustment was the rapidly increasing exports of the economies of Japan, Western Europe (particularly the Federal Republic of Germany), and a small number of developing countries relative to the United States.(6)

This situation was reflected in a continuing decline in the United States trade performance and a resulting large outflow of dollars.(7) The adjustment process failed to work because the position of the United States dollar as a world medium of exchange enabled the United States to support an outflow of finance in excess of its balance on current account, the difference being offset by the accumulation of foreign-owned dollar balances. This system is known as borrowing short and lending long. It can only be maintained so long as there is nothing else to substitute as a means of international exchange.(8)

On the deficit side, the international role of the dollar enabled the United States to postpone what would have been an economically and politically costly adjustment. On the surplus side, there was no effective mechanism in the Bretton Woods system to pressure Japan and Germany to curb their growing current-account surpluses. And those countries, whose economies were based on export-led growth, did not see it in their political or economic interests to do so.(9) Therefore disequilibrium continued until the United States finally decided such a situation was becoming very unstable (in large part due to the short-term capital flows from the Eurocurrency market) and forced the abandonement of the adjustable-peg exchange rate system in August 1971. However, even with the subsequent realignment of currency values and the change to managed floating after the abandonment of an agreed set of international monetary rules, structural adjustment in the world economy has not occurred.(10)

An integral part of this breakdown in the world adjustment process has been a rapid and continued increase in international liquidity, primarily attributable to the liquidity-creating effects of the United States external payments deficit and the subsequent growth in the Eurocurrency market.(11) It was this development that laid the foundation for the growth of the private external indebtedness of developing countries in the 1970s. The rapid increase in funds available in the international financial market (Eurocurrency market) expanded the opportunity and need for banks to diversify their international business. These supply side pressures, combined with the traditional demand of developing countries for net inflows of money capital, resulted in the growth of private bank lending to these countries for the first time in the post-World War II era.

Although the data are imperfect, approximately one-third to two-fifths of expanded international lending by commercial banks since 1970 has been to the non-OPEC developing countries.(12) From 1971 to 1976, net lending by commercial banks to developing countries grew at a rapid pace. The World Bank estimates that "net lending by private financial institutions to governments and to the private sector against government guarantees increased by about 50 percent a year."(13) From a sum of less than $1 billion in 1970, gross borrowing by developing countries from commercial banks reached approximately $92 billion at the end of 1977. However, their net position vis-a-vis foreign banks stood at approximately $30 billion.(14)

Another factor of major significance, in addition to the rapid increase in gross borrowing, is the extreme concentration of private bank lending among a few developing countries. Table 13.1 details this concentration of borrowing

Table 13.1. External Financial Position of Nonoil-Developing Countries by Rank Order
(billions of dollars, position end = 1977)

	Gross Borrowing From Banks	Cumulative	Cumulative (percent)
1. Brazil	22.9	22.9	24.8
2. Mexico	19.3	42.4	45.8
3. South Korea	5.3	47.5	51.5
4. Argentina	4.5	52.0	56.4
5. Taiwan	3.4	55.4	60.1
6. Peru	3.0	58.4	63.3
7. Philippines	2.8	61.2	66.4
8. Thailand	2.0	63.2	68.5
9. Columbia	1.7	64.9	70.3
10. Chile	1.4	66.3	71.9
Total Nonoil Developing Countries	92.2	92.2	100

Source: Bank for International Settlements, <u>48th Annual Report</u>, (Basle, Switzerland, June 1978), pp. 94-95.

showing that the top ten countries accounted for 71.9 percent of gross borrowing; Brazil, Mexico and South Korea account for over 50 percent of the total.

The ability of a small number of developing countries to use the Eurocurrency capital market to obtain either real resources or greater liquidity is an important development not only for those countries, but for the world economy in general.

Throughout the post-World War II era, there had been

only two major sources of external capital available to developing countries. These were the multilateral lending institutions such as the World Bank group and the regional development banks or the multinational corporation. This system of international financial intermediation predominated both because of the exigencies of international politics and the fact that developing countries were judged as not being sufficiently competitive to obtain foreign exchange in order to pay back debts.(15)

In the 1970s, the increased access to Eurocredits has changed this system of financial intermediation and expanded the financial options open to a number of developing countries. The financial transactions are "carried out in a cold, standoffish commercial spirit that contrasts sharply with the tangled emotional relations surrounding concessional finance."(16) Thus, developing countries have an important interest in this continuation and expansion of private bank lending that is characterized by competitiveness, free access and depoliticization.

The fact that the bulk of private bank lending to developing countries is concentrated among just a few countries is no accident. These countries, while still having significant internal development problems, are semi-industrialized countries with a rapidly expanding capacity to generate exports of manufactured goods to hard currency markets and thereby earn sufficient foreign exchange to service their debt.(17) Indeed, the export of manufactured goods from developing countries is just as concentrated as their private international borrowing. The top five international borrowers (Brazil, Mexio, South Korea, Argentina and Taiwan) accounted for 42.7 percent of total developing country manufactured exports in 1976. If the exports of Hong Kong and Singapore, two major offshore financial centers, are added to those of the five other countries the total share of manufactured exports in 1976 increases to 68 percent.(18)

The vast majority of private bank lending to developing countries through mid-1978 had proved to be on a sound basis. All of the concern voiced in the aftermath of the oil price increases in 1973-1974 and the world recession of 1974-1975 has been forgotten. Indeed the developing countries as a group, and the heavy borrowers from the international banking sector in particular, have adjusted much better to world economic changes since 1973 than have the developed countries.(19) As a result, the developing countries which had borrowed a net amount of $30 billion between 1974-1976, supplied a net amount of $1.6 billion to the banks in international markets in 1977.(20)

It appears that international bank lending did not discourage serious efforts toward balance-of-payments adjustment. Indeed those developing countries that have been the largest borrowers of funds from the international banking sector have shown the largest improvement in current-account balances in 1976 and 1977. Brazil, Mexico, South Korea, Argentina, and Taiwan - all of which have pursued restrictive domestic policies and rapid export expansion - improved their current-account positions by about $5 billion in 1977.(21)

The growth of private bank lending has had beneficial results for the international economic position of a small number of developing countries. It is equally obvious that this nontraditional source of international financial intermediation has not really affected the low-income and middle-income developing countries because domestic economic conditions effectively seal them off from this source of funds. Their capacity to service debt remains very limited and they must continue to rely on official development assistance at highly concessional terms.(22)

It has been shown that, for a small number of semi-industrialized developing countries, access to international financial markets has expanded their financial options and maneuverability in the world economy.

This result was brought about by the rapid expansion in international liquidity consequent upon the conflict over the distribution of global adjustment costs and the disintegration of the Bretton Woods exchange rate system. The implication of this recent economic development for the future process of global economic adjustment will now be examined.

GLOBAL PARAMETERS OF DEBT AND ADJUSTMENT

The ability of the semi-industrialized developing countries to access international financial markets in the 1970s has allowed them to maintain development plans and rates of economic growth that would not have been possible in the absence of such international borrowing. However the rapid increase in borrowing at higher commercial rates has meant a rapid increase in contractually fixed debt service payments. This situation has magnified the need for these countries to accelerate the expansion of their exports of manufactured foods to developed countries in order to earn foreign exchange for the servicing of international debt.

While the expansion of borrowing from international financial markets has provided new options for these countries, it has also enforced new necessities upon them. The necessity not just to export, but to expand the rate of growth in manufactured exports will mean that these dozen or so developing countries will increasingly be compelled to allow the exigencies of external balance dictate national economic policy. The establishment of free-trade zones, incentives to attract new investment for export production and other such policies can be expected to increase in the coming years.(23) Whether or not the increase in the export of manufactured products can be maintained will depend crucially upon the dynamics of adjustment in the developed countries; specifically whether the state of internal and external balance allows these countries to adjust to the rate of export expansion of the semi-industrialized developing countries.

The developed countries have not adjusted well to the oil price rise of 1973-1974 and the recession of 1974-1975. And the adjustment which has occurred externally has been very asymmetrical.

Figure 13.1 puts the recent economic situation among developed countries in historical perspective. The current economic condition of the developed countries has no precedent in the postwar era. Compared with the output trend over the period 1960-1973, the present "growth recession" is the longest and deepest yet experienced.(24) This has meant that the total increase in unemployment since 1974 has been the largest since the war. Inflation and the level of external imbalance have reached new peaks since the oil crisis and global recession, although inflation has declined somewhat recently. The lower section of Fig. 13.1 is the absolute sum of the current-account positions of the OECD countries expressed as a percent of gross domestic product. While a very crude measure of current-account imbalances, it does highlight the fact that the disequilibria in the international payments positions of these countries is at record levels. While all four of these factors (growth, employment, prices and external balance) are highly interrelated, the crucial point for the present analysis is that all are at unacceptable levels simultaneously.

The amount of international payments imbalance among the OECD countries is a reflection of the high degree of asymmetry in the external balance of a few important developed countries; these include the United States, Japan, Germany and Switzerland.(25) In 1977 the United States registered a current--account deficit of $15.2 billion. This is projected to rise to approximately $21 billion for 1978. The other three countries have registered large and growing current-account surpluses in recent years. For Japan, the surplus was $10.9 billion in 1977 and is projected to increase to about $17 billion in 1978. The figures for Germany and Switzerland for 1977 are $3.9 billion and $4 billion, respectively, and are projected to increase in 1978 to $5.5 billion and $4.5 billion.

A crucial structural factor underlying the deterioration in the United States current-account balance has been the recent emergence of the semi-industrialized developing countries as important exporters of manufactured goods. United States imports of manufactured products from these countries have

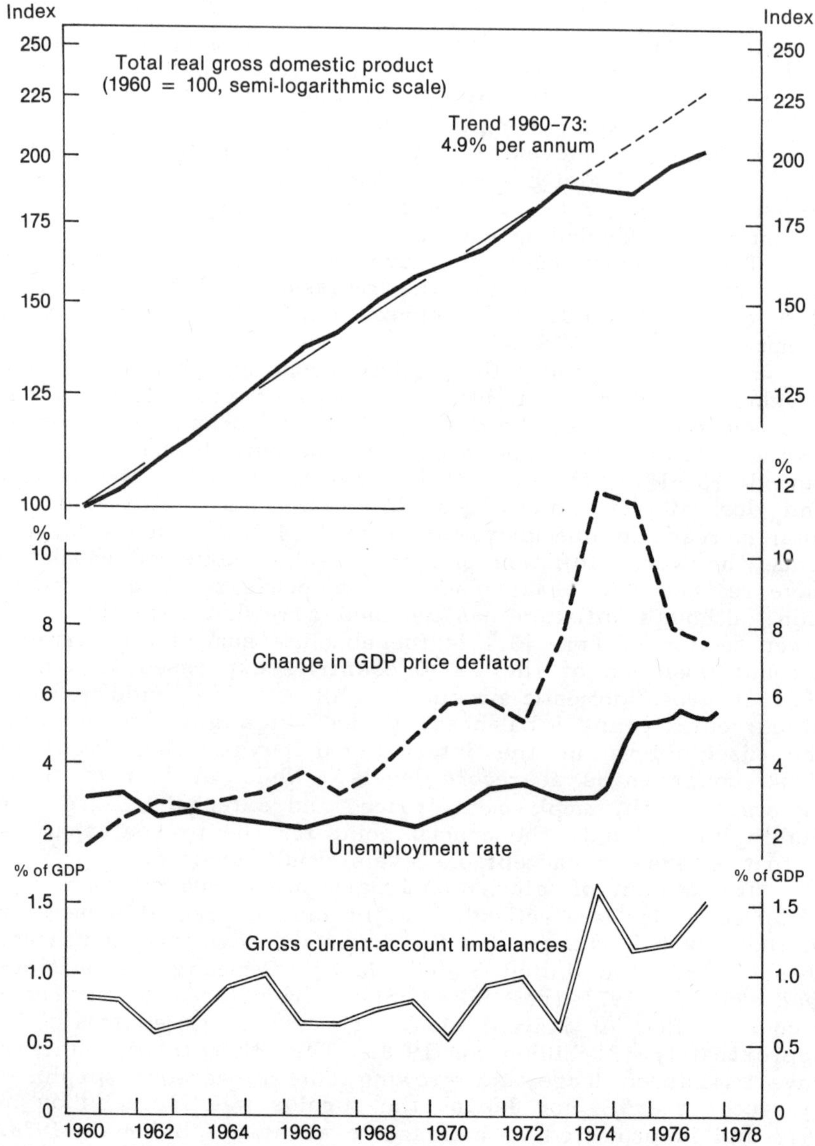

Source: Bank for International Settlements, *48th Annual Report,* Basle, Switzerland, June 1978, p. 41.

Fig. 13.1. OECD countries: growth, inflation, unemployment and external imbalance.

Fig. 13.1. OECD countries: growth, inflation, unemployment and external imbalance.

Source: Bank for International Settlements, Report, (Basle, Switzerland, June 1978), p. 41.

been increasing at rates of about 25 percent or more a year.(26) This factor contributed to a $5.5 billion trade deficit with the nonoil developing countries in 1977 - the first United States bilateral trade deficit with these countries since World War II. "The traditional or structural deficit of LDCs characteristic of the development process is narrowing and trade competition with traditional United States exporters is widening."(27)

While the rapid shift in the structure of manufactured goods trade with these developing countries is not the only factor underlying the United States deficit position, it is of important significance in the context of the problems outlined above.(28) As the rapid increase in exports from the semi-industrialized developing countries continues, the trade positions of the top developed countries will be under heavy competition. Already in Japan and Germany, less clearly in other major countries, there is a shift away from the production of standard unsophisticated products toward increasingly high-technology and luxury goods.(29) This process will intensify international competition in product lines that have been mainly dominated by United States manufacturers - computers, antipollution equipment, sophisticated electronics, high-technology machinery, etc. The rapid expansion in the exports of a small group of developing countries, and their increasing share in the world output of manufactured goods, will therefore affect the dynamics of trade and adjustment among the developed countries themselves. Thus, the growing importance of manufactured exports from a small number of developing countries, along with the slowing growth trend in output of the industrialized countries and the size of their external, asymmetrical imbalance, has major implications for the ability of the United States and other industrial countries (including the surplus countries) to adequately adjust to the medium-term current-account prospects.

The imbalances, by themselves and in any given year, are not necessarily a major problem. A country's balance on current account is a residual item (however, more so for the United States than for a country with a high proportion of international to domestic economic transactions like West Germany) that reflects the interaction of many international and domestic economic factors. There is no need for a country to have balanced trade - either for total trade, by commodity category or by country. What matters is not the particular balance on current account but the factors that determine it. "A particular value for the balance is satisfactory only if it is associated with an acceptable configuration of other, more important, national and international objectives."(30) As was pointed out above, for OECD countries as a whole, the state of external balance is associated with an <u>unacceptable</u> configuration of other national and international objectives. This can be illustrated by briefly examining the United States economy.

In 1978, the United States ran a very large current-account deficit, despite the fact that for a period of economic recovery the rate of output growth was lower and unemployment rate higher than historical norms. Additionally, the rate of inflation was accelerating and the value of the dollar on foreign exchange markets was depreciating in relation to other major currencies. Thus the position of the current account was not associated with an accceptable configuration of other national and international objectives. The policy dilemma was choosing between lower inflation and preserving the international value of the dollar or even slower growth and more unemployment.(31) In November 1978 international financial events forced the Carter administration to choose policy measures to try to implement the former choice.

The results of the actions to support the dollar and lower the inflation rate remain to be observed. In monetary and fiscal restraint prove effective, this should slow the rate of inflation by reducing the output growth rate and increasing the amount of unemployment. A decline in the growth rate of national income, however, will also mean a contraction in approximately 30 percent of the market for developing country exports of manufactured goods. Higher unemployment in the United States will also make it difficult to resist protectionist pressures in various sectors of the United States economy because alternative employment opportunities will be even more scarce than previously. Finally a decline in the United States growth rate of national income, relative to major trading partners, will tend to dampen the stimulus to those economies from sales to the United States. The economic problems are highly interrelated and any attempt to rely on uncoordinated unilateral action for solution to external economic problems can only worsen the overall international situation. This applies especially to policy effects on developing country exports, ignoring their need for foreign exchange to service debt and pay for needed imports.

This brief exposition of recent trends in the world economy brings out the very difficult international adjustment problems that have to be dealt with by various nation-states. It also highlights the potential obstacles concerning the ability of the semi-industrialized developing countries to maintain their rate of export-led growth and thereby their capacity to service further accumulation of international private bank debt. For the continued failure of the macroeconomic management of the capitalist world economy to increase output and lower rates of unemployment and inflation mean that adjustment costs will be very high for many countries and will be resisted by those most directely affected. The agonizingly slow pace of the Tokyo round of the multilateral trade negotations and the spread of a host of actions to restrict and regulate trade in recent years are an indication of the difficulties that nation-states are experiencing in their external economic position. These restrictive actions increased to such an extent that in September 1977, the General Agreement on Tariffs and Trade (GATT) secretariat warned that the spread of protectionist policies had reached a point where "the continued existence of an international order based on agreed and observed rules may be said to be open to question."(32)

The present surge in the exports of manufactured goods from the semi-industrialized developing countries is based upon the provision of external capital and technology, supplied by international banks and corporations, and an elastic supply of labor, which holds down wages and maintains profits and investments. While such a strategy of export-led growth has been seriously questioned by development economists in recent years, there is also the more immediate problem of the creation of too much labor-intensive production and an oversupply of these goods - the problem of "banana republics becoming pyjama republics."(33) The issue appears to be diversification into more capital-intensive production so that this type of dependency can be overcome. Hong Kong, Singapore and South Korea have started in this direction, but it is questionable how many developing countries can follow such a path. And the success of these countries is still dependent upon the ability and willingness of the developed market economies to absorb increasing imports.

The basic conclusion that arises from the above analysis of trends in the global economy is that the present state of external imbalance and domestic unemployment in developed economies places constraints on the continued ability of the semi-industrialized developing countries to expand their market share in manufacturing products at rates of the recent past. If this is the case, the ability of these countries to obtain and service more international debt will be constrained. It also means that the access of other developing countries to international financial markets will be limited.

The fundamental factor that will determine the ability of developing countries to continue to borrow on international capital markets and service their accumulated debt will be the way in which economic adjustment to the present state of global imbalance is carried out. This, more than any other factor, will determine the capacity of developing country borrowers to continue to service past and future debt and eventually to develop surpluses in their balance of trade with the rest of the world to pay off the debt. Thus the actions taken by developed country governments to internal and external adjustment will be much more important for the repayment and borrowing prospects of developing countries than various ad hoc proposals such as improved surveillance of international lending or more involvement by the International Monetary

Fund in directing a country's economic and financial policies.

The countries of the European Economic Community, the United States and Japan account for approximately 56 percent of the developing countries' export market (52 percent of their market for manufactured exports).(34) The economic adjustments problems they presently face are very real and very difficult. Likewise the need for the semi-industrialized developing countries to maintain their growth rate of manufactured exports is crucial for their immediate financing and growth requirements. The problem is to move toward an international arrangement that does not disproportionately distribute the costs of adjustment onto any particular country or group of countries. To reach such a solution requires the recognition that there is no automatic free-trade equilibrium. The world's trading system requires conformity by the various nations to agreed-upon rules of behavior to prevent some countries from trying to maximize the benefits from trade and investment, causing serious economic injury to others and thereby destroying any possible basis for a liberal trading regime. In the context of the problem being considered, it should be clearly understood that any actions which by design or result (e.g., trade restrictions or economic recession) limit the export growth of major developing country borrowers will severely strain their ability to service the debt and other contractually fixed obligations they have incurred. If the means for repayment is closed off, then either major debt relief will be required or else defaults will occur, affecting the economic stability of the defaulting country, the profitability of major international banks and causing a contraction in international liquidity.

In the longer term, developing countries may want to reevaluate their present policies of relying on developed country financial and product markets to the degree that they have in the recent past. Access to finance that, in the short run, increases a country's economic options may, in the long run, prove undesirable if international events make those options extremely costly.(35)

NOTES

1. Unless otherwise stated, defined as the non-OPEC, non-OECD, non-Socialist countries. See OECD <u>Economic Outlook</u>, no. 23 (July 1978) p. 42, Table 27.

2. One of the most comprehensive studies in Dragoslav Avramovic et al., <u>Economic Growth and External Debt</u>, (Baltimore: Johns Hopkins University Press, 1964). For a more recent analysis see UNCTAD, <u>Report of the Intergovernmental Group of Experts on the External Indebtedness of De-</u>

veloping Countries. (United Nations, TD/B/685/Add. 1, December 29, 1977), especially annex I, part B.

3. For example, see Charles N. Stabler, "Emerging Nations Use Private Lenders More, Causing Some Worries," Wall Street Journal, September 28, 1976; and Robert J. Samuelson, "When the Run on the Bank Leads toward the United States and the IMF," National Journal, December 11, 1976. For a summary of this whole issue, see Howard M. Wachtel, The New Gnomes: Multinational Banks in the Third World (Washington, D.C.: Transnational Institute, 1977).

4. Benjamin J. Cohen, Adjustment Costs and the Distribution of New Reserves, Princeton Studies in International Finance, no. 18 (Princeton, N.J.: Princeton University Press, 1966): 3.

5. Ibid., pp. 5-15. For a summary of reasons for adjustment failure under fixed exchange rates see Gus Edgren, "Employment Adjustment to Trade Under Conditions of Stagnating Growth," International Labor Review 117, (May-June 1978): 293-94.

6. It is not the purpose of this chapter to analyze the breakdown of the Bretton Woods System. For a good analysis, see Sidney E. Rolfe and James L. Burtle, The Great Wheel: The World Monetary System, part II (New York: McGraw-Hill 1975), and C. Fred Bergsten, The Dilemmas of the Dollar, part I (New York: New York University Press, 1975).

7. P.T. Ellsworth and J. Clark Leith, The International Economy, chapter 25 (New York: Macmillan 1975).

8. Joan Robinson, "The Need for a Reconsideration of the Theory of International Trade," in Collected Economic Papers vol. 4 (New York: Humanities Press, 1973), p. 20. ff.

9. Rolfe and Burtle, The Great Wheel.

10. This development suggests that more is involved in the deterioration of the United States trade balance than an overvalued dollar. See C. Michael Aho and Richard D. Carney, "United States Export Performance in the Post-Devaluation Period: Continuation of a Secular Decline" (Submitted to the Subcommittee on International Finance of the United States Senate Committee on Banking, Housing and Urban Affairs, February 23, 1978).

11. See various issues of the Bank for International Settlements, Annual Report, for detailed data on the growth of liquidity in international financial markets. A good overview article is by Reinhold Harringer, "The Development of International Debt," Aussenwirtschaft 33, Jahragang, Heft I, II (March/June 1978): 11-51.

12. See Joseph D. Wood, "Risks Associate with External Debt: The Borrowers Perspective," in Harringer, Development of International Debt, pp. 106-07.

13. World Bank, World Development Report, 1978, p. 23.

14. Banks for International Settlements, Forty-Eighth Annual Report (Basle, Switzerland, 1978), p. 92.

15. See Gunnar Myrdal, The Challenge of World Poverty, part 3 (New York: Vintage Books, 1970).
16. Carlos F. Diaz-Alijandro, Less Developed Countries and the Post-1971 International Financial System, Essays in International Finance, no. 108 (Princeton, N.J.: Princeton University Press, 1975), p. 16.
17. Some countries, like Peru and Chile, are also considered good risks because of their natural resource base.
18. Data calculated from World Development Report, Annex, Tables 6 and 7.
19. A brief note on the cost of oil factor in developing country debt analysis may be in order at this point. The topic has been extensively treated in many places and need not be treated again here. In the context of the analysis being presented the OPEC price increases reinforced and accelerated the trend to non-traditional sources of financing for the semi-industrialized countries. The OPEC phenomenon did not initiate this trend. In terms of affecting current account balances, the primary impact of OPEC was on the developed countries which consume the vast majority of oil. The developed countries have not adjusted adequately to the OPEC price increases and the United States in particular has financed its current account deficits by printing more dollars, thus increasing even more the gross amount of world liquidity. See IMF Survey, May 16, 1977, pp. 147-51.
20. Bank for International Settlements, Forty-Eighth Annual Report.
21. Ibid., p. 84. For a detailed analysis of external adjustment by Korea and Taiwan see Hang-Steng Cheng, "Alternative Balance-of-Payments Adjustment Experiences: Korea and Taiwan, 1973-77," Federal Reserve Bank of San Francisco Economic Review, Summer 1978, pp. 37-48.
22. World Development Report, p. 24.
23. Folker Frobel, Jurgen Heinrichs, and Otto Kreye, "The New International Division of Labour," Free Labour World, September/October 1978, pp. 15-18.
24. Bank of International Settlements, Forty-Eight Annual Report, pp. 40-42. This section is based upon the BLS analysis.
25. A very good analysis of these developments is in Morgan Guaranty Trust Company, World Financial Markets, July 1978. The data that follow in the text comes from this source.
26. Ibid., p. 5.
27. Rudiger Dornbusch, "International Adjustment and Surveillance" (Statement before the Joint Economic Committee of Congress, July 18, 1978), p. 11.
28. Morgan Guaranty Trust Co., World Financial Markets, pp. 4-5.
29. Citibank, "Unit Labor Costs - Trade Rivals, Checklist," Monthly Economic Letter, September 1978, pp. 11-15.

30. Robert Z. Lawrence, "An Analysis of the 1977 U.S. Trade Deficit," Brookings Papers on Economic Activity, no. 1 (1978), p. 184.

31. Carlos M. Canal Jr., "Balance of Payments and Market Discipline" (Speech delivered at the 65th National Foreign Trade Convention, November 14, 1978).

32. GATT, International Trade 1976/1977 (Geneva, 1977), p. 22. See also Richard Blackhurst, Nicolas Marian, and Jan Tumlir, Trade Liberalization Protectionism and Interdependence, GATT Studies in International Trade, no. 5 (Geneva, November 1977).

33. Gyorgy Adam, "Multinational Corporations and Worldwide Sourcing," in International Firms and Modern Imperialism, Hugo Radice, ed. (New York: Penguin Books, 1975), p. 102. For a critique of export-oriented industrialization of developing countries see Folker Frobel, Jurgen Heinrichs, and Otto Kreye, Die neue internationale Arbeilsteilung: Strukterelle Arbeilslosigkeit in Industrieländern und Industrialesierung in Entwicklungsländern (Hamburg: Rowohlt Taschenbuch Verlag, 1977).

34. Calculated from UNCTAD, Handbook of International Trade and Development Statistics - Supplement 1978 (New York: United Nations, 1978); Tables A.1, A.6, A.9, A.10. Manufactured goods are defined as SITC categories 5, 6, 7, 8 less 67, 68.

35. Perhaps governments will reconsider the arguments presented by John Maynard Keynes, "National Self-Sufficiency," Yale Review 22 (June 1933): 755-69.

14 Debt, Trade, and the Prospects for World Economic Growth

Lawrence G. Franko

There are various reasons why countries - or individuals for that matter - become large-scale debtors. First among them, however, is the desire to maintain and, if possible, increase a desired standard of living.

During the late 1960s and early 1970s a large number of developing countries had grown accustomed to relatively significant rates of growth in real income and product. Much of this growth was predicated on a similar growth in real imports, the vast majority of which, apart from oil, came not from other LDCs, but rather from the developed OECD world, in the form of manufactured investment or intermediate goods.

By historical standards, this growth took place at a rapid rate. Moreover, it was quite widely spread across LDCs. The middle- and upper-income LDCs did best, with real growth averaging around 6 percent, and in some cases, substantially exceeding this rate. But even the poorest LDCs (those with per capita incomes less than $250 in 1976) experienced real annual growth rates averaging some 3.6 percent.(1) This unprecedented growth of the 1960s was accompanied by a growth in LDC imports - especially of goods purchased from advanced, OECD countries - of 6.6 percent per annum in the case of the middle and higher income LDCs, and of 4.6 percent in the case of the poorer countries.(2)

By the early 1970s these growth habits had become translated into seemingly realistic aspiration levels. There was little that then seemed utopian about the 6 percent per annum growth target for LDCs for the 1970s, enshrined in United Nations resolutions.

Between 1973 and 1975 these aspirations were subjected to a series of shocks in the nonoil-exporting LDCs. The first and greatest was the oil-price increase, but increases in the prices of other LDC imports contributed as well: grain prices tripled, and monetary expansion and the pass-through of energy-price increases raised the prices of capital goods and intermediates supplied by advanced countries to the LDCs. (See Table 14.1 for United States State Department estimates of the bases for LDC current account deficits between 1973 and 1975.)

Table 14.1. Basis for the Increased Trade Deficits of Nonoil LDCs: 1973 to 1975

	Percent of Increased Deficit*
TOTAL CHANGE	100%
PRICE CHANGES	111
a) increased import prices	170
1) Energy	93
2) Food	9
3) Other Primary Commodities	8
4) Manufactures	60
b) decreased export prices (increase is -)	-60
1) to OECD countries	-43
2) to other countries	-17
VOLUME CHANGES	-10
a) increase in imports volume (decrease is -)	5
1) from OECD countries	20
2) Oil	-14
3) Other	-1
b) decrease in export volume (increase is -)	-15
1) to OECD countries	-10
2) to other countries	-4

*Figures may not add to totals due to rounding and some unallocated flows.

Source: U.S. Department of State, Bureau of Intelligence and Research, "LDC Current Account Deficits May Affect Growth," Report no. 725, February 14, 1977, p. 3.

In the first instance these massive price increases added directly to the LDCs' total import-bill. Then, those who profited from these increased prices - especially the handful of OPEC countries in surplus - proceeded to save roughly half of the proceeds of their action. What the OPEC surplus countries (Saudi Arabia, Kuwait, the United Arab Emirates, and Libya) did spend, was spent primarily on advanced products from developed countries; thus OPEC purchases produced no LDC export boom by which the nonoil LDCs could offset their increased payments for imports.

The OPEC savings (and the savings of some of the capital goods exporters such as Japan and Germany) then dealt LDC exports yet another blow. The unspent OPEC and other surpluses had a contractionary effect on the world economy as a whole. In particular, the oil price increase acted much like an increase in taxes on all oil-consuming nations. Had the post-October 1973 price increases for oil not occurred, these sums would have been part of purchasing power in the oil-consuming countries - and part of that purchasing power would have spilled over on to imports for LDCs exports of manufactured goods and raw materials. Instead, a near depression occurred in the developed oil-consuming countries, and it provoked a slump in demand for LDC exports. The slump turned out to be temporary and limited to 1975 for the manufactures produced by Brazil, Mexico, Korea, and other newly industrializing LDCs: it was much more durable for raw materials exported by primary producers such as Zaire, Peru, Zambia, Jamaica, and Morocco.

BORROWING FOR GROWTH

In theory, increased prices for imports and reduced earnings for exports did not have to mean lower growth for LDCs. LDCs could - and those few with access to private capital markets did - maintain their capacity to import the capital, intermediate and agricultural goods needed to maintain growth by borrowing for as long as it might take to adapt their economies gradually to less reliance on high-cost imports of oil and grain. After all, although the deficit LDCs may be necessitous borrowers, OPEC and other surplus countries are necessitous lenders. OPEC receipts did not disappear into mattresses or the sands of Araby; they were deposited with banks bearing names like Chase Manhattan and Citicorp.

The collection of articles in this book bears witness to the fact that a good deal of borrowing to maintain growth did take place: many OPEC surplus petrodollars did get recycled. Moreover, and contrary to the view that LDCs in general are profligate wastrels, most borrowing countries, most of the time, supported not just growth in current consumption, but growth in investment for future growth (see Chapter 2).(3) In the immediate aftermath of the 1973 increases in oil and grain prices, the view therefore gained currency in the advanced world that the large trade deficits of the nonoil LDCs did not create a financial problem, or even that much of a development problem.

On the contrary, the private banking sector seemed to view some LDC deficits as a financial opportunity. The banks and the Eurocurrency markets were receiving large and growing supplies of funds from OPEC and other surplus governments at a time when demand from traditional borrowers was slackening off as a result of the recession in the developed countries. The banks appeared only too willing to seek new outlets for their funds. The "petrodollar recycling problem" was declared solved by the flexibility of the private capital markets, and LDC current account deficits of some $29 billion in 1974, $38 billion in 1975, and $26 billion in 1976 and $23 billion in 1977 were financed with only a modest increase in bilateral government-to-government aid from non-OPEC sources (see Table 14.2).

During 1974 and 1975, a general optimism prevailed about the private capital markets' ability to finance the nonoil LDCs deficits. Even at that time however, careful observers were noting a theme often sounded in this collection: that the bulk of private lending to LDCs (and, for that matter, to poorer OECD borrowers) was going to only a few countries; countries who were among the best off of the LDCs, such as Brazil and Mexico. Nearly 90 percent of the private bank and capital market lending to LDCs recorded by the World Bank has gone to LDCs with per capita incomes in excess of $500 per annum. Thus the financial needs of only a handful of LDCs were being met; others solved their inability to get funds from private lenders either through recourse to what little public foreign aid was available, or - more often - through lower growth.

The pressure to reduce imports and growth was strongest on the poorest countries (those with per capita incomes of less than $250 per year as of 1976). The Joint Development Committee of the IMF and World Bank asserts that these countries have maintained debt-service-to-export ratios at reasonable levels since 1973 only by cutting their imports in real terms by 20 percent below levels prevailing in the late 1960s.(4) These are the same countries which have had virtually no growth in per capita income since 1970.

Table 14.2. External Capital Flows to Non-OPEC Developing Countries, 1973-1978*
(in billions of dollars)

	1973	1974	1975	1976	1977
Deficit on Goods, Services and Private Transfers(a)	$ 10	$ 29	$ 37	$ 26	$ 23
Change in Reserves	+ 8	+ 3	- 1	+11	+ 9
NET EXTERNAL FLOWS	$ 18	$ 32	$ 36	$ 37	$ 32
Net Official Flows	$ 10	$ 15	$ 18	$ 20	$ 22
(of which: Goods)	(4)	(5)	(6)	(7)	(9)
Bilateral DAC Grants, Loans, & Credits(b)	6	7	7	9	10
Bilateral Socialist Grants Loans & Credits	1	1	1	1	1
OPEC Grants, Loans and Credits	1	3	5	5	5
Traditional Multilateral Grants, Loans & Credits(b)	2	4	5	5	6
Net Private Flows	$ 8	$ 16	$ 15	$ 15	$ 10
Direct Investment	4	3	3	4	5
Private Credit	4	13	12	11	5
Reserve-Related Flows	$ --	$ 1	$ 3	$ 2	$ --
IMF and other Credit	0	1	3	2	0
YEAR-END RESERVES	$ 28	$ 31	$ 30	$ 41	$ 50

*79 Developing countries exclusive of OECD members, Israel, South Africa, non-market countries and certain others.

(a) Including technical cooperation and military transactions that are unreported by recipient countries.

(b) Including technical cooperation grants, military grants and loans, and official export credits. (Guaranteed credits appear under private credit.)

Source: U.S. Treasury Department, "Report on the External Debt of Developing Countries and on Debt Relief Provided by the United States," Annual Submission to the U.S. Congress, January 31, 1978.

AVOIDING EXCESSIVE INDEBTEDNESS

Avoiding excessive or even any significant indebtedness to the private capital markets by restricting demand and import growth was an easy, if not always pleasant choice for the poorest LDCs. As a result of dwindling real supply of official development assistance, poor export abilities and prospects, and their being perceived an unstable, hence uncreditworthy, by private capital markets, the poorest had no alternative. But they were not alone. The number of countries that could borrow the often quoted substantial sums of LDC debt was so limited that pressures to limit real growth in imports (and therefore often domestic aggregate demand, including investment) were felt even by higher income, nonoil LDCs. Higher income LDCs such as Argentina, Uruguay, Jamaica, Chile, Columbia, Zambia, and Liberia all had negative real-growth rates of imports during the first six years of the 1970s, and countries such as the Philippines (indebted as it was), the Ivory Coast, and Costa Rica experienced substantial declines in their rates of import growth.(5)

The countries like Peru which borrowed on the basis of anticipated, but not yet (or never to be) realized raw materials wealth also cut back on their growth and imports when they woke up to what had happened to them - or when IMF conditionality, with its relative insensitivity to needs for long-term structural adjustment through more, but different investment (not less), forced them to do so. Some had borrowed to consume, and those countries perhaps should have been allowed to face the consequences or the error of their ways. But others had borrowed to invest and has guessed wrong: and one wrong guess seemed to be enough to limit the supply of funds for a second try.

Indeed, even the industrializing LDCs, those new exporters of manufactures who were able to go heavily into debt, were not immune to the pressures to cut imports, and (given limited import-substitution options) consumption and investment growth. To point to the recent deterioration in the United States (and other OECD countries) trade balances with the upper-tier, borrower LDCs, as is done elsewhere in this volume, is also to point to the dramatic improvement in these upper-tier LDCs (UTLDCs) trade and current account balances, and reserve positions.(6) (See Table 14.3.) These developments in the UTLDCs largely accounted for the dramatic shift in the industrialized countries' trade balances with the nonoil LDCs from a (positive) $19.7 billion in 1975 to a (positive) $5 billion in 1977.(7) Much of the recent deterioration in United States (and other countries) trade balances with the UTLDCs is explainable by the fact that several of the UTLDCs had rates of economic growth below historic averages

Table 14.3. Trends in the Trade Balances and Foreign Exchange Reserve Positions of the UTLDCs, 1975-1977: Improvements across the Board

	Imports as a percent of Exports(a)			Foreign exchange reserves as a percent of imports(b)		
	1975	1976	1977	1975	1976	1977
Taiwan	105	88	85	20	21	17
Korea	133	102	95	21	34	40
Singapore	141	129	119	37	37	37
Brazil	140	119	n.a.	30	48	55
India	127	91	92	22	62	55
Mexico	218	166	127	23	21	31
Argentina	119	69	67	11	53	76

n.a. Not available.

Sources:
(a) Calculated from IMF, International Financial Statistics, Washington, D.C., various issues.
(b) Calculated from IMF, Directions of Trade, Annual, 1970-1976 issues.

while United States growth in particular continued unabated. Mexico, Brazil, and Singapore, for example, had real rates of growth of GNP in 1977 which were a third to one-half the 10 to 12 percent rates these countries experienced during the 1963-1973 decade.(8) This lower growth, however, did not just happen. Policy makers in those UTLDCs chose - or felt, obliged by the balance of payments constraints they saw - to reduce growth, and to restrict imports and promote exports.

By 1977, the fears of too much debt had led private markets to gradually reduce their net lending to nonoil LDCs, and had led the borrower LDCs themselves to reduce their aspiration levels, as well as to increase their reserves for a rainy day. United States Treasury figures indicate a decline from $11 billion to $5 billion in private net lending to nonoil LDCs (or of 55 percent between 1976 and 1977. (See Table 14.2.) Although many proposals were advanced to supplement short-term, risk-averse private lending with longer-term, public facilities or guarantees, the OECD Financial Support Fund failed in the United States Congress and final appropriation of the proposed Witteveen expansion of IMF resources has long been held up in the same body.

LDC indebtedness grew at slower and slower rates, largely because countries such as Brazil, followed advice to tighten their belts and initiated a policy of import reduction by levying large new tariffs or by tightening quantitative or government purchasing restrictions on top of already existing high-tariff protective structures. Because of the very short maturity terms of the debts incurred by the borrower LDCs, these countries attempted to accelerate the already rapid growth of their exports of manufactures in order to earn the foreign exchange with which to pay back these debts. Export subsidies and incentive contracts holding the profitability of affiliates of multinational firms hostage against export performance proliferated.(9)

From the point of view of the United States and other developed countries, it could be asserted that the upper-tier borrower LDCs have succeeded all too well in coping with the difficult economic management problem handed to them by the OPEC oil-price revolution. Although Brazil and Mexico continue to have debt service-to-export ratios which are considered high by historical standards,(10) the much vaunted LDC debt problem has - at least insofar as the industrializing UTLDCs are concerned - turned into a trade problem for the United States and other OECD countries.

FINANCE, TRADE AND GROWTH

In fact, the structure of financial market interactions, with nonoil developing countries as a whole has created not one but two trade problems for the advanced countries. The extraordinarily rapid growth of exports of manufactures from the handful of industrializing, borrower LDCs - so reassuring to lenders, and so inconvenient to organized labor and small business in the developed world - is the most visible of the two. But the other, less visible problem of the excessively slow growth of OECD exports to nonoil LDCs is surely the ultimately more important one.

Other chapters in this book have posed a relatively stark policy choice between a need to allow the indebted LDCs exports access to advanced country markets in order to allow them to earn the foreign exchange needed to pay back the banks, <u>versus</u> a need to provide a more or less indefinite series of reschedulings, rollovers and new loans. A more emphatic policy point can be made however. Slow growth (especially in Europe), and Third World competition have already begun to bear protectionist fruit.(11) If this movement continues, the first, market-access policy option may simply not be available, unless relatively steady, real, noninflationary, growth in the industrialized world can be reestablished.

LDCs AS ENGINES OF GROWTH?

One of the few politically and socially feasible routes to getting noninflationary growth started again in the advanced world may well be that of expanding OECD exports of capital goods and intermediates - sectors in notorious overcapacity (underdemand) in much of the OECD world - to the nonoil LDCs. A recent article put the point in the form of a rhetorical question with an implied negative answer: "Can the Rich World Prosper Without the Progress of the Poor?"(12) Thus, it is more than somewhat possible that the solution to the first trade problem and ultimately the debt servicing problem, may require a solution to the second.

How much of an engine of growth could the LDCs be if LDCs other than the charmed circle of 10 had access to funds, and if in addition, those 10 had access to loans with longer maturities? One estimate has been made using a large scale econometric model of the Wharton School of the University of Pennsylvania (the LINK model). This estimate suggests that, other things being equal, an increase of three percentage points in the annual growth rates of the nonoil LDCs alone (to something approximately the six percent originally targeted by the United Nations for the rest of the decade) could increase the annual growth of the OECD economies taken as a group by one percentage point.

Another estimate is possible by asking the question: what size would OECD exports to the nonoil LDCs have been in 1977, had the nonoil LDCs share of world imports from the OECD stayed at the 10 to 11 percent it occupied in the 1960s - instead of declining to 8.6 percent in 1977?(13) Had the nonoil LDCs market share remained constant, LDCs would have imported an additional $25 to $35 billion of OECD goods. Assuming the usual multiplier effects in OECD economies, such exports would have added, say $60 billion to a total North America plus EEC Gross Domestic Product in 1977 of roughly $3,600 billion, or perhaps 1.6 percent.

But perhaps that incremental growth figure should be added not to the total OECD GDP, but rather to the GDP of slow growth Europe alone; a GDP of $1,575 billion, for a growth increment of some 4 percent. The United States, after all, <u>was</u> growing again in 1977 and 1978: it did not face the same balance of payments constraint as others. As has been noted in Chapter 13, only the United States could bid oil away from others by spending its own currency.

FINANCING THE LDC GROWTH ENGINE

Unfortunately, promoting a high general level of world economic activity through long-term finance aimed at alleviating balance of payments constraints to productive investment is a public good. Private lenders will not, and could not be expected to bear the risks of providing funds on the necessary scale, or to the necessary borrowers, especially since others - exporters - would be the prime beneficiaries of such lending. No reasonable amount of social responsibility on the part of the banks or Euromarkets would likely be sufficient to engender the requisite lending to uncreditworthy countries.

Just what institutional instruments would be necessary or appropriate to the provision of this global public good is a subject worthy of discussion on its own.(14) So is the question of whether the United States could or should undertake such a responsibility on its own - as it did during the time of the Marshall Plan - or whether it should act as principal promoter of an international intergovernmental consortium.

Whatever the institutional vehicle or vehicles for such measures might be, they could well include public guarantees for private risk taking in the form of the provision of loans with maturities longer than those generally available from the private markets; they might also include a much expanded World Bank or IMF.(15) Whatever the framework, the institution(s) would require considerably more resources (at least in the form of guarantees) than those projected for the Witteveen Facility or for the next increase in IMF quotas - for it would act like the structurally and investment-sensitive lender of last resort which, as C.R. Neu points out in his contribution to this volume, the IMF is not.

DOOMSDAY SCENARIOS

To be sure, policy forecasts and choices need not be polarized simply between acceptance of the current stagflation (alleviated by occasional breakouts of growth in individual countries - offset by others stagnation), and promoting measures to make investment by the LDCs the engine of advanced countries growth. Other scenarios are possible.

One would be the trading of slow, erratic, and occasionally relieved contractionary pressures for a fast descent into global depression. Fortunately, one of the possible routes to this fate, the 1930s inspired scenario of a massive domino effect series of LDC defaults, followed by an indiscriminate refusal of banks to lend to other LDCs, has been well examined and found unlikely in a world in which the differences in borrowers real abilities to service debt through foreign-exchange earnings are recognized. Moreover, although the IMF may be in no position to be a true lender of last resort, it nonetheless exists, and it is a lender (and implicit guarantor to private lenders) of some resort. IMF contractionary conditionality may sometimes be questionably overzealous both from the point of view of the political health of IMF wards, and of the economic health of would be exporters to countries under IMF care. If I interpret Robert McCauley's survey of countries in trouble in this volume correctly, a more of the same, current policy option will leave us lurching along from near-failure to near-success, punctuated by occasional riots. But it should not sound too cold-blooded to point out that there are worse imaginable alternatives for both wards and exporters. The analysis presented in this book argues that these are unlikely.

A somewhat less rapid, but almost as dangerous spiral into world depression could come about from a cancerous spread of protectionism. Protectionism has been clearly on the rise during 1977 and 1978. The available, although far from adequate, compilations of protectionist trends sadly suggest that the best known law of Newtonian physics may be all too effectively in process: the dramatic acceleration in LDC manufactured exports, especially during 1976, has been met by an opposite (if not yet equal) reaction in the form of tightened "orderly marketing arrangements in textiles; selective, discriminatory safeguards in footwear and electrical appliances; trigger-pricing barriers to import in steel; a vast increase in antidumping actions - sometimes with ill-disguised exclusionary, and not just fair trade intent; and the negotiation (imposition?) of (perhaps many) informal, little or unpublicized voluntary export restraints.(16)

Moreover, the dramatic increases since 1974 in the current subsidization of industry in advanced countries such as Sweden, Canada, the United Kingdom, Italy, and Holland(17) almost certainly had some real, if difficult to quantify, trade-distorting impact on the export prospects of the LDCs.

Fortunately for world trade as a whole, as well as for the ability of the LDCs most indebted to the private banks to service debt, manufactured exports from LDCs continue to grow - seven to eight percent in 1977 - albeit at a slower pace than the 30 percent of 1976.(18) Moreover, there is reason to believe that the resurgence of protectionism is not the whole story of advanced country commercial and industrial policy. Instances of trade liberalization do exist. Certain sectors of LDC comparative advantage, notably electronics and many electrical appliances, especially in the United States, have thus far remained relatively open to LDC export penetration - perhaps because many of the most important institutional agents of the LDC manufactured-exports boom are either import and retail houses, or affiliates of multinational manufacturing firms, headquartered in the advanced countries.(19) Thus, something of a political counterweight in favor of LDC exports exists to offset (some) protectionist pressure; all the more so since some of the same multinational manufacturing firms are also diversified exporters (or potential exporters) of capital and intermediate goods to LDCs, who are just beginning to divine that LDCs with access to more foreign exchange (via more exports, more debt, or debt with longer maturities) could be their best customers in the future.

Despite these more hopeful signs, however, protectionism seems more, rather than less likely to spread if global growth continues to do no more than sputter along.

ENERGY CONSERVATION, SUPPLY AND STRUCTURAL ADJUSTMENT

It may provide a happy ending to this collection to state that doomsday appears not only undesirable, but also unlikely. However, stagflationary muddling through with a possibility of progressively protectionist contraction seems highly likely, and hardly very attractive. Muddling through not only is causing strains within and between OECD countries with overcapacity/underdemand pains, but also appears to be imposing unpleasant political and human rights costs in various LDCs around the globe (see Chapters 7 and 8). Yet, the most promising alternative route, increasing the debt (especially the long-term debt) of the nonoil LDCs to allow them to be the new engines of growth may be an idea whose time has not yet come. Is there any other alternative?

Hardly a day goes by without a call from Washington, Paris, or EEC headquarters in Brussels, for getting investment going again in the OECD countries. And getting investment going again certainly would be an alternative were it practically and politically feasible. But attempts to get investment going again in capital and intermediate goods sectors subject to global underdemand have had, are having, and doubtless will continue to have about the same result as pushing on a string. Investors, particularly private investors, see little return from adding to capacity in industry where capacity is currently ample, to say the least. (Unless, of course, the potential markets for these investment good in the LDCs were to materialize.)

Nevertheless, there clearly is at least one sector where there is global undercapacity, even at current levels of economic activity. It is a sector which brings us back to where the mushrooming of developing country debt began: energy.

If the phrase "structural adjustment" means anything at

all, it means that the world economy as a whole (not just the United States, or the OECD) must sooner or later change its production apparatus or its life style - or the structural workings of its financial markets - as a consequence of one political and one social, and therefore two structural facts. The first is that OPEC oil producers, and most notably Saudi Arabia, will only pump so much oil per year. The second is that at actual and desired levels of world economic activity, they cannot or will not spend what they receive in payment on real consumption or investment goods. If sound financial practice limits the recycling of the petrodollar financial assets of surplus countries to potential puchasers of the goods the world is currently set up to supply, world economic activity must decline or stagnate (as it has), or inflation of the currency in which those assets are held must provide the means to reduce the real oil price (as it has), or more energy must be produced outside OPEC countries, or less energy must be consumed. Failing a major reduction in OPEC surpluses by one or more of these events, the efforts of individual oil-importing countries to stimulate their domestic economies will (as they have) end up producing inflation and/or shifts in trade patterns and exchange rates which may shuffle the misery around, but will not alleviate its causes.

Structurally, therefore, getting investment going again in the absence of more petrodollar recycling (and therefore debt), first and foremost means investment in energy-saving processes, products and life-styles, and in the production of energy from non-OPEC oil sources. But are these structural options available in the developed world alone on a scale or within a time frame which would matter?

There isn't much non-OPEC oil in the OECD area (or so it seems despite a quantum leap in exploration). Would be investors in coal production face a daunting gaunlet of environmentalist pressures, litigation, legislation, and regulation. Nuclear power, if not dead, is in a state of near coma as a result of similar factors. Other alternative sources may be of use only toward the year 2000. Still by some estimates a good deal of progress has been made in energy conservation. But the United States in particular, a country some have called "the Saudi Arabia of oil consumption," has been notably unwilling to much alter its energy-intensive life style in order to alleviate, say, Jamaica's oil-price-imposed negative rate of growth.

Yet, all is not bleak: for some action on the structural, energy front is by no means mutually exclusive with the notion of the LDCs as an engine of growth. Some developing country debt is going to finance investment in oil and gas exploration and development. If Mexico should indeed turn out to be sitting on 300 billion barrels of oil, not only Mexico, but quite a few other countries may have less worry about developing country debt, or about future OPEC price increases causing a yet worsened oil price import-constraint to growth. Moreover, in what may turn out to be the greatest paradox of all, it appears increasingly probable that developed country governments who find it politically impossible to insure would be investors in coal, oil, shale-oil or nuclear energy against the manifold political risks that face at home, will find it easier to insure and promote such investment abroad. The new support by the World Bank and the United States Overseas Private Insurance Corporation (OPIC) for LDC energy exploration and development is getting investment going again - abroad; with developing country debt. The few new nuclear energy power plants being built are being built largely in LDCs, and financed by debt.

In the final analysis, the issue of developing country debt is ultimately the issue of developing country growth. In a world in which developed countries are unwilling or unable to alleviate the primary cause of the massive increase in developing country debt, this debt is also ultimately the question of developed country growth. The import and export trade problems LDC debt engenders for the advanced countries will see to that. This dependence on the South by the North (even facing squarely the option of severing it) will take some getting used to in the developed world, particularly in a United States that once needed neither to fear nor welcome domestic repercussions of what it did or did not do abroad.

NOTES

1. World Bank, World Development Report, 1978, p. 78.
2. Ibid., p. 86.
3. Ibid., p. 82 shows annual rates of growth in investment in the principal borrowing countries typically exceeding 10 percent during the 1970s.
4. Ibid., p. 86.
5. Ibid., pp. 82-83. Not surprisingly, rate of growth in gross domestic investment - except in the Philippines and Liberia -dropped as well.
6. For a detailed examination of the trade and payments behavior of the UTLDCs between 1973 and 1977 see L. G. Franko, "Trade Policies and Practices of Developing Country Exporters of Manufacturers: Must Export-Oriented Development be Disruptive?" (Washington, D.C.: National Planning Association, April 1979).
7. Calculated from GATT, International Trade.
8. World Bank Data.
9. On the Brazilian use of multinational firms affiliates as instruments of export promotion see Wall Street Journal, "Hot

Time in Rio," October 8, 1976, p. 1; Stefan H. Robock, "Controlling Multinational Enterprises: The Brazilian Experience," Journal of Contemporary Business, Autumn 1977.

10. Estimates of gross interest and amortization due on external public and private debt, as a percentage of exports of goods and services, range as high as 41 percent in the case of Brazil and 46 percent in the case of Mexico for 1977. (Discussions with World Bank and OECD officials.) Debt-service ratios for the Far Eastern UTLDCs all dropped under 10 percent by 1977. From the viewpoint of the world economy, it is to be regretted that they did so: the main result was fewer OECD exports to these countries than otherwise would have occurred.

11. IMF, The Rise in Protectionism, IMF Pamphlet Series no. 24, Washington, D.C., 1978.

12. John Sewell, "Can the Rich Prosper Without the Progress of the Poor?" Development 20 (1978); see also what was perhaps the seminal article along these lines, at least for the United States, Van Dorm Ooms and Arnold Packer, "The International Economy and the Federal Budget," U.S. Senate Budget Committee, December 1976.

13. For export share data see GATT, International Trade, 1977-78, p. 6.

14. For one effort along these lines, see Lawrence G. Franko, "Policy and Budget Options for International Economic Recovery," in Export Policy, Part 3, Hearings before the U.S. Senate Subcommittee on International Finance of the Committee on Banking, Housing and Urban Affairs, March 9, 1978, p. 294.

15. Or, better yet, something between the two - perhaps in the airspace over 19th Street.

16. IMF, The Rise In Protectionism.

17. OECD, National Accounts of OECD Countries, 1976; Eurostat National Accounts, ESA Aggregates.

18. GATT, International Trade, 1977/78, p. 7.

19. For an examination of the relationship between multinational firms investment and export activities in LDCs and the question of debt see Lawrence G. Franko, "Financing Economic Development," Journal of World Trade Law 12 (March/April, 1978): 127-31.

Index

About the Contributors

JOHN J. CAVANAUGH recently began his second term in the Congress of the United States representing the Second Congressional District of Nebraska.

As a member of both the House Banking Subcommittee on International Trade, Investment and Monetary Policy and the House International Relations Subcommittee on International Economic Policy and Trade, Congressman Cavanaugh is in a unique position to assist in shaping the legislative initiatives required in response to the new world economic order.

JANE D'ARISTA is an analyst in the National Security and International Affairs Division of the Congressional Budget Office. She was previously on the staff of the House Banking, Finance, and Urban Affairs Committee and has written studies on the development of Federal Reserve open-market operations, foreign bank activities in the United States, and United States bank operations overseas.

LAWRENCE G. FRANKO is a member and coholder of the United States Professorship of the Corporation and Society at the Center for Education in International Management in Geneva, Switzerland where he was formely director for Continental Europe of the Harvard Multinational Enterprise Project. He previously was with the Carnegie Endowment for International Peace and served as Adjunct Professor at the Georgetown University Center for Foreign Service. He formerly was Deputy Assistant Director for International Affairs, U.S. Congressional Budget Office.

CHARLES S. GANOE is Senior Executive Vice President and Director of The Fidelity Bank, Philadelphia, Pa. He was in charge of their international department for 15 years, and he served as President of the Bankers' Association for Foreign Trade in 1973-74. Mr. Ganoe has authored numerous articles for financial and banking journals.

ROBERT N. McCAULEY is a Teaching Fellow and doctoral candidate in the economics department, Harvard University. He was a traveling scholar from June 1978 to January 1979 while working for the National Security and International Affairs Division of the Congressional Budget Office on an analysis of International Monetary Fund lending.

NEIL J. McMULLEN is Vice President with responsibility for international studies at the National Planning Association. He was previously with the World Bank and has authored studies on economic development and international economic issues.

CARL R. NEU is a principal analyst in the National Security and International Affairs Division of the Congressional Budget Office. He was formerly a member of the economics department of the Rand Corporation.

WILLIAM A. NOELLERT is an international economist in the Bureau of International Labor Affairs of the United States Department of Labor. He previously did research on industrial organization for the Small Business Administration and was an Instructor of International Economics at American University. Mr. Noellert specializes in international investment and multinational enterprises, industrial organization and international labor standards.

J. DANIEL O'FLAHERTY, a political scientist, is currently a program officer at the Carnegie Endowment for International Peace. He is a former aide to the Senate Intelligence Committee, and is the author of articles and studies on the conduct of United States foreign policy.

ROBERT W. RUSSELL is currently Counsel to the Subcommittee on International Finance of the Senate Banking Committee. He is on leave from Northern Illinois University where he holds an appointment as Associate Professor of Political Science. Dr. Russell has authored several articles on international economic policy which have appeared in academic journals and conference proceedings.

MARILYN J. SEIBER is a financial economist in the Office of International Finance and Investment of the United States Department of Commerce. She was formerly Deputy Executive Director of the Rent Advisory Board, United States Price Commission (1971-73), was on the staff of the Secretary of Housing and Urban Development, and served in the Philippines with the Peace Corps. Ms. Seiber is a specialist in economic development policy and Southeast Asian systems.

ROBERT SOLOMON is a Senior Fellow in the Foreign Policy Studies Program at the Brookings Institutions. Mr. Solomon has served as economist and advisor to the Federal Reserve Board; Vice Chairman of the Deputies of the Committee on Reform of the International Monetary System and Related Issues (Committee of Twenty); Senior Staff Economist at the Council of Economic Advisors; and as the United States representative of the Group of Ten's Study Group on the Creation of Reserve Assets which led to the establishment of special drawing rights.

Pergamon Policy Studies

No. 1 Laszlo—*The Objectives of the New International Economic Order*
No. 2 Link/Feld—*The New Nationalism*
No. 3 Ways—*The Future of Business*
No. 4 Davis—*Managing and Organizing Multinational Corporations*
No. 5 Volgyes—*The Peasantry of Eastern Europe, Volume One*
No. 6 Volgyes—*The Peasantry of Eastern Europe, Volume Two*
No. 7 Hahn/Pfaltzgraff—*The Atlantic Community in Crisis*
No. 8 Renninger—*Multinational Cooperation for Development in West Africa*
No. 9 Stepanek—*Bangladesh—Equitable Growth?*
No. 10 Foreign Affairs—*America and the World 1978*
No. 11 Goodman/Love—*Management of Development Projects*
No. 12 Weinstein—*Bureaucratic Opposition*
No. 13 DeVolpi—*Proliferation, Plutonium and Policy*
No. 14 Francisco/Laird/Laird—*The Political Economy of Collectivized Agriculture*
No. 15 Godet—*The Crisis in Forecasting and the Emergence of the "Prospective" Approach*
No. 16 Golany—*Arid Zone Settlement Planning*
No. 17 Perry/Kraemer—*Technological Innovation in American Local Governments*
No. 18 Carman—*Obstacles to Mineral Development*
No. 19 Demir—*Arab Development Funds in the Middle East*
No. 20 Kahan/Ruble—*Industrial Labor in the U.S.S.R.*
No. 21 Meagher—*An International Redistribution of Wealth and Power*
No. 22 Thomas/Wionczek—*Integration of Science and Technology With Development*
No. 23 Mushkin/Dunlop—*Health: What Is It Worth?*
No. 24 Abouchar—*Economic Evaluation of Soviet Socialism*
No. 25 Amos—*Arab-Israeli Military/Political Relations*
No. 26 Geismar/Geismar—*Families in an Urban Mold*
No. 27 Leitenberg/Sheffer—*Great Power Intervention in the Middle East*
No. 28 O'Brien/Marcus—*Crime and Justice in America*
No. 29 Gartner—*Consumer Education in the Human Services*
No. 30 Diwan/Livingston—*Alternative Development Strategies and Appropriate Technology*
No. 31 Freedman—*World Politics and the Arab-Israeli Conflict*
No. 32 Williams/Deese—*Nuclear Nonproliferation*
No. 33 Close—*Europe Without Defense?*
No. 34 Brown—*Disaster Preparedness*

No. 35 Grieves—*Transnationalism in World Politics and Business*
No. 36 Franko/Seiber—*Developing Country Debt*
No. 37 Dismukes—*Soviet Naval Diplomacy*
No. 38 Morgan—*Science and Technology for Development*
No. 39 Chou/Harmon—*Critical Food Issues of the Eighties*
No. 40 Hall—*Ethnic Autonomy—Comparative Dynamics*
No. 41 Savitch—*Urban Policy and the Exterior City*
No. 42 Morris—*Measuring the Condition of the World's Poor*
No. 43 Katsenelinboigen—*Soviet Economic Thought and Political Power in the U.S.S.R*
No. 44 McCagg/Silver—*Soviet Asian Ethnic Frontiers*
No. 45 Carter/Hill—*The Criminal's Image of the City*
No. 46 Fallenbuchl/McMillan—*Partners in East-West Economic Relations*
No. 47 Liebling—*U.S. Corporate Profitability*
No. 48 Volgyes/Lonsdale—*Process of Rural Transformation*
No. 49 Ra'anan—*Ethnic Resurgence in Modern Democratic States*
No. 50 Hill/Utterback—*Technological Innovation for a Dynamic Economy*
No. 51 Laszlo/Kurtzman—*The United States, Canada and the New International Economic Order*
No. 52 Blazynski—*Flashpoint Poland*
No. 53 Constans—*Marine Sources of Energy*
No. 54 Lozoya/Estevez/Green—*Alternative Views of the New International Economic Order*
No. 55 Taylor/Yokell—*Yellowcake*
No. 56 Feld—*Multinational Enterprises and U.N. Politics*
No. 57 Fritz—*Combatting Nutritional Blindness in Children*
No. 58 Starr/Ritterbush—*Science, Technology and the Human Prospect*
No. 59 Douglass—*Soviet Military Strategy in Europe*
No. 60 Graham/Jordon—*The International Civil Service*
No. 61 Menon—*Bridges Across the South*
No. 62 Avery/Lonsdale/Volgyes—*Rural Change and Public Policy*
No. 63 Foster—*Comparative Public Policy and Citizen Participation*
No. 64 Laszlo/Kurtzman—*Eastern Europe and the New International Economic Order*
No. 65 United Nations Centre for Natural Resources, Energy and Transport—*State Petroleum Enterprises in Developing Countries*